Introduction to DevOps with Kubernetes

Build scalable cloud-native applications using
DevOps patterns created with Kubernetes

Onur Yılmaz and Süleyman Akbaş

Introduction to DevOps with Kubernetes

Authors: Onur Yılmaz and Süleyman Akbaş

Technical Reviewer: Hasan Turken

Managing Editor: Aditya Datar

Acquisitions Editor: Aditya Date

Production Editor: Samita Warang

Editorial Board: David Barnes, Mayank Bhardwaj, Ewan Buckingham, Simon Cox, Mahesh Dhyani, Taabish Khan, Manasa Kumar, Alex Mazonowicz, Douglas Paterson, Dominic Pereira, Shiny Poojary, Erol Staveley, Ankita Thakur, Mohita Vyas, and Jonathan Wray

First Published: May 2019

Production Reference: 1210519

ISBN: 978-1-78980-828-5

Published by Packt Publishing Ltd.

Livery Place, 35 Livery Street

Birmingham B3 2PB, UK

Table of Contents

Introduction to Kubernetes   69

Creating a Kubernetes Cluster

Deploy an Application to Kubernetes

Updating and Scaling an Application in Kubernetes   189

Troubleshooting Applications in Kubernetes   223

Preface

About

This section briefly introduces the author, the coverage of this book, the technical skills you'll need to get started, and the hardware and software required to complete all the included activities and exercises.

About the Book

Kubernetes and DevOps are the two pillars that can keep your business at the top by ensuring high performance of your IT infrastructure.

Introduction to DevOps with Kubernetes will help you develop the skills you need to improve your DevOps with the power of Kubernetes. The book begins with an overview of Kubernetes primitives and DevOps concepts. You'll understand how Kubernetes can assist you with overcoming a wide range of real-world operation challenges. You will get to grips with creating and upgrading a cluster, and then learn how to deploy, update, and scale an application on Kubernetes. As you advance through the chapters, you'll be able to monitor an application by setting up a pod failure alert on Prometheus. The book will also guide you in configuring Alertmanager to send alerts to the Slack channel and trace down a problem on the application using kubectl commands.

By the end of this book, you'll be able to manage the lifecycle of simple to complex applications on Kubernetes with confidence.

About the Authors

Onur Yılmaz is a senior software engineer in a multinational enterprise software company. He is a certified Kubernetes administrator and works on Kubernetes and cloud management systems. He is a keen supporter of cutting-edge technologies, including Docker, Kubernetes, and cloud-native applications. He has one master's degree and two bachelor's degrees in engineering and is pursuing a doctorate degree.

Süleyman Akbaş is a senior software engineer in a multinational enterprise software company. He is also a certified Kubernetes administrator and works on open source, cloud-native projects using Kubernetes. He is passionate both about developing and managing cloud-native applications. He has a bachelor's degree with honors in computer science and is now pursuing his master's degree in computer science in one of the top European universities, the University of Helsinki.

Objectives

- Create and manage Kubernetes clusters in on-premises systems and the cloud

- Exercise various DevOps practices using Kubernetes

- Explore configuration, secret, and storage management techniques, and exercise them with Kubernetes

- Perform different update techniques and apply them on Kubernetes

- Use the built-in scaling feature in Kubernetes to scale your applications up and down

- Use various troubleshooting techniques and have a monitoring system installed on Kubernetes

Audience

Introduction to DevOps with Kubernetes is for you if you want to gain a solid understanding of DevOps and how to apply DevOps practices using Kubernetes. It's a handy book for those with no experience with DevOps or Kubernetes and for experienced DevOps engineers to broaden their views of using Kubernetes for DevOps practices.

Approach

Introduction to DevOps with Kubernetes takes a hands-on approach to understanding DevOps practices with Kubernetes. It contains multiple activities that use real-life business scenarios for you to practice and apply your new skills in a highly relevant context.

Hardware Requirements

For an optimal student experience, we recommend the following hardware configuration:

- Processor: Intel Core i5 or equivalent

- Memory: 8 GB RAM (16 GB Preferred)

- Hard disk: 10 GB available space

- Internet connection

Software Requirements

You'll also need the following software installed in advance:

- Sublime Text (latest version), Atom IDE (latest version), or another similar text editor application

- Git

Conventions

Code words in text, database table names, folder names, filenames, file extensions, pathnames, dummy URLs, user input, and Github handles are shown as follows: Click on the **Create** button, and you will be redirected to the new repository page.

A block of code is set as follows:

```
FROM ubuntu:18.10

RUN apt-get update
RUN apt-get install -y nodejs npm
RUN npm install -g http-server

WORKDIR /usr/apps/hello-world/

CMD ["http-server", "-p", "8080"]
```

New terms and important words are shown in bold. Words that you see on the screen, for example, in menus or dialog boxes, appear in the text like this: "Click **Add a column** and add these three columns: **Backlog**, **WIP,** and **Done**."

Installation and Setup

Installing Git

Please follow the steps for your operating system to install Git: https://docs.gitlab.com/ee/topics/git/how_to_install_git/

Additional Resources

The code bundle for this book is also hosted on GitHub at: https://github.com/TrainingByPackt/Introduction-to-DevOps-with-Kubernetes

We also have other code bundles from our rich catalog of books and videos available at https://github.com/PacktPublishing/ Check them out!

1

Introduction to DevOps

Learning Objectives

By the end of this chapter, you will be able to:

- Identify the benefits of DevOps for organizations
- Define DevOps toolchain steps in detail
- Create a modern DevOps pipeline running on GitHub

This chapter gives an introduction to DevOps. This chapter will briefly explain what DevOps is and the concepts around it

Introduction

In the last decade, several comprehensive paradigm shifts have taken place in the software industry. These changes have made it possible for millions of people to chat on their mobile phones at the same time and stream their favorite movies while traveling throughout the world. When changes in software development and operations are reviewed, two prominent, mutually reinforcing paradigms come to the forefront: **DevOps** and **cloud-native architecture**. DevOps created a cultural change by establishing more open communication between teams. This cultural change led to practices such as continuous integration, testing, and deployment, which shaped today's software development methodology. Likewise, cloud-native architecture created an open environment with scalable microservices capable of serving millions of customers. In order to manage this scalability, container technologies have evolved for the development, testing, and deployment of applications. These two paradigm shifts have enabled today's robust, scalable, and easy-to-manage software applications to change the technological, social, and industrial face of the world.

Before diving into innovative software development methods, let's have a glance at a conventional approach. Traditionally, software development was similar to manufacturing a passenger aircraft. Considerable investments in infrastructure and personnel followed the collection of requirements, design, and planning. There were teams identical to production-line engineers and workers that specialized in a particular topic and delivered parts of the aircraft for the next stages. There were even companies with organizational structures including teams named "production line." Prodigious output was delivered to customers following formal acceptance tests. After that, it was the customer's responsibility to make the aircraft fly with its team of engineers and operators. Further requests and upgrades were part of another substantial project.

Today, software development has evolved and become more customer-oriented. It has moved away from making customers buy software products by having customers subscribe to software services. A similar thing could be said for the aircraft analogy: software applications are smaller and more flexible, like drones. Requirements are collected at every stage, and the product is configured to the customer's environment "on the fly." Since customers also buy the product as a service, maintenance and keeping drones in the air is the job of the producer. In order to manage these services, microservice orchestrators such as Kubernetes make these small drones run in harmony to achieve more complex air shows. These changes in software development and operations owe their success to the cultural shift of DevOps and containerized cloud-native technologies.

DevOps' Effect on Industry

Leading companies such as PayPal, Facebook, and Netflix have very strong DevOps success stories that have evolved over the years. For instance, Paypal has more than 200 million active users, with nearly 5,000 developers. In 2013, creating a new application on PayPal required opening dozens of tickets and following their complex statuses for months instead of writing code. To resolve this problem, PayPal developed a software development lifecycle system to manage the complete lifecycle of software, going from planning to production in a couple of weeks.

Likewise, Facebook focused on code ownership, automation, and continuous improvement way before DevOps became popular. Today, Facebook uses the Chef configuration management tool to manage all of its infrastructure and backend systems. Similarly, Netflix created an environment where thousands of changes are made to production each day. It both decreased the time taken to fix problems and increased its market responsiveness.

When old and new software development practices are compared, it is evident that the old mindset of conventional software development is doomed to fail. Running scalable, reliable, and robust applications on cloud providers that can scale to serve millions of customers requires learning and applying new methodologies. The basics of

these methodologies include learning the basics of DevOps culture and toolchain and container technology. Following that, it is essential to learn and exercise how to install, configure, scale, and monitor containerized applications inside the de facto container orchestrator, Kubernetes.

In this chapter, the inception of the DevOps cultural shift and its value toolchain are explored. How DevOps changed the software development environment and potential benefits for organizations are covered. Following that, every step of a complete DevOps toolchain will be discussed, starting from the plan for a software project to monitoring an installed application. All toolchain steps are presented and experimented on with a modern cloud-native application suitable for today's software trends.

DevOps Culture and its Benefits

Traditional software development focused on planning, developing, testing, and delivering software systems with separate teams focused on the respective areas. The outputs and expectations of teams were defined in detail beforehand, and each team was responsibile for its deliverables. For instance, the planning team, consisting of seasoned planning managers and industrial engineers, would calculate the working-hour requirements and delivery dates for their output. The development team would create software, and the testing team would test the output of the development team.

Finally, the delivery team would visit a customer on site and install the software systems according to the customer's needs. These consecutive stages were huge, and they were done with minimal inter-team communication. The state of mind was based on not interfering with the business of other teams involved in the development process. With this style of development, many IT projects were undertaken; however, most of them failed. To make it clear with actual numbers, according to research on "*The Impact of Business Requirements on the Success of Technology Projects*", by IAG Consulting, in 2008, **68%** of IT projects failed as they were impractical due to lack of communication between the various teams.

What made the software projects impractical was a lack of proper requirement analysis and inter-team communication. Planning and consulting teams would collect requirements without the collaboration of development teams. With the same kind of flawed approach, development teams did not cooperate with the operations teams responsible for configuring, installing, and monitoring applications for customers. This lack of formal inter-team communication resulted in development teams having minimal knowledge about the runtime environment. On the other hand, operations teams had practically no concrete understanding of the requirements and features of the applications they were deploying. With enormous barriers between these teams, they created applications that did not concurrently consider the runtime environment and software requirements. Consequently, both development and operations teams were held responsible for many failures, thus leading to financial losses.

As the term DevOps derives from the combination of development and operations, the DevOps culture came in to being to increase the collaboration between development and operations teams. With DevOps' cultural change, companies now form DevOps teams consisting of engineers from development and organizational backgrounds. These new teams help developers to realize both operational and customer requirements. On the other hand, operations engineers gain insights into applications and development requirements. With the barriers between teams having collapsed, requirements are collected efficiently, quality is fostered, and lead times are reduced. The benefits of this cultural shift have led to DevOps being adopted in organizations of various sizes, from start-ups to enterprise companies.

Note

The term DevOps was coined by Patrick Debois in 2009 and was first used at a devopsdays conference in Belgium. Devopsdays focuses on software development and IT infrastructure operations and events are organized worldwide throughout the year. You can read more about this at:

https://www.devopsdays.org/

With the successful implementation of DevOps, not only has communication between teams increased, but software delivery speed, reliability, and scalability have also been enhanced. Firstly, DevOps culture indicates better requirement collection and better utilization of those requirements in the product design. Therefore, it is expected to have decreased the time taken to deliver new product features to the market. Secondly, with continuous integration and testing, more robust and reliable applications are expected. Finally, DevOps also enhances operations including configuring, deploying, and monitoring.

With infrastructure-as-a-code practices and metrics from production environments, it is expected to have scalable applications. DevOps culture is capable of providing organizations with various advantages. However, before implementation, understanding the current company's culture and creating a feasible action plan for introducing DevOps is crucial. In the following sections, the DevOps toolchain is explained in detail to illustrate how DevOps' cultural shift has evolved into a value chain for software development.

The DevOps Toolchain

The DevOps toolchain consists of practices that connect development and operations teams, with the aim of creating a value chain. The stages of the DevOps chain and their interconnectivity is presented as follows:

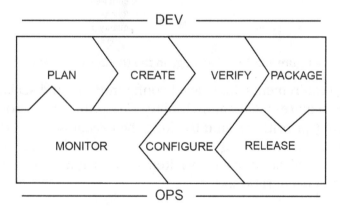

Figure 1.1: The DevOps toolchain

The DevOps toolchain is a continuous chain of streamlined activities that can be grouped into two: development and operations. DevOps tries to remove the barriers between development and operations and its toolchain also emphasizes the association of activities and teams. For the successful implementation of a DevOps culture, it is crucial that each stage is executed and communicated transparently. In the following sections, each step is presented along with its interaction with other stages and modern real-life software application examples.

Plan

Planning is the first step in most software development projects and is also a critical step that should be revisited for long-term ongoing projects. Planning a modern, cloud-native software application requires more than calculating person-hour requirements, and it is a crucial step between the monitor and create stages. If planning is considered a black box, it should take production and busines metrics from the monitoring stage as inputs. As depicted in Figure 1.2, it should produce requirements, release schedules, and quality standards for the create stage:

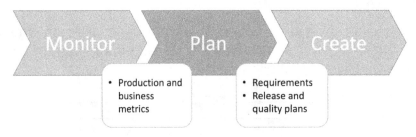

Figure 1.2: The plan stage in the DevOps toolchain

With everchanging requirements, high-level configurations, and scalability, planning today's applications requires agility and visibility. The principal approach for planning is based on classifying, prioritizing, and tracking the execution of work on issue boards. Issue boards help to manage backlog and work-in-progress items by following statuses collaboratively. The overall state of all work items is available to anyone, following the main idea of DevOps: collaboration.

Work items are created in project management systems such as **JIRA**, **GitHub Issues**, or **GitLab** Issues and classified with labels such as **bug**, **enhancement**, or **needs help** based on the content and requirements of the issues. In *Figure 1.3*, the issue list of the Kubernetes project is shown with labels near to the issue names:

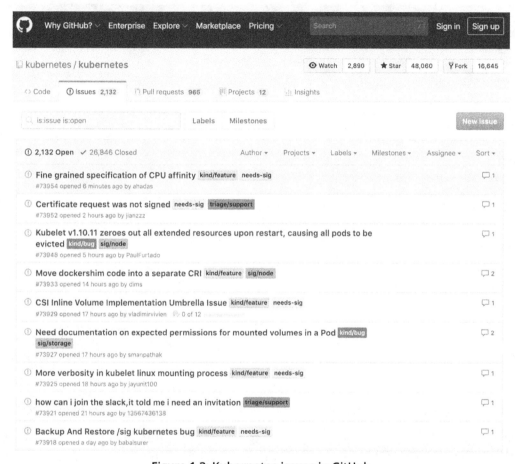

Figure 1.3: Kubernetes issues in GitHub

Being the most popular project in GitHub, there are more than 2,000 open issues in the Kubernetes repository and more than 26,000 closed ones. Besides, Kubernetes **Special Interest Groups** (**SIGs**) are used within issue labels to specify the main group responsible.

The second level of classifying is based on the planning timeframe of issues, and the most common groups are **Backlog**, **WIP** (Work in progress), and **Done**. For the Kubernetes repository, the **CustomResourceDefinition** project board can be checked:

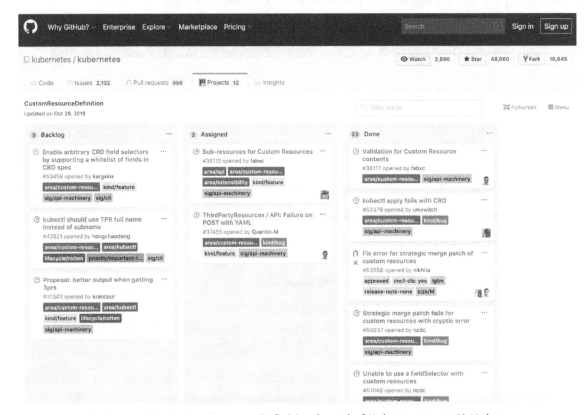

Figure 1.4: CustomResourceDefinition board of Kubernetes on GitHub

This project board consists of issues related to the **CustomResourceDefinition** feature (formerly known as **ThirdPartyResource**) in Kubernetes. Compared to all issue lists, this provides a more focused and manageable list of topics. There are three blocks, named **Backlog**, **Assigned**, and **Done**. **Backlog** items consist of things that the team has not started working on yet, whereas **Assigned** items are in progress. As expected, this project aims to move all issues into the **Done** block eventually.

Project boards and issues are conventionally created and tracked using code repositories such as GitHub and GitLab. This makes it easier to mention bugs in code and failing test cases, and also increases the developers' contributions to boards, since they are already dealing with the code repository daily. However, the most critical input of planning using project boards, according to DevOps culture, is providing an overview of a project's status, which is created and followed collaboratively. In the following exercise, you will open and create a repository in GitHub and add your first item to a project board.

> **Note**
>
> If you do not have a GitHub account, you need to create one before starting the exercise. GitHub is a free service, and you can register with your email, choosing a username and password, at https://github.com/join.

Exercise 1: Creating a Repository and Project Board on GitHub

In this exercise, we'll create a new repository in GitHub and start the planning stage by adding our first backlog items to the project board.

> **Note**
>
> The code files for the exercises in this chapter can be found at https://github.com/ TrainingByPackt/Introduction-to-DevOps-with-Kubernetes/tree/master/Lesson01.

To successfully complete the exercise, we need to ensure the following steps are executed:

1. Click **+** in the header menu in GitHub and choose **New Repository**:

Figure 1.5: Header menu in GitHub

2. Fill **Repository name** with **devops-blog** and ensure that **Public** is selected. Click **Create Repository**:

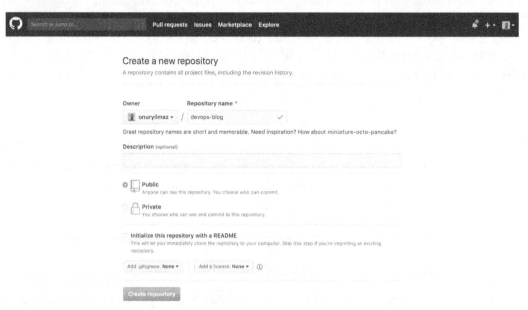

Figure 1.6: Creating a repository in GitHub

You will be redirected to the new repository:

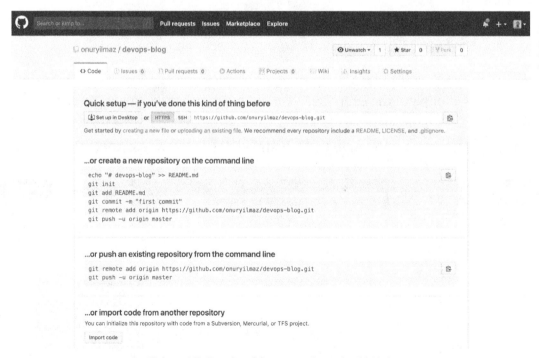

Figure 1.7: DevOps blog repository in GitHub

3. Click **Projects** in the repository view and then choose **Create a Project**:

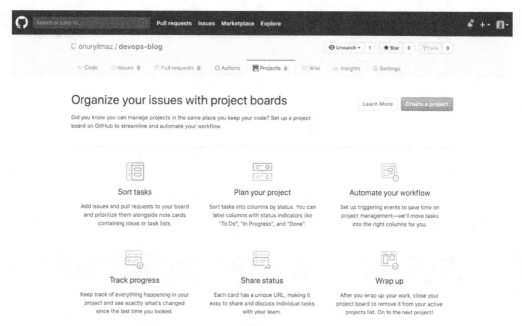

Figure 1.8: Projects view in GitHub

4. Fill **Project board name** with **First Version** and click **Create Project**:

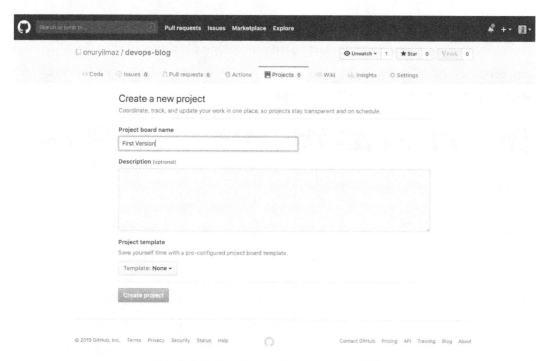

Figure 1.9: Creating a new project in GitHub

You will be redirected to the new project board:

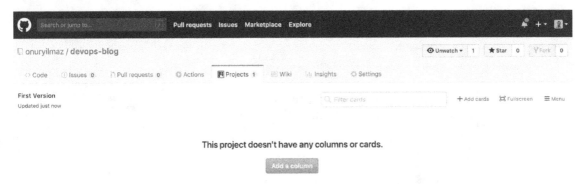

Figure 1.10: Project board in GitHub

5. Click **Add a column** and add these three columns: **Backlog**, **WIP**, and **Done**:

Figure 1.11: Project board with columns in GitHub

6. Click the **+** icon in the **Backlog** column add two new items: **Create the first working blog** and **Connect CI/CD pipeline**:

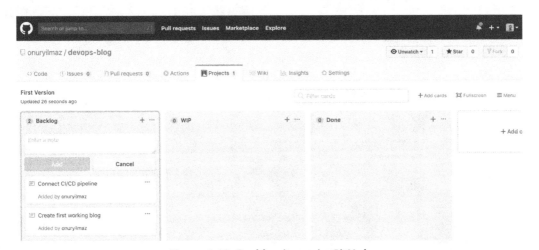

Figure 1.12: Backlog items in GitHub

7. Move **Create the first working blog** into the **WIP** column from the **Backlog** column since we have started working on it:

Figure 1.13: WIP items in GitHub

With the GitHub repository set up, now it is possible to add some backlog items to the project board and start planning. In the next section, planning requirements and issues will be utilized while creating the software according to DevOps practices.

Create

With a detailed planning stage carried out, there are items in **Backlog** ready to be assigned to teams so that the software creation can start. When this stage is modeled as a black box, as in *Figure 1.14*, it takes inputs from the plan stage as requirements and release dates, and creates the source code of the application, which should be verified in the next step:

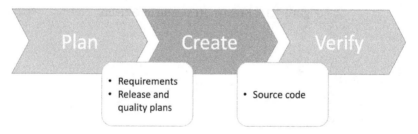

Figure 1.14: Create stage in the DevOps toolchain

Modern software applications are developed by geographically distributed teams of developers collaboratively, with clear communication channels. Therefore, the de facto path is to keep all source code, configuration, and sensitive data in distributed version control systems as Git repositories. All popular tools, such as GitHub, GitLab, and Bitbucket, provide Git repositories to manage source code securely, and developers commit their changes to repositories as frequently as possible.

For an open source project such as Kubernetes, which is developed by different people from various organizations and in various time zones, there are more than 74,000 commits by almost 2,000 contributors in the repository:

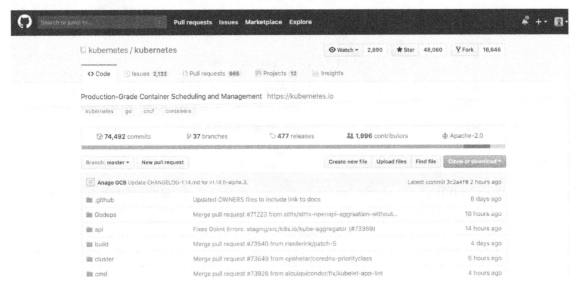

Figure 1.15: Kubernetes code in GitHub

The create stage in DevOps culture is the stage at which collaborative work is converted into a single source code. It is important to have clear communication and transparency between teams, and the popular Git repositories facilitate these requirements. When the active branches are checked in *Figure 1.16*, there are seven active branches for the Kubernetes repository. This indicates that more than one copy of the primary source code is in progress and some future commits will be part of these branches:

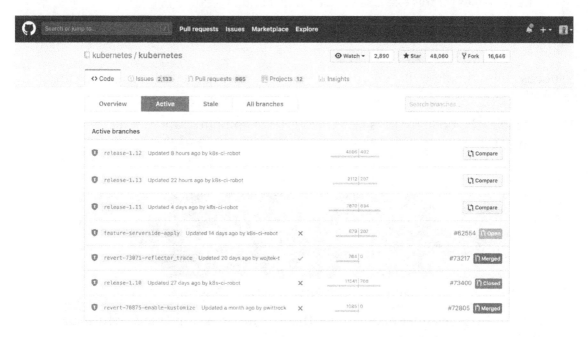

Figure 1.16: Active branches for Kubernetes in GitHub

In the following exercise, the source code for a DevOps blog will be uploaded to the GitHub repository created in the previous section.

Exercise 2: Creating a DevOps Blog

In this exercise, we'll create the source code of a DevOps blog and maintain it in the GitHub repository created in *Exercise 1, Creating a Project Board on GitHub*.

> **Note**
>
> The code files for this exercise can be found at https://github.com/TrainingByPackt/ Introduction-to-DevOps-with-Kubernetes/tree/master/Lesson01.

To successfully complete this exercise, we need to ensure the following steps are executed:

1. Download the code for **Lesson01** to your local computer and open it in the terminal:

    ```
    $ ls Lesson01
    ```

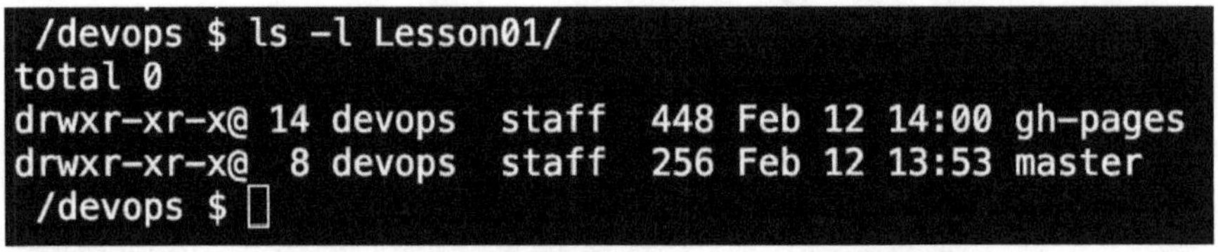

    ```
    /devops $ ls -l Lesson01/
    total 0
    drwxr-xr-x@ 14 devops  staff   448 Feb 12 14:00 gh-pages
    drwxr-xr-x@  8 devops  staff   256 Feb 12 13:53 master
    /devops $ 
    ```

    Figure 1.17: Contents of the Lesson01 folder

2. Go to the **master** folder and commit the files in the **master** folder into GitHub with the following commands:

    ```
    $ cd Lesson01/master
    $ git init && git add -A && git commit -m "first commit"
    $ git remote add origin https://github.com/<USERNAME>/devops-blog.git
    $ git push -u origin master
    ```

```
/devops $ git init && git add -A &&  git commit -m "first commit"
Initialized empty Git repository in /Users/i313226/Downloads/Lesson01/master/.git/
[master (root-commit) 4b4e477] first commit
 6 files changed, 71 insertions(+)
 create mode 100755 .gitignore
 create mode 100755 .travis.yml
 create mode 100755 README.md
 create mode 100755 config.toml
 create mode 100755 content/_index.md
 create mode 100755 content/post/2019-02-01-kubernetes-deployment.md
/devops $
/devops $ git remote add origin https://github.com/onuryilmaz/devops-blog.git
/devops $
/devops $ git push -u origin master
Enumerating objects: 10, done.
Counting objects: 100% (10/10), done.
Delta compression using up to 8 threads
Compressing objects: 100% (7/7), done.
Writing objects: 100% (10/10), 1.38 KiB | 1.38 MiB/s, done.
Total 10 (delta 0), reused 0 (delta 0)
To https://github.com/onuryilmaz/devops-blog.git
 * [new branch]      master -> master
Branch 'master' set up to track remote branch 'master' from 'origin'.
/devops $
```

Figure 1.18: Committing the master branch into GitHub

3. Go into the **gh-pages** folder and commit the files in **gh-pages** folder into GitHub with the following commands, one by one:

```
$ cd ../gh-pages
$ git init && git checkout --orphan gh-pages
$ git add -A && git commit -m "first commit" --quiet
$ git push https://GitHub.com/<USERNAME>/devops-blog.git gh-pages
```

```
/devops $ cd ../gh-pages
/devops $ git init && git checkout --orphan gh-pages
Initialized empty Git repository in /devops/Lesson01/gh-pages/.git/
Switched to a new branch 'gh-pages'
/devops $ git add -A && git commit -m "first commit" --quiet
/devops $
/devops $ git push https://github.com/onuryilmaz/devops-blog.git gh-pages
Enumerating objects: 72, done.
Counting objects: 100% (72/72), done.
Delta compression using up to 8 threads
Compressing objects: 100% (63/63), done.
Writing objects: 100% (72/72), 1.12 MiB | 765.00 KiB/s, done.
Total 72 (delta 15), reused 0 (delta 0)
remote: Resolving deltas: 100% (15/15), done.
remote:
remote: Create a pull request for 'gh-pages' on GitHub by visiting:
remote:      https://github.com/onuryilmaz/devops-blog/pull/new/gh-pages
remote:
To https://github.com/onuryilmaz/devops-blog.git
 * [new branch]      gh-pages -> gh-pages
/devops $
```

Figure 1.19: Committing the gh-pages branch into GitHub

4. Open the GitHub repository in the browser and ensure that there are two branches with code inside them:

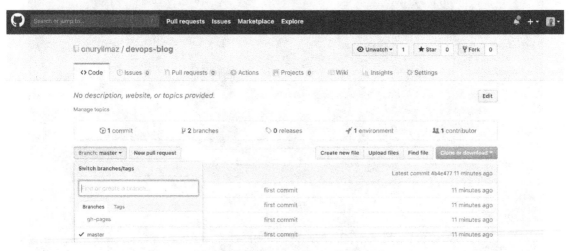

Figure 1.20: GitHub repository for a DevOps blog

In this exercise, source code for a DevOps blog has been created and pushed to a Git repository. The next step, verification, focuses on the requirements for accepting and validating changes.

Verify

Verification in DevOps software development culture is based on the idea of manual and automated testing of changes for acceptance or rejection from the source code. Manual verification includes reviewing code changes by other developers, to comment on and discuss them in an open environment. Automated testing consists of multiple levels, starting from static code analysis to end-to-end scenario tests. Sets of commits, from development branches to active release branches, are accepted when a set of criteria is passed, and code reviews are marked as approved by other developers.

As a black-box model, verification processes potential changes to source code from the create stage and creates a confirmed source code, ready to be packaged in the next step:

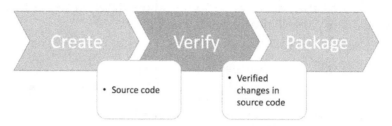

Figure 1.21: Verify stage in the DevOps toolchain

Practically, sets of commits are grouped into **pull-requests**. When a developer opens a **pull request** (PR), it indicates that the included commits are ready to be reviewed by other developers and tests can be run including these new changes. For the Kubernetes repository, there are almost 1,000 open and 44,000 closed PRs. Open ones are still in discussion or waiting to be approved. On the other hand, closed PRs could be accepted and merged into active branches or entirely rejected by reviewers:

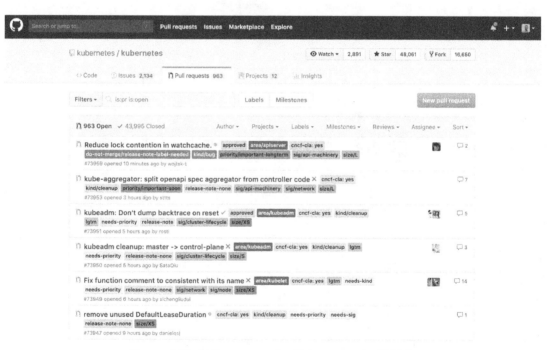

Figure 1.22: Pull requests for Kubernetes in GitHub

The automated testing of changes is handled by continuous integration and testing systems, such as Travis CI, Jenkins, and GitLab CI/CD. On these cloud systems, the source code of new PRs is retrieved, and test operations are undertaken. If any of these test steps fail, it returns the status to PR and does not allow it to be merged. For instance, PR **#73854** has passed all 16 checks, as follows:

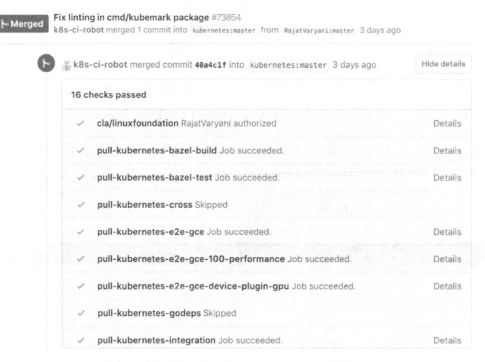

Figure 1.23: PR checks for Kubernetes in GitHub

Unfortunately, PR **#73953** failed some tests and cannot be merged before they are solved:

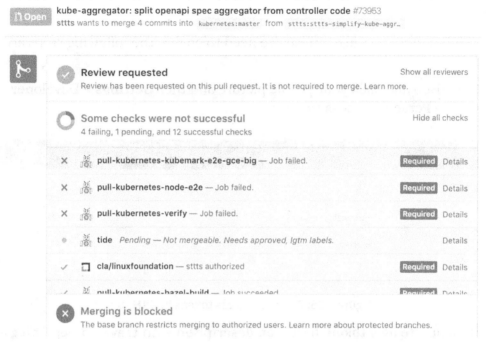

Figure 1.24: PR checks for Kubernetes in GitHub

Verification by automated testing removes the burden of building and testing every PR locally and decreases the time taken to review them. Without automation and streamlined results, it would not be possible to merge 44,000 PRs in less than 5 years. In other words, extensive reviews and the automated verification of changes made it possible to create the de facto container orchestration tool, which enables running applications on the cloud. In the following exercise, a method for connecting a cloud CI/CD system, Travis CI, to the DevOps blog is presented.

> **Note**
>
> If you do not have a Travis-CI account, you need to create one before starting the exercise. Travis-CI is a free service, and you can register with your existing GitHub account at https://travis-ci.org/.

Exercise 3: Connecting the DevOps Blog to a CI/CD System

In this exercise, we'll connect the DevOps blog to a CI/CD system for automated testing and builds. We will use Travis-CI, which is a free cloud-service providing CI/CD capabilities.

To successfully complete the exercise, we need to ensure the following steps are executed:

1. Open GitHub and click your profile picture and then **Settings** > **Developer settings** > **Personal access tokens**:

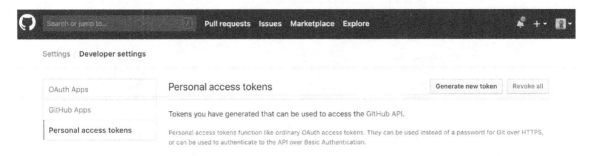

Figure 1.25: Personal access tokens in GitHub

2. Click **Generate new token**, fill **Token description** with `travis-devops-blog` and ensure that the **repo** scope is selected:

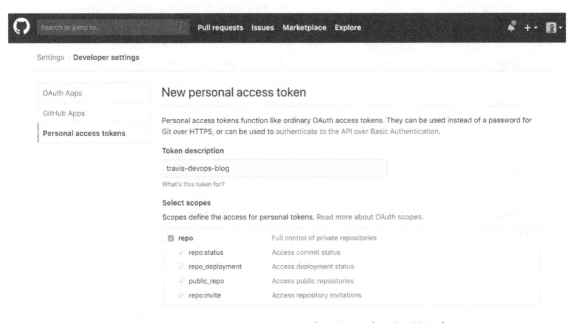

Figure 1.26: Generating a personal access token in GitHub

3. Click **Generate token** and you will be redirected to your new token page:

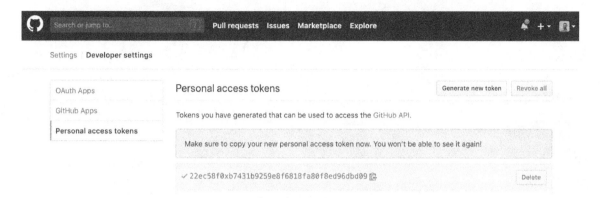

Figure 1.27: New personal access token in GitHub

4. Copy the token highlighted in green to use in Travis-CI in the next steps.

5. Open Travis-CI (https://travis-ci.org/) and click the **+** icon on the left-hand menu, next to **My Repositories**, and search for **devops-blog**:

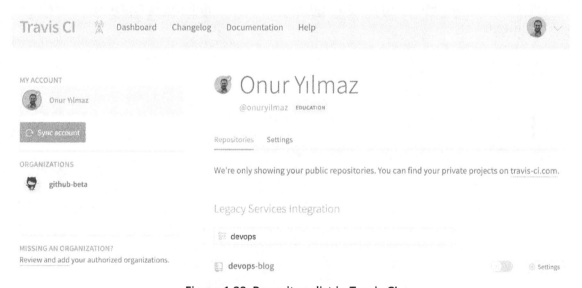

Figure 1.28: Repository list in Travis-CI

6. Enable **devops-blog** by checking the slider:

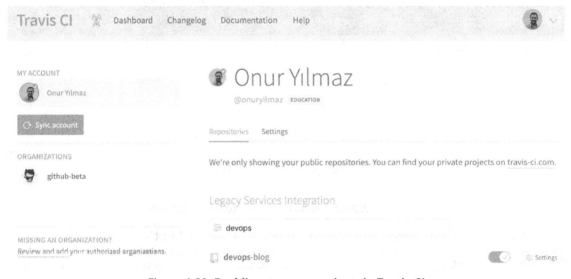

Figure 1.29: Enabling a new repository in Travis-CI

7. Click on **devops-blog** and on the redirected page, click **More Options** > **Settings** in the menu:

Figure 1.30: Repository view in Travis-CI

8. Ensure that **Build pushed branches** and **Build pushed pull requests** are checked at the top. In addition, **Add** a new environment variable below with the name **GITHUB_TOKEN** and the value you copied in step 4:

Figure 1.31: The settings view in Travis-CI

With this exercise, continuous integration is now possible for the DevOps blog. In the next section, verified changes in release branches will be packaged and delivered to end users.

Package

Packaging is the last step in the development part of the DevOps toolchain. In this final step, the verified and accepted source code changes are gathered and end-user packages are created:

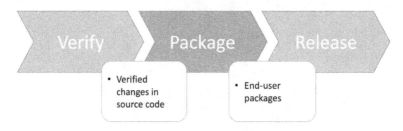

Figure 1.32: Package stage in the DevOps toolchain

For modern cloud-native applications, there are two main approaches to packaging and delivering end products. The first is for the client or on-premise applications to be installed on local systems. Executables of these applications are made available in GitHub releases or GitLab artifacts sections. The second is containerized applications that run on cloud systems such as Kubernetes. These applications are packaged as containers and managed inside container registries such as **Docker Hub**, **Google Cloud Platform Container Registry**, and **GitLab Registry**. For instance, **Minikube** is a local Kubernetes solution, and its releases are available on GitHub:

Figure 1.33: Minikube packages on GitHub

Since Minikube is expected to be downloaded and installed on local systems, it is acceptable to have a list of executables in the GitHub releases section. However, **kubernetes-dashboard** is the official dashboard for Kubernetes clusters, and it is expected to be installed on clusters. Therefore, it is a containerized application, and its versions are available on the **Google Cloud Platform - Container Registry**:

Figure 1.34: Kubernetes Dashboard releases on GCP

With these packaged artifacts available in different formats, operation team tasks start. In the next section, the first task – releasing artifacts – will be explained.

Release

Releasing is the first step in the operations part of the DevOps toolchain. In this step, packaged and versioned applications from the previous step are put into the end-user service:

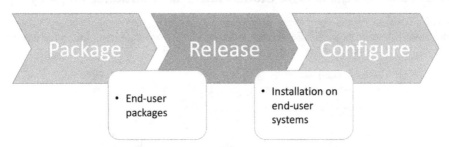

Figure 1.35: Release stage in the DevOps toolchain

Modern cloud-native applications are delivered to end users or cloud systems by considering three essential characteristics – downtime, targeting, and infrastructure costs:

- **Downtime:** While offering applications, it is possible to have downtime, in which no instances of the application are serving user requests.

- **Targeting:** With an enormous user base, it is vital to differentiate between customers and target them with specific feature sets, such as geolocations and device models.

- **Infrastructure costs:** As applications scale to millions of users, the cost of infrastructure and investment is an inevitable characteristic to consider for the delivery of systems.

While some of these characteristics are given more importance, some sacrifices are made based on business requirements. For instance, for a banking application, downtime is not acceptable; however, high infrastructure cost is bearable. Likewise, it is critical for a marketing start-up to classify and target users without increasing infrastructure costs dramatically. With an appropriate deployment strategy and automation, it is possible to deploy and update cloud-native microservices in the cloud reliably. In the following exercise, the DevOps blog will be released for the first time, on GitHub Pages. **GitHub Pages** is a service provided by GitHub to host websites directly from a GitHub repository.

Exercise 4: Releasing the DevOps Blog

In this exercise, we'll release the DevOps blog to the entire world by using GitHub Pages. To successfully complete the exercise, we need to ensure the following steps are executed:

1. Open the **devops-blog** repository in GitHub and click **Settings**:

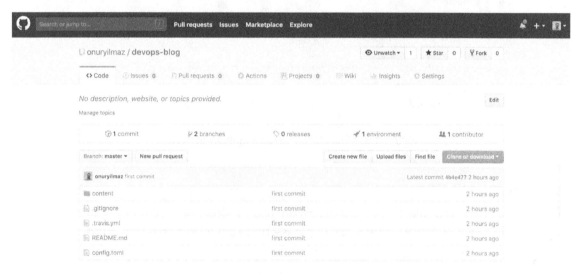

Figure 1.36: Settings in the devops-blog repository in GitHub

2. Scroll down to GitHub Pages, select **"gh-pages branch"** in the Source section, and click "**Save**":

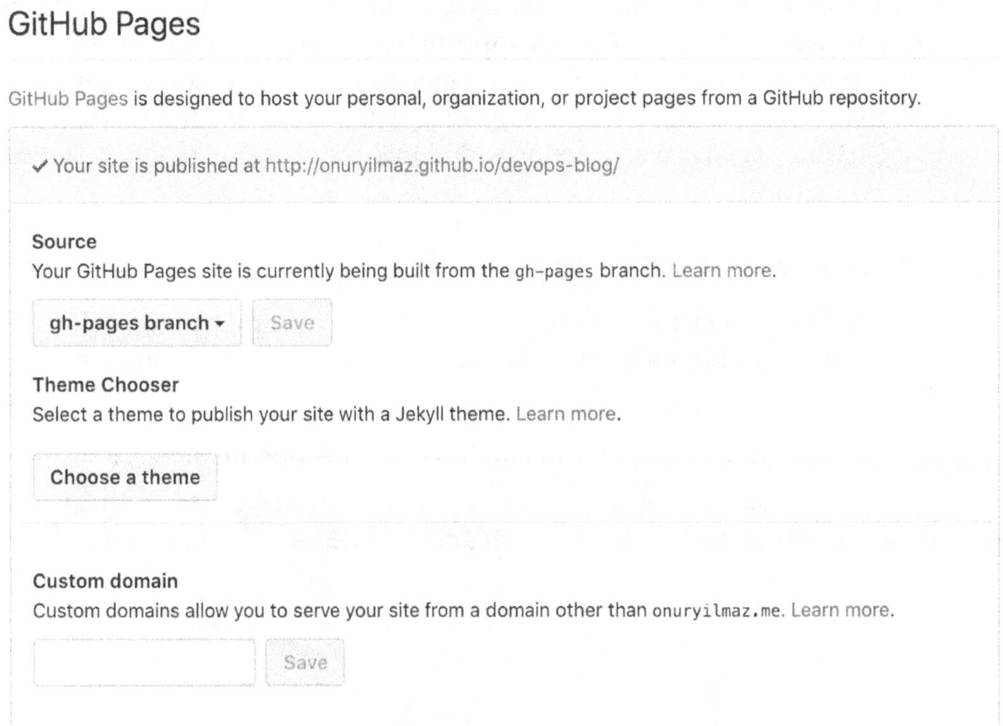

GitHub Pages

GitHub Pages is designed to host your personal, organization, or project pages from a GitHub repository.

✓ Your site is published at http://onuryilmaz.github.io/devops-blog/

Source
Your GitHub Pages site is currently being built from the gh-pages branch. Learn more.

gh-pages branch ▾   Save

Theme Chooser
Select a theme to publish your site with a Jekyll theme. Learn more.

Choose a theme

Custom domain
Custom domains allow you to serve your site from a domain other than onuryilmaz.me. Learn more.

Save

Figure 1.37: Enabling GitHub Pages in GitHub

Note

It could take a couple of minutes to resolve the subdomain for your username. If you receive a 404 error from GitHub, please try again in a couple of minutes.

3. Open http://<USERNAME>.github.io/devops-blog in the browser:

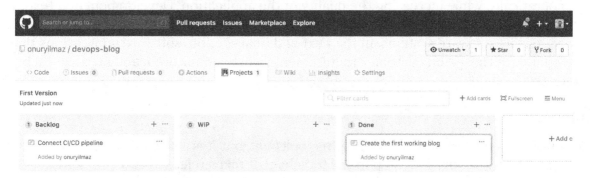

Figure 1.38: DevOps blog is up and running

4. Open the project board created in Exercise 1 and move the "**Create the first working blog**" item to "**Done**," since the blog is up and running now:

Figure 1.39: Done items in GitHub

With this exercise, the very first version of the DevOps blog is released to the world.

Configure

The configuration step focuses on managing all the custom configuration required for the generic application released in the last step:

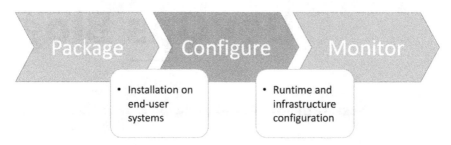

Figure 1.40: Configure stage in the DevOps toolchain

The configuration of modern cloud-native applications consists of two parts: runtime configuration for the application and infrastructure configuration definition. Both of these configurations are created, managed, and tracked as code in Git repositories. This approach increases the visibility of requirements to all teams while strengthening the DevOps culture. For instance, if there is a requirement for a replica of the PostgreSQL database, it should be declared in the respective configuration files in the repository. This makes it easy for not only the operations team but also developers to know about runtime requirements. It removes the barrier between teams and distributes knowledge democratically, while increasing the quality of the application. Development and testing teams can create their testing environment based on this requirement, resulting in more reliable software systems. In the next and final section, software applications that are configured based on customer requirements will be monitored, and metrics will be collected.

Monitor

Monitoring is the last step in the DevOps toolchain, but it is also a critical step to feed planning, the very first step in the toolchain. It takes released and configured applications and provides business-critical metrics for the planning stage:

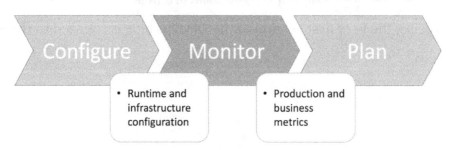

Figure 1.41: Monitor stage in the DevOps toolchain

For cloud-native applications, monitoring enables the tracking of key performance indicators and indicates the status of applications compared to goals. Besides this, monitoring is critical for troubleshooting production systems to find problems and resolve them proactively.

Within the framework of the DevOps toolchain, monitoring is the only step that shows the impact of changes made in the previous steps. In other words, it is now possible to show how newly developed, verified, packaged, released, and configured changes will affect production systems. For current, cloud-native monitoring, there are three crucial aspects to consider:

- **Logging**: Collecting, storing, and making logs searchable to troubleshoot problems in the long run.

- **Error tracking**: Receiving and collecting key details about errors that have occurred in running systems. These errors could indicate misconfiguration, undesired user behavior, and malicious activities.

- **Cluster monitoring**: Tracking the health of clusters based on master and worker health statuses, applications running on them, and scalability.

With the monitoring stage, all seven steps in the DevOps toolchain are presented with real-life examples and exercises. In the following activity, an automated pipeline running in the cloud will be set up to show how DevOps culture is practically converted into a pipeline.

Activity 1: CI/CD Pipeline for the DevOps Blog

The aim of this activity to create an automated pipeline to verify, package, configure, and release the DevOps blog. Until now, the DevOps blog has been generated locally, and HTML files have been uploaded to the gh-pages branch. GitHub Pages hosts the pages in this branch and makes the blog available to the public. It should verify, generate, and configure the blog from the source code automatically, so that when a new blog post is added, the pipeline should update the running website.

All previous exercises in this chapter will need to have been completed to complete this activity. The GitHub repository, the source code in the master branch, and Travis-CI should be utilized with a pipeline to achieve automation. Once completed, you should have a complete pipeline running in Travis-CI and successfully passing:

Figure 1.42: Successful run in Travis-CI

As expected, the blog should be up and running:

Figure 1.43: DevOps blog is up and running

When a new blog post is added to the **content/post** folder in the source code, the pipeline should run automatically and update the website with the new post:

Figure 1.44: Automated updates in the DevOps blog

Execute the following steps to complete this activity:

1. Create a file with the name `.travis.yml` in the master branch of the repository including the Travis-CI definition.

2. Commit the `.travis.yml` file into the **master** branch.

3. Trigger a build in Travis-CI for the **master** branch.

4. Add a new blog post to the **content/post** folder. An example of blog content could be as follows, in a file named **2019-02-02-kubernetes-scale.md**.

5. Wait for Travis-CI to trigger an automated build with the new material.

6. Check for the blog on the browser for the new content once the build is completed.

7. Move the **Connect CI/CD pipeline** item to **Done** in the project board created in *Exercise 1, Creating a Project Board on GitHub*.

> **Note**
>
> The solution of this activity can be found on page 298.

Summary

In this chapter, we first described conventional software development methods and discovered their boundaries. Precisely, we explained how conventional methods failed to encourage collaboration between development and operations, ultimately resulting in failures. Then, we discussed the motivation for the DevOps cultural shift.

We then progressed to introduce the DevOps toolchain in detail. Each stage of the toolchain was explained, firstly as a black box, and later, cloud-native modern implementations were discussed. We mentioned that each stage of the DevOps toolchain aims to increase collaboration and create a successful software project. Through the chain, a DevOps blog was planned, created, and released. At the end of the chapter, this DevOps blog was automated with a CI/CD pipeline within an activity.

The DevOps toolchain and DevOps practices discussed in this chapter will be revisited in later chapters to be implemented inside Kubernetes. In the next chapter, we will be describing the fundamentals of cloud-native technologies, microservices, and containers. These concepts are essential, since they are the building blocks of container orchestration and Kubernetes.

Introduction to Microservices and Containers

Learning Objectives

By the end of this lesson, you will be able to:

- Summarize the basics of microservice architecture
- Demonstrate the fundamental concepts of Docker
- Build and release Docker containers
- Run and share volumes and ports using Docker containers

This lesson gives an introduction to microservices and containerization.

Introduction

Microservices are one of the most recent and prominent trends in software development and architecture. Nowadays, applications are designed as a set of loosely-coupled services in microservice architecture. These "micro" services are expected to be developed independently, and they focus on a small subset of business functionalities. For instance, let's imagine developing a banking application with a web frontend for its customers and multiple backend services. It is expected to run frontend and backend services independently, and the frontend finds the IP address of the backend from discovery services to send queries. Each service focuses only on its business functionality and does not directly depend on other services. This architecture enables faster development, bug-fixing, and customer responsiveness. Therefore, it is inevitable for competitive organizations to engage in microservice architecture.

Creating single and large applications, namely, monolithic architecture, was a common approach in the past. All the functionalities of an application were packaged into a single process and delivered to customers as a single binary. It was easy to build, deploy, and update; however, it lacked horizontal scalability. For instance, let's assume that you have purchased a human-resources system such as a monolith application and installed it into costly servers in your data center. Within a couple of months, you realize that everything works, but the payroll systems are not responding fast enough because complex calculations are required for your company. The most straightforward solution is to buy another high-priced server and run two instances of the complete HR system. Although you only need faster payroll operations, it will cost you more than double since you must upgrade the whole system. This is the main problem with monolith applications; that is, without proper scalability based on usage levels, monolithic architecture is doomed to fail in the long run.

On the other hand, microservice architecture puts each business functionality into a separate service so that you can quickly increase the number of "only" payroll service replicas. Even better than this is that it can scale itself automatically with the usage level – since the microservice architecture will not span the complete resources of the servers. The scalability of microservices makes them the ultimate choice for the successful applications of today and the future compared to the monolithic architecture of yesterday.

Using traditional methods and tools for a new architectural style of microservices is impractical. Dramatic changes are needed for the development, build, testing, and runtime environment due to the requirements of microservice architecture. Prior to the last decade, the only solution for this was to actually run applications on physical servers. Since our applications are now "micro" services, it is possible to run multiple services on the same host.

However, this comes with its own risks, such as conflicting dependency libraries or causing a chaotic domino effect of failing applications in the same host. Virtualization is the solution to this problem; it creates multiple virtual servers or virtual machines (VMs) on the same physical server. It is a very well established and popular technology, and it is the fundamental service provided by all cloud providers, such as AWS, Google Cloud, Azure, and Alibaba Cloud. However, a fine level of virtualization is required considering the scalability and the high number of microservices in a complex application. Containerization technology provides a high level of virtualization as a de facto runtime solution for microservices:

A lightweight runtime: VMs partition the physical server by using a comprehensive operating system as their runtime environment. Considering the scope of microservices, using one VM for one microservice results in heavy infrastructure costs. In addition, there is theoretically no need for a completely "new" operating system to run an application. In order to reach the scalability required by microservices, virtualization is moved one level closer to the application. Containerization focuses on virtualization at the operating system level so that multiple containers are able to share the same operating system without interfering with each other. *Figure* 2.1 shows how VMs and containers are structured as layers on top of the infrastructure. Each microservice running in its container creates a separate execution environment while reducing the overhead and enabling scalability. Compared to VMs, containers – with their lightweight runtime environments – are a better option for running microservice applications.

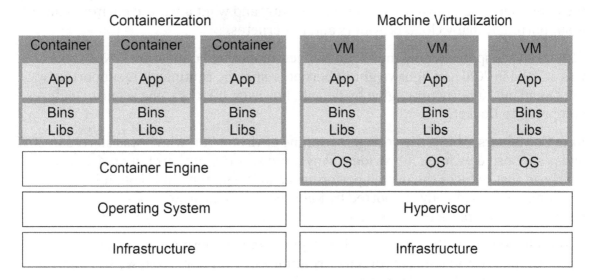

Figure 2.1: The VM and container layers on top of the infrastructure

The build and run speed: Hypervisors start VMs on physical servers, and it could take a couple of minutes to bootstrap and start a complete operating system. In order to solve this issue, some additional idle VMs could be initialized and kept ready for workloads, but this will come with extra costs. On the other hand, microservices are started inside an operating system with less overhead and in a couple of seconds. Today's applications are expected to react more quickly to spikes in usage levels, and so waiting a couple of minutes is not acceptable in most cases. Containers are a better option compared to physical servers and VMs to run scalable, reliable, and robust applications when considering these performance concerns.

Microservice architecture focuses on the design and operations of multiple services but does not indicate any runtime choice. Containers are the most appropriate runtime environment considering the requirements of scalability, reliability, and responsiveness of today's applications. It is best if you start your microservices journey from scratch. However, it is also acceptable if you have a well-established system such as Netflix running an entire microservice architecture on AWS instances instead of containers. Container runtimes are standardized under the Container Runtime Interface (CRI) so that container orchestrators such as Kubernetes can support different runtimes. There are open source and licensed container runtimes available in the market, such as Docker Engine, CRI-O, and Kata Containers:

Docker Engine: This was started in 2013 and is currently being supported by Docker Inc. It is the most widely adopted, popular, and mature environment, which has been tested by a huge number of users and organizations. It is the best choice if you started the containerization of your applications recently and want a mature environment that is supported by many cloud providers and Kubernetes.

CRI-O: This is sponsored by the Cloud Native Computing Foundation (CNCF) and was started in 2016 as a lightweight Kubernetes-specific runtime. It is supported by the OpenShift Kubernetes engine by default; however, it lacks some security features compared to Docker.

Kata Containers: This is the youngest runtime environment, which was started in 2017 and is supported by Intel. It provides many more security options but creates extra overhead that reduces the overall performance of the system. Although it is a young environment, it is already supported by Kubernetes and is promising for enterprises because of its extra security options.

In this chapter, we will focus on Docker Engine, since Kubernetes support it and it is the most mature and popular container runtime environment. First, we will introduce Docker using a "Hello World" container. Second, we will explain container images and image repositories. We'll then continue by presenting methods that can be used to share resources between the host system and the containers. Finally, we will perform an activity to run a WordPress blog using a database connection inside a Docker container.

Introduction to Docker

Docker is an open source container runtime system based on Linux containers. Linux containers use Linux kernel features such as namespaces, control groups (cgroups), and layered filesystems:

- **Namespaces:** Namespaces isolate each application from the host and other applications by creating separate environments.

- **cgroups:** In Linux, cgroups are used to limit applications for a specific set of resources such as memory or processing power.

- **Layered filesystems:** Layered filesystems consist of reusable layers stacked on top of each other to form the base of a root filesystem. They are the primary technology that enables containers to be lightweight.

Namespaces and cgroups surround the containers that are to be isolated and limited; whereas a layered filesystem consists of what is shared and packaged inside the containers. When you consider the popularity of Docker, the following three essential features make it prominent:

- **Speed:** Docker containers are lightweight, and their engines work quickly not only on data center servers but also on developer laptops. Therefore, they shorten the time that is required to debug problems, test fixes, and release new versions.

- **Ecosystem:** The Docker ecosystem enables newcomers to build and run containerized applications. It is possible to find, download, and start a Docker container from the Docker Hub registry in a couple of seconds. Docker Hub is a free-to-use Docker container registry, which is similar to the mobile application store in Apple or Android.

- **Usability:** Docker makes it easier to run containers for everyone, including developers, quality teams, and operators. It made the motto of Java "build once run everywhere" real with its easy-to-use client and API.

The speed, vibrant ecosystem, and usability features of Docker make it the container runtime that comes to mind first. In order to learn about Docker in detail and use it, we need to cover some fundamental concepts next.

> **Note**
>
> You are required to have Docker Engine installed on your local system before starting on the fundamental concepts and the exercise. Download and install the Docker Desktop based on your local operating system from the Docker website at https://www.docker.com/products/docker-desktop.

The Fundamental Concepts of Docker

In this section, the basic concepts of Docker are explained in detail as some of them are used interchangeably in various blogs and tutorials. Starting from the operating system part of Docker itself to the containers, the fundamental concepts are visualized in *Figure 2.2*, as follows:

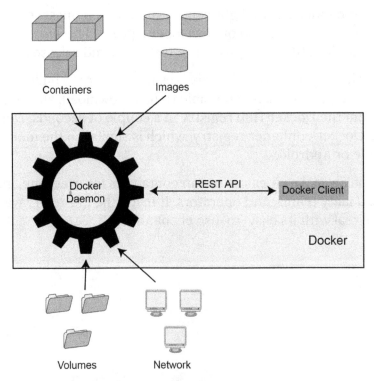

Figure 2.2: The fundamental concepts of Docker

Docker Engine

Docker Engine is the layer on top of the operating system where the containers run. It consists of the **Docker Daemon** running in the host system and the **Docker Client** in order to communicate with its daemon service.

Docker Daemon

Docker Daemon is the service that runs on the host system and manages the containers and their interactions with external systems. We can easily check whether the daemon is installed and running on the Docker system by executing the following command:

```
ps aux |grep docker
```

```
/devops $ ps aux |grep docker
    1 root      0:00 dockerd --host=unix:///var/run/docker.sock --host=tcp://0.0.0.0:2375
   20 root      0:01 containerd --config /var/run/docker/containerd/containerd.toml --log-level info
/devops $ 
```

Figure 2.3: The process status output filtered for Docker

If you cannot see any process items for Docker in the process status output, you could check for them by restarting the daemon with the commands based on your operating system. If you see a couple of items like in Figure 2.3, it shows that the daemon is working and is accessible by Docker Client.

Docker Client

Docker Client is the tool that is used for interacting with Docker Daemon and, by default, it is accessible by a Docker command in the Terminal. In a system where Docker is installed and running, the version and API information can be checked using the following command:

```
docker version
```

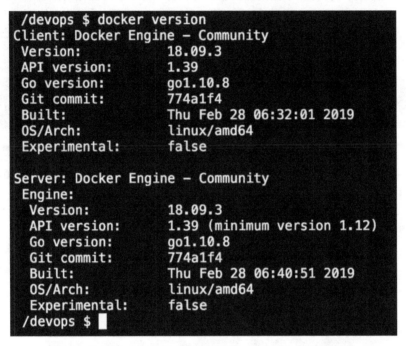

```
/devops $ docker version
Client: Docker Engine - Community
 Version:           18.09.3
 API version:       1.39
 Go version:        go1.10.8
 Git commit:        774a1f4
 Built:             Thu Feb 28 06:32:01 2019
 OS/Arch:           linux/amd64
 Experimental:      false

Server: Docker Engine - Community
 Engine:
  Version:          18.09.3
  API version:      1.39 (minimum version 1.12)
  Go version:       go1.10.8
  Git commit:       774a1f4
  Built:            Thu Feb 28 06:40:51 2019
  OS/Arch:          linux/amd64
  Experimental:     false
/devops $ █
```

Figure 2.4: The output of the docker version command

This lists the version of the client and server with the corresponding API versions and further information about the runtime environment. This command is helpful if any unexpected API mismatches occur between the client and the daemon.

Docker Images

Docker images are read-only packages, which can include operating system libraries and application requirements, if necessary. Docker images are defined using Dockerfiles which include stepwise actions on the base image. Dockerfiles are used when Docker images are built, and each step that is specified in a Dockerfile is executed on the base image. Official and community-maintained images are designed to be stored in the Docker registry, and Docker Hub is the official one; for instance, Ubuntu images can be checked in the Docker registry, as follows:

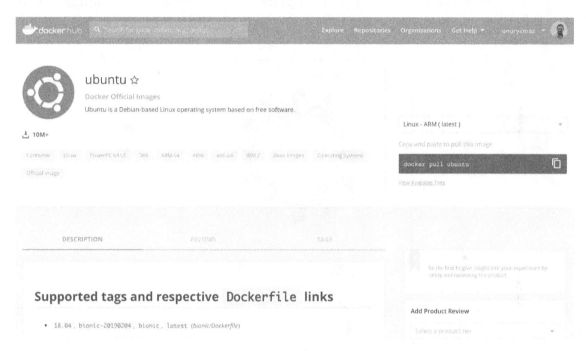

Figure 2.5: The official Ubuntu Docker image in Docker Hub

The Docker registry page for Ubuntu lists all of the available versions and quick-start information to run containers using an Ubuntu image. It is possible to download any Docker image from the Docker registry in a couple of seconds, and it is one of the reasons that makes the Docker environment a popular one.

Docker Containers

Docker containers are running instances of Docker images that consist of an execution environment for applications. They are expected to run many instances of the same Docker image; in other words, multiple Docker containers. Two essential features are added to containers in addition to the images; first, since Docker images are read-only, Docker containers include an additional filesystem layer to enable read-and-write capabilities. Additionally, a network interface is attached to those containers with an available IP so that containers are reachable from the host system and from outside. The flow of Docker images to the registry, and then to the containers is summarized in Figure 2.6:

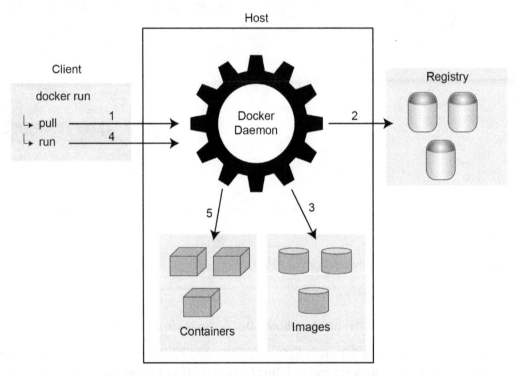

Figure 2.6: The flow of the Docker container and image

In the following exercise, we will combine these fundamental concepts in order to run and manage a "Hello World" container in Docker.

Exercise 5: Creating a "Hello World" Container in Docker

In this exercise, we aim to create and manage a "Hello World" container in Docker Engine.

To complete the exercise, we need to ensure the following steps are executed:

1. Ensure that Docker is working as expected by running the following command:

    ```
    docker version
    ```

```
/devops $ docker version
Client: Docker Engine - Community
 Version:           18.09.3
 API version:       1.39
 Go version:        go1.10.8
 Git commit:        774a1f4
 Built:             Thu Feb 28 06:32:01 2019
 OS/Arch:           linux/amd64
 Experimental:      false

Server: Docker Engine - Community
 Engine:
  Version:          18.09.3
  API version:      1.39 (minimum version 1.12)
  Go version:       go1.10.8
  Git commit:       774a1f4
  Built:            Thu Feb 28 06:40:51 2019
  OS/Arch:          linux/amd64
  Experimental:     false
/devops $
```

Figure 2.7: The output of the docker version command

Here, you should see both the client and server version with their matching API versions in order to operate in harmony. In Figure 2.7, both the client and server have the same version of 18.09.3 and the same API version of 1.39, which indicates that our Docker engine is working.

2. Create a **hello-world** container by running the following command:

    ```
    docker run hello-world
    ```

    ```
    /devops $ docker run hello-world
    Unable to find image 'hello-world:latest' locally
    latest: Pulling from library/hello-world
    1b930d010525: Pull complete
    Digest: sha256:2557e3c07ed1e38f26e389462d03ed943586f744621577a99efb77324b0fe535
    Status: Downloaded newer image for hello-world:latest

    Hello from Docker!
    This message shows that your installation appears to be working correctly.

    To generate this message, Docker took the following steps:
     1. The Docker client contacted the Docker daemon.
     2. The Docker daemon pulled the "hello-world" image from the Docker Hub.
        (amd64)
     3. The Docker daemon created a new container from that image which runs the
        executable that produces the output you are currently reading.
     4. The Docker daemon streamed that output to the Docker client, which sent it
        to your terminal.

    To try something more ambitious, you can run an Ubuntu container with:
     $ docker run -it ubuntu bash

    Share images, automate workflows, and more with a free Docker ID:
     https://hub.docker.com/

    For more examples and ideas, visit:
     https://docs.docker.com/get-started/

    /devops $ ▮
    ```

    Figure 2.8: The output of docker run hello-world

In *Figure* 2.8, the first line indicates **Unable to find image 'hello-world: latest' locally**, which is to be expected if this container image is never used locally. In the following lines, the Docker image is downloaded from the registry, which is indicated by "**latest: Pulling from library/hello-world**". After downloading, **Hello from Docker!** shows the first outputs of the running containers. These stages are also described in the four steps in the output.

3. Check the Docker process status by executing the following command:

    ```
    docker ps
    ```

Figure 2.9: The output of docker ps

Since the **hello-world** container has been started and completed, there is no container listed in the output. When the same command is used with the **--all** flag to show all the containers, the **hello-world** container is expected to be listed:

```
docker ps --all
```

Figure 2.10: The output of docker ps --all

The container with **ID b06d40f39b58** has an **Exited (0) 3 minutes ago** status, which shows that it was completed successfully.

In this exercise, we have demonstrated how to run a simple Docker container and check its status. In addition, we have shown how the Docker image is downloaded from the Docker registry automatically and is ready to reuse locally. In the following section, we will explain how to build a Docker container and publish it to the Docker registry in order to show how applications are built and released as Docker containers.

Building Docker Images

Docker images consist of applications with their dependencies and they are ready to be launched at scale. In addition, they are suitable to run on cloud servers and data centers because of their lightweight architecture. Docker images are created from the steps defined in **Dockerfile**, where each instruction forms a layer on top of the previous one. This layered design of images is the prominent feature that makes Docker images lightweight and quick to start. The underlying technology of layered Docker images is the **union file system (UFS)**. The UFS can be considered as stackable layers of files and directories. Each layer is traceable back to its parent layer in a tree structure so that different branches can share the same root. In other words, if two container images have the same base image of **ubuntu:18.10**, this base image will not be replicated twice; Docker Engine will reuse the same base image to run these two containers. In the next sections, we will present Dockerfiles, how containers are defined, and how they are released in registries.

Dockerfiles

A Dockerfile consists of the necessary commands that are required to build a Docker image in a sequential scheme. Docker Engine uses the text file in **Dockerfile** format to create the Docker image and this file consists of the steps defined with the commands including but not limited to:

- **FROM:** The base image for the container as a starting phase

- **ADD:** To copy files from the host system into the container filesystem

- **ENV:** The environment variables for the container

- **RUN:** To execute commands in the container, such as running commands in the Terminal

- **WORKDIR:** The working directory to run the container commands

- **CMD:** The executable command to run every time the container starts

> **Note**
>
> A complete list of supported commands in Dockerfile is available in the official reference document at https://docs.docker.com/engine/reference/builder/.

An example **Dockerfile** is defined for a web server using the following script:

- The base image of **ubuntu:18.10**.

- The **RUN** commands to update the **apt-get** repositories, install **nodejs** and **npm**, and install **http-server**.

- **WORKDIR** is defined as the **/usr/apps/hello-world/** folder that is used for HTML files in the future.

- The executable command to run **http-server** on port **8080**. Since **WORKDIR** was defined previously, the **CMD** command will run in the **/usr/apps/hello-world/** folder:

```
FROM ubuntu:18.10
RUN apt-get update
RUN apt-get install -y nodejs npm
RUN npm install -g http-server

WORKDIR /usr/apps/hello-world/

CMD ["http-server", "-p", "8080"]
```

The Docker Registry

Docker registries are the solution for building and delivering containers in a cloud-native way. A Docker registry is a content delivery and storage solution for Docker images, which are tagged, given specific versions, and different tags of the same Docker image are kept in the same repository. Docker registries play a crucial role in continuous delivery and deployment. They make it possible to run hundreds of instances in a distributed cluster by storing them efficiently and delivering them in a scalable fashion. Cloud registries provide a high level of security features that could work for startups and large enterprises. There are various cloud registry services, and some of the most popular ones are as follows:

- Docker Hub: https://hub.docker.com/

- Quay: https://quay.io/

- AWS EC2 Container Registry: https://aws.amazon.com/ecr/

- Google Container Registry: https://cloud.google.com/container-registry/

In the following exercise, we will build a Docker image and push it to the Docker registry. This will demonstrate how to build and deliver images in a cloud-native way, which is a prerequisite for running containerized microservices in cloud systems such as Kubernetes.

> **Note**
>
> You will need a Docker Hub account to push the images into the registry in the following exercise. Docker Hub is a free service and you can sign up to it at https://hub.docker.com/signup.

Exercise 6: Building a Docker Image and Pushing it to Docker Hub

In this exercise, we aim to build and push a web server container to Docker Engine.

To complete the exercise, we need to ensure the following steps are executed:

1. Create a text file with the **Dockerfile** name, and include the following content:

    ```
    FROM ubuntu:18.10

    RUN apt-get update
    RUN apt-get install -y nodejs npm
    RUN npm install -g http-server
    WORKDIR /usr/apps/hello-world/

    CMD ["http-server", "-p", "8080"]
    ```

    > **Note**
    >
    > Dockerfile is already available at https://github.com/TrainingByPackt/Introduction-to-DevOps-with-Kubernetes/blob/master/Lesson02/Dockerfile.

2. Build the Docker image with the tag including your Docker Hub username:

    ```
    docker build -t <USERNAME>/webserver:latest .
    ```

    ```
    Step 4/6 : RUN npm install -g http-server
     ---> Running in 0f396b76aec2
    /usr/local/bin/http-server -> /usr/local/lib/node_modules/http-server/bin/http-server
    /usr/local/bin/hs -> /usr/local/lib/node_modules/http-server/bin/http-server
    + http-server@0.11.1
    added 26 packages from 28 contributors in 1.828s
    Removing intermediate container 0f396b76aec2
     ---> af58852bddf1
    Step 5/6 : WORKDIR /usr/apps/hello-world/
     ---> Running in ec186c8af514
    Removing intermediate container ec186c8af514
     ---> 8fe41aafe5fd
    Step 6/6 : CMD ["http-server", "-p", "8080"]
     ---> Running in c58344f16572
    Removing intermediate container c58344f16572
     ---> 1e54f0e11db7
    Successfully built 1e54f0e11db7
    Successfully tagged onuryilmaz/webserver:latest
    ```

    Figure 2.11: The output of docker build (end of the run)

Building the image includes installing various libraries, therefore, a long output is to be expected. At the end of the build, you will see **Successfully built 1e54f0e11db7** and **Successfully tagged onuryilmaz/webserver:latest** on the screen, which indicate successful completion.

3. Create a repository in Docker Hub with the webserver name:

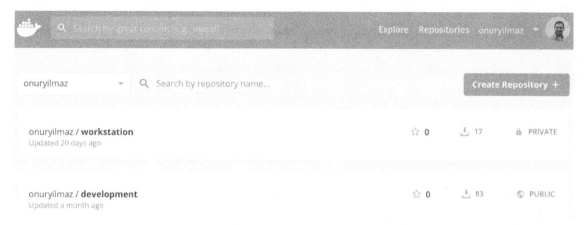

Figure 2.12: The repository view in Docker Hub

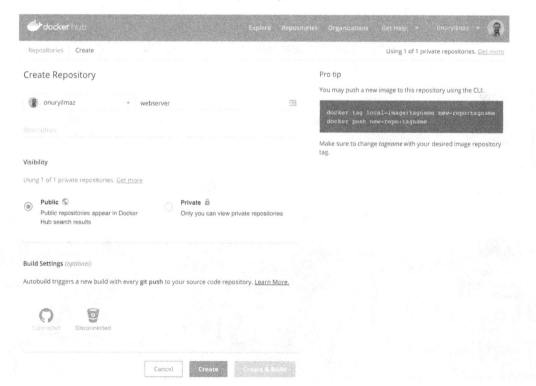

Figure 2.13: Create a repository in Docker Hub

Fill the name field with webserver and ensure that you select **Public** under Visibility. Click on the **Create** button, and you will be redirected to the new repository page:

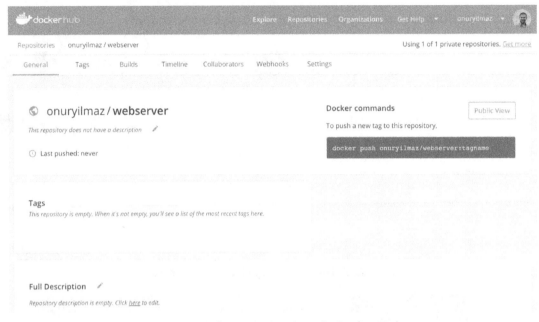

Figure 2.14: The new repository in Docker Hub

> **Note**
>
> If this is the first time that you are using Docker client with your Docker Hub account, you need to log in using the **docker login** command from the Terminal.

4. Push the image to the Docker hub registry, as follows:

```
docker push <USERNAME>/webserver
```

```
/devops $ docker push onuryilmaz/webserver
The push refers to repository [docker.io/onuryilmaz/webserver]
f3c7a67296fc: Pushed
aecb98836ce4: Pushed
c078b95af013: Pushed
907e8eef2e88: Pushed
ea19f72c880c: Mounted from library/ubuntu
aa01286a0869: Mounted from library/ubuntu
587d38c9e2dd: Mounted from library/ubuntu
ed787fb1c1c4: Mounted from library/ubuntu
latest: digest: sha256:5bfef3935a1c3a1dd3ce9332822cf6a998f3197bd59b938fd02975bc7fd406fc size: 1993
/devops $
```

Figure 2.15: The output of docker push

Following successful completion, all layers inside the Docker image should be uploaded. The new image with the **latest** tag can be checked from the Docker Hub in the Tags section of the repository:

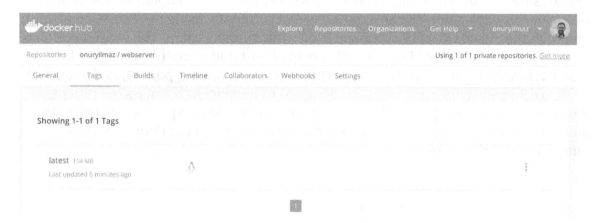

Figure 2.16: Tags of the new repository in Docker Hub

In this exercise, we demonstrated how to build a Docker image and push the image to the Docker registry in Docker Hub. In the following section, we will explain how you can run a Docker container and share resources from the host system in order to demonstrate the fundamentals of managing containers in the cloud.

Running Docker Containers

Containers in Docker are considered ephemeral environments where executables are run, and no state is kept. This is partially true, since the data generated inside the container is only available in the same container. However, Docker Engine provides methods that allow you to share data between the host system and containers. In addition, the services inside the containers are reachable between the host system and other containers.

In this section, we will explain how to run Docker containers using volume and port mapping in order to show how containers are used for stateful services. Running a container starts by running processes, which are packaged as Docker images, as isolated containers. This could be initiated by the **docker run** command, or programmatically by using the Docker API on local or remote host systems. Docker Engine provides more than just running processes and it can attach networks or volumes, ensure runtime constraints on resources, or add Linux privileges. In this section, the two fundamental capabilities that are presented are **port mapping** and **volume mapping**:

Port Mapping: Docker Engine allows containers to connect to the outside world by default, however, it does not allow incoming traffic to containers. There are a couple of **docker run** options to allow incoming traffic to containers; the first option is to use the **--publish-all=true** flag to enable all the ports exposed in the container. The required ports for this application can be exposed in Dockerfiles by using the **EXPOSE** command, and then the **--publish-all** flag can be used while running them. The second option is to explicitly use the **--publish** flag with a map of host and container ports; for instance, **--publish=8080:80** will map the host port **8080** to the container port **80**, as demonstrated in Figure 2.17. Since microservices are designed to implement business operations, having an API and being reachable from the outside world is expected behavior. Docker and container orchestration tools provide reliably-running containers while also enabling network access:

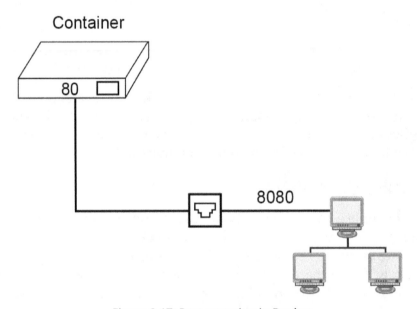

Figure 2.17: Port mapping in Docker

Volume Mapping: Docker is designed so that containers do not contain persistent data. If any data is stored in the writable layer of a container, it will be unavailable when the container is stopped. In order to solve this issue, Docker provides volume-mounting options in the **docker run** command. It is possible to mount a file or folder from the host filesystem to a running command using the **--volume** flag. For instance, the **--volume=/var/data:/db/data** flag will mount the **/var/data** folder of the host system to the **/db/data** folder of the container. Mounted files and folders are writable from inside the container so that they are reusable when the containers are restarted.

Mounted volumes from the host system and ephemeral temporary storage in memory are demonstrated in Figure 2.18. Although containers are considered for ephemeral business operations, containerization with volume capabilities makes it possible to run and manage stateful applications such as databases:

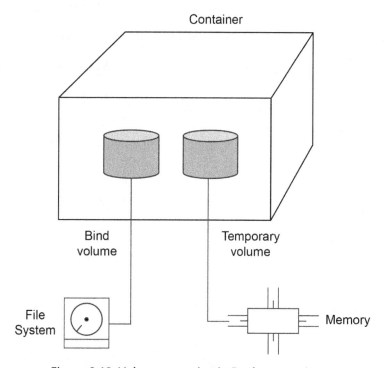

Figure 2.18: Volume mapping in Docker containers

In the following exercise, we will run the Docker image of the web server from the previous exercise using host volume mapping and port sharing. By doing so, we will demonstrate how you can manage the data and networking of containers when they run at scale.

Exercise 7: Running Docker Containers, Volume Mapping, and Port Sharing

In this exercise, we aim to run the web server container using host volume mapping and port sharing.

To complete this exercise, we need to ensure the following steps are executed:

1. Create a text file with the **index.html** name, and the following content.

    This file consists of a simple HTML page with a **Hello DevOps World** header:

    ```
    <html>
        <body>
            <h1>Hello DevOps World</h1>
        </body>
    </html>
    ```

    > **Note**
    >
    > **index.html** is already available at https://github.com/TrainingByPackt/
    > Introduction-to-DevOps-with-Kubernetes/blob/master/Lesson02/index.html

2. Start the container using the following command:

    ```
    docker run -it \
    -p 8080:8080 \
    -v ${PWD}:/usr/apps/hello-world/ \
    <USERNAME>/webserver:latest
    ```

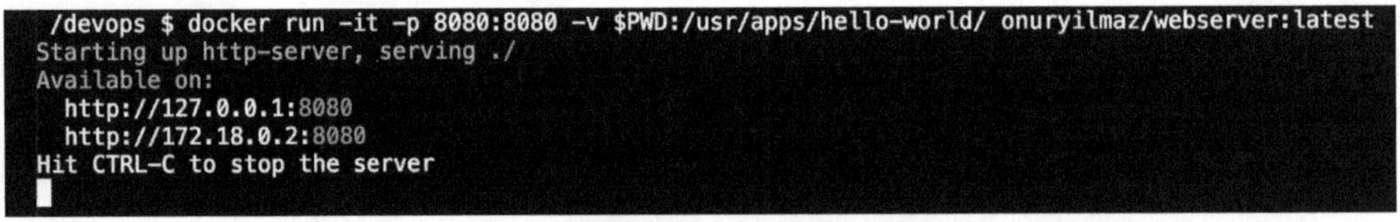

    ```
    /devops $ docker run -it -p 8080:8080 -v $PWD:/usr/apps/hello-world/ onuryilmaz/webserver:latest
    Starting up http-server, serving ./
    Available on:
      http://127.0.0.1:8080
      http://172.18.0.2:8080
    Hit CTRL-C to stop the server
    ```

Figure 2.19: The output of the docker run command

Using this command, a volume is mapped from the pathname of the current Working Directory **($PWD)** to **/usr/apps/hello-world/**, where the web server inside the container is running. Additionally, port **8080** from the host system is mapped to port **8080** of the container. This indicates that the container will be reachable from the **8080** port of the host system.

3. Check the running containers in another Terminal, as follows:

```
docker ps
```

Figure 2.20: The output of the docker ps command

You can expect to see an instance of **<USERNAME>/webserver** with a status that is similar to **Up About a minute** and the published ports.

4. Open **http://localhost:8080** in a browser, as follows:

Figure 2.21: The web server in the browser

This shows that the web server is working and that the container is reachable through host port mapping. In addition, the output shows the file created in Step 1, which also indicates that volume mapping is working.

5. Stop the container started in *Step 2* using the *Ctrl + C* command.

In this exercise, we demonstrated how you can run a stateful container that is reachable from the host system. In the following activity, we will create a stateful database instance using Docker containers and a WordPress blog instance to connect to the database and run coherently.

Activity 2: Installing a WordPress Blog and Database Using Docker

The aim of this activity is to install and manage a **MySQL** database and **WordPress** blog using Docker containers. **WordPress** is based on **PHP** and is a free and open source content management system. It needs a MySQL database as its data source for user and content management. In this activity, both the database and blog containers should be ephemeral, however, persistent data should be kept on the host system. Additionally, these two containers should interact with each other using Docker functionalities.

> **Note**
>
> WordPress is the most popular content management system on the internet, and it is used by more than 60 million websites, including 30.6% of the top 10 million websites as of April 2018. It can be found at https://wordpress.org/.
>
> MySQL is an open source relational database, which was first released in 1995, and is still one of the most popular database management systems with more than six million installations. It can be found at https://www.mysql.com/.

Using the Docker commands from the previous exercises in this chapter, you can expect to have two containers running and communicating with each other. With the successful start of the WordPress container, you should see the setup screens as follows:

Figure 2.22: The setup steps for installing WordPress

After setup, the new blog should be up and running, as follows:

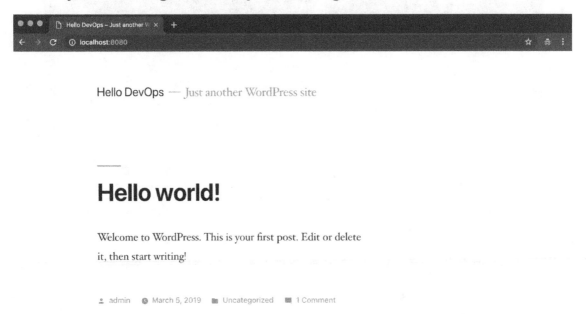

Hello DevOps — Just another WordPress site

Hello world!

Welcome to WordPress. This is your first post. Edit or delete it, then start writing!

admin   March 5, 2019   Uncategorized   1 Comment

Figure 2.23: The home page of the WordPress blog

Execute the following steps to complete this activity:

1. Create a folder named **data**. This folder will keep the stateful state of the database in the next steps.

2. Start a MySQL container using the official Docker image and the following specifications:

   Use the data folder from Step 1 as the database file. Publish port 3306 to the local system. Set the **MYSQL_ROOT_PASSWORD** environment variable as rootPassword. Set the **MYSQL_DATABASE** environment variable as database. Set the **MYSQL_USER** environment variable as user. Set the **MYSQL_PASSWORD** environment variable as password. Use **mysql** as the name of the container. Use the **mysql:5.7** container image

   Wait for the MySQL container to be ready using a similar logline to **[Note] mysqld: ready for connections**.

3. Start a WordPress container using the following specification:

   Publish port **80** of the container to port **8080** of the host system. Link the **mysql** container using the **db** name. Set the **WORDPRESS_DB_HOST** environment variable as **db:3306**. Set the **WORDPRESS_DB_NAME** environment variable as **database**. Set the **WORDPRESS_DB_USER** environment variable as **user**. Set the **WORDPRESS_DB_PASSWORD** environment variable as **password**. Use **WordPress** as the name of the container. Use the **latest** WordPress container image.

4. Open **http://localhost:8080** in the browser and fill out the WordPress setup form.

5. Open **http://localhost:8080** in the browser and check that your new blog is running in the containers.

6. Stop the running containers and remove the data folder.

> **Note**
>
> The solution of this activity can be found on page 304.

In this activity, we have presented how to operate a WordPress blog and its database on the same host using Docker. With this basic activity of running a single instance blog, you can imagine how difficult it is to run and manage hundreds of blogs and databases in a cloud environment. For instance, it is a fundamental problem if two blog containers are using the same HTTP ports and running on the same host. Additionally, consider running a database container with volume mapping and what will happen if the node is broken; in this instance, the container could start running on another node, but its node will not have the data at all. Operational problems like this and many more are already being embraced by Kubernetes in order to run reliable and scalable applications, and this will be explained in *Chapter 3, Introduction to Kubernetes*.

Summary

In this chapter, we first described the microservice architecture and compared it to monolith applications. We discussed how traditional methods for the development, building, testing, and runtime environments could fail for running microservices in a cloud-native environment. Then, we explored containers in detail and explained why they have become the de facto solution for microservices. Following this, we presented different container runtime environments and introduced Docker. The fundamental concepts of Docker containers were covered, including Docker Engine, client, image, and container terminology. Following the theoretical background, we built Docker images and stored them in registries. Finally, we ran Docker containers by sharing volumes and ports from host systems. At the end of the chapter, we used Docker containers to create a stateful popular MySQL database and a WordPress blog in order to show how multiple containers can work in harmony.

Docker concepts and operational knowledge was discussed throughout the chapter, and we will be revisiting this in the following chapter on Kubernetes. Since Docker is the default container runtime for Kubernetes, it is crucial to have fundamental knowledge of Docker and some practical hands-on experience, as covered in this chapter.

3

Introduction to Kubernetes

Learning Objectives

By the end of this chapter, you will be able to:

- Acquaint yourself with the various sections of Kubernetes architecture

- Install a local Kubernetes solution and create a cluster

- Access a Kubernetes cluster graphically and by using the command-line interface (CLI)

- Work with the building-block concepts of Kubernetes

- Install a real-life application in a Kubernetes cluster

This chapter gives an introduction to Kubernetes. We will cover Kubernetes history, architecture, and important Kubernetes concepts required for further chapters.

Introduction

Running microservice applications in containers solves problems related to scalability, reliability, and robustness; however, it comes with own its drawbacks. In the previous chapter, a database and blog application were run in Docker containers. If you want to run multiple databases and blogs across numerous servers, there are a couple of issues to consider. For instance, networking should be configured to enable communication between database and blog instances. In addition, the storage of the database instances should be handled so that no data is lost. Furthermore, there should be a method to handle failures at the application and hardware levels. Kubernetes is the answer to solve all these problems, plus many more to run microservice applications in containers in a scalable, reliable, and robust way. In this chapter, the history and architecture of Kubernetes are presented first. After that, accessing Kubernetes clusters is covered, and, finally, Kubernetes concepts and resources are introduced.

What is Kubernetes?

Kubernetes is actually a Greek word meaning ship captain. As ships carry a vast number of containers overseas, it is an excellent analogy for managing containers in the massive ocean of data centers. Kubernetes is also abbreviated as **k8s** to indicate the eight letters between "k" and "s" in both developer communities and source code. Kubernetes started as an open source project backed by Google in 2014. It is the outcome of 15 years of experience in managing containers for almost every Google product, such as Search or Gmail.

From a technical point of view, Kubernetes is a platform for running and managing containers. Kubernetes enables the running of microservice applications, defined as a set of containers on a Kubernetes cluster. It focuses on the complete life cycle of containers to provide scalability and high availability. With Kubernetes, it is possible to define the number of instances of a database application and interaction points with the outside world. You can also scale up or down manually or with usage level, roll out new updates, or redirect customer traffic. Kubernetes provides building blocks to define and manage complex cloud-native applications with a high level of flexibility and reliability.

There are many container orchestration tools in the market, such as Mesos, Docker Swarm, Amazon Elastic Container Service, and Kubernetes. All of these tools have an active community and many organizations adopt them. However, Kubernetes puts itself forward among others with Google support, a significant amount of popularity, and many success stories, including GitHub, GoDaddy, and Workday.

With more than 76,000 commits and nearly 50,000 stars on GitHub, Kubernetes is the most popular open source repository, as shown in *Figure* 3.1. Its vast popularity and fast adoption in the industry made Kubernetes the de facto container management solution:

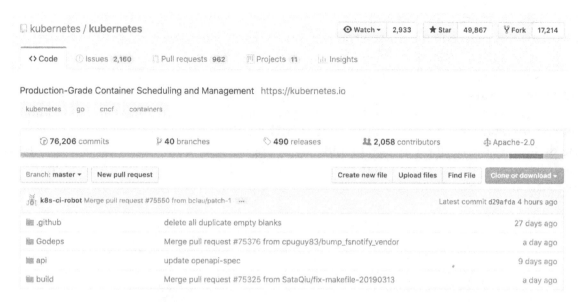

Figure 3.1: Kubernetes GitHub repository

In the following section, the Kubernetes architecture is discussed to give an overall idea of how Kubernetes manages microservices in containers.

Kubernetes Architecture

Kubernetes is a sophisticated platform consisting of various components that enables us to run production-ready container applications robustly and reliably. It is crucial to learn about its architecture and design to understand how it works and why it is so successful. Kubernetes is designed to run applications on clusters on the cloud or on-premise systems. Virtual or physical server instances are used with a shared network in these clusters to operate in harmony. This is the actual environment where all Kubernetes components and user applications are configured and run.

Servers in a Kubernetes cluster are given two essential roles: **master** or **node**. If a server is assigned with the master role, it is expected to run centralized logical components of Kubernetes. It is possible to have more than one master server to achieve high availability, and the master servers run the Kubernetes API server, key/value store, scheduler, and controllers. These components create the brain of Kubernetes that interacts with the outside world and makes decisions based on the changes in the cluster or user demands. Other servers in the clusters are assigned the node role to run the workload as containers. Node servers receive the definition of the workload from the master and create, update, or delete the containers accordingly. In addition, nodes form the required networking and storage for the containers and forward the traffic between them.

Kubernetes with master and node components work on the desired state of applications provided by the Kubernetes API. For example, it is possible to send a declarative **JSON** or **YAML** definition of a workload to the Kubernetes API in master servers. Master components enrich these definitions for the required storage, networking, and computing resources and these are then sent to nodes for execution. Node instances execute the plan by running containerized applications and checking application statuses continuously. To sum up, the Kubernetes cluster tries to achieve the desired state, defined in **JSON** or **YAML**, by changing and testing the actual state. In the following sections, components in the master and node servers are described in more detail, as shown in *Figure 3.2*:

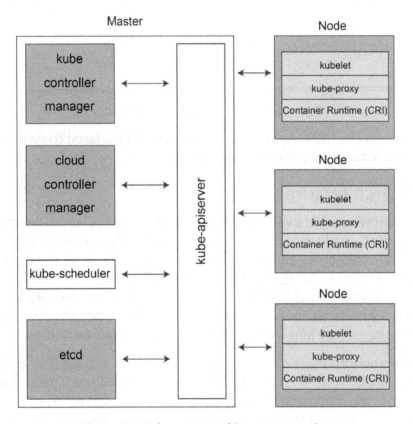

Figure 3.2: Kubernetes architecture overview

Master Components

Master components of Kubernetes, also called the **control plane**, is the primary set of services that provide the API operations, authentication, scheduling, and networking. It is possible to install these components on a single server or distribute across servers. Control plane components and their interaction with each other are as follows:

etcd

etcd is the data store of Kubernetes where all configuration, runtime information, and statuses are stored. The actual statuses and the desired states of resources are stored in **etcd**, which is the only stateful component in the master components. **etcd** is an open source key/value store developed by CoreOS, and is one of the crucial components that make Kubernetes reliable. **etcd** can be installed in multiple master servers, as well as being reachable inside the Kubernetes cluster.

kube-apiserver

The API server is the central management interface in the Kubernetes cluster for user interactions and status information. It is possible to send and receive data from **kube-apiserver**, since it is a RESTful API server. Every workload definition is sent to this API server, and it handles the storing the data in **etcd**. Since Kubernetes is an API-driven platform, **kube-apiserver** is the most critical component in the control plane.

kube-controller-manager

The controller is a general pattern in Kubernetes to manage the life cycle of resources. Controllers are expected to read the new information when a change is seen. Then, they implement the required changes to achieve the desired state. For instance, when an application is scaled up by the user, the data is sent to **kube-apiserver** and persisted in **etcd**. The controller manager of the corresponding resource handles the creation of additional instances. **kube-controller-manager** consists of such controllers to manage the Kubernetes resources.

kube-scheduler

The scheduler is responsible for assigning workload containers to the nodes, taking into account capacity, requirements, and the infrastructure environment. It can be regarded as a continuous loop for checking unassigned workloads and finding appropriate nodes.

cloud-controller-manager

Kubernetes is designed to be installed into any cloud provider that implements required interfaces. It is possible to run Kubernetes on AWS, Google Cloud, Azure, Alibaba Cloud, or on-premise OpenStack systems. Cloud controller managers are the set of bridges that connect Kubernetes resources to the cloud providers. For instance, they manage the storage and networking requirements based on the cloud environment. It is possible to have portable and robust applications running in Kubernetes with the help of cloud controller managers.

Node Components

Node components are responsible for running workloads in Kubernetes. Thus, it is expected to manage containers, networking, and storage operations of the workload assigned to the node. Node components and their interaction with the control plane are as follows:

Container runtime

The container runtime is required to run the workload as containers in the node servers. It is expected to implement the **Container Runtime Interface** (CRI) and **Docker**, **rkt**, and **runc**, which are the notable container runtimes for Kubernetes environment. The main functionality of the container runtime is to start, check the status, and delete containers according to the desired state in Kubernetes.

kubelet

kubelet is the primary service running on the servers that collect information from the control plane and manage the resources in the node. It is expected that kubelet will communicate with the control plane to get desired states and send commands to the container runtime to convert the actual state into the desired one.

kube-proxy

kube-proxy is the service responsible for networking on the node servers. Since containers and the host system are isolated in terms of networking, this is the service that forwards requests to the containers and makes them reachable from the outside world.

In the following exercise, a local Kubernetes solution will be installed, and a cluster will be started to show all master and node components in action.

> **Note**
>
> In the following exercise, the official local Kubernetes solution, namely `minikube`, will be used. It uses a virtual machine (VM) to run all Kubernetes clusters, therefore, it is required that a hypervisor, such as **VirtualBox**, is installed:
>
> https://kubernetes.io/docs/tasks/tools/install-minikube/#install-a-hypervisor

Exercise 8: Installing and Starting a Local Kubernetes Cluster

In this exercise, we aim to install and start a local Kubernetes solution and check for all master and node components.

To complete the exercise, we need to ensure that the following steps are executed:

1. Download the **minikube** executable based on your operating system by running the commands in your local Terminal:

   ```
   # Linux
   curl -Lo minikube https://storage.googleapis.com/minikube/releases/latest/
   minikube-linux-amd64
   # MacOS
   curl -Lo minikube https://storage.googleapis.com/minikube/releases/latest/
   minikube-darwin-amd64
   ```

2. Make the downloaded **minikube** executable and move to the following path:

   ```
   chmod +x minikube
   sudo mv minikube /usr/local/bin
   ```

3. Start the **minikube** cluster:

   ```
   minikube start
   ```

   ```
   /devops $ minikube start
   😄  minikube v0.35.0 on darwin (amd64)
   🔥  Creating virtualbox VM (CPUs=2, Memory=2048MB, Disk=20000MB) ...
   💿  Downloading Minikube ISO ...
    184.42 MB / 184.42 MB [===============================================] 100.00% 0s
   📶  "minikube" IP address is 192.168.99.100
   🐳  Configuring Docker as the container runtime ...
   ✨  Preparing Kubernetes environment ...
   🚜  Downloading kubeadm v1.13.4
   🚜  Downloading kubelet v1.13.4
   🚜  Pulling images required by Kubernetes v1.13.4 ...
   🚀  Launching Kubernetes v1.13.4 using kubeadm ...
   ⌛  Waiting for pods: apiserver proxy etcd scheduler controller addon-manager dns
   🔑  Configuring cluster permissions ...
   🤔  Verifying component health .....
   💗  kubectl is now configured to use "minikube"
   🏄  Done! Thank you for using minikube!
   /devops $ ▊
   ```

   Figure 3.3: Starting the minikube cluster

With this command, the VM image is first downloaded, as mentioned by **Downloading Minikube ISO**. Then, the Kubernetes environment is set inside this VM with the **Preparing Kubernetes environment** line. All required images and tools are downloaded into the VM and a one-node cluster is started.

4. Check for the status and wait for the cluster to be **Running**:

   minikube status

```
/devops $ minikube status
host: Running
kubelet: Running
apiserver: Running
kubectl: Correctly Configured: pointing to minikube-vm at 192.168.99.100
/devops $
```

Figure 3.4: minikube status output

5. Connect to the **minikube** VM using SSH:

   minikube ssh

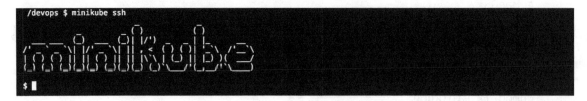

Figure 3.5: Minikube status output

With this command, you are running the commands in the VM that was started in *Step 3*.

6. List the running Docker containers to check the master components:

   docker ps --format 'table {{.Image}}\t{{.Command}}'

```
$ docker ps --format 'table {{.Image}}\t{{.Command}}'
IMAGE                                         COMMAND
gcr.io/k8s-minikube/storage-provisioner       "/storage-provisioner"
k8s.gcr.io/pause:3.1                          "/pause"
fadcc5d2b066                                  "/usr/local/bin/kube…"
k8s.gcr.io/pause:3.1                          "/pause"
f59dcacceff4                                  "/coredns -conf /etc…"
f59dcacceff4                                  "/coredns -conf /etc…"
k8s.gcr.io/pause:3.1                          "/pause"
k8s.gcr.io/pause:3.1                          "/pause"
k8s.gcr.io/kube-addon-manager                 "/opt/kube-addons.sh"
dd862b749309                                  "kube-scheduler --ad…"
3cab8e1b9802                                  "etcd --advertise-cl…"
40a817357014                                  "kube-controller-man…"
fc3801f0fc54                                  "kube-apiserver --au…"
k8s.gcr.io/pause:3.1                          "/pause"
k8s.gcr.io/pause:3.1                          "/pause"
k8s.gcr.io/pause:3.1                          "/pause"
k8s.gcr.io/pause:3.1                          "/pause"
k8s.gcr.io/pause:3.1                          "/pause"
$
```

Figure 3.6: Running containers in minikube

With this command, all Docker containers are listed with their **Image** and **Command** fields. It is possible to find the following master components:

Component	Image	Command
etcd	3cab8e1b9802	etcd --advertise-cl...
kube-apiserver	fc3801f0fc54	kube-apiserver --au...
kube-controller-manager	40a817357014	kube-controller-man...
kube-scheduler	dd862b749309	kube-scheduler --ad...

Figure 3.7: Master components with their respective commands

There is only one master component missing, and it is the cloud-controller-manager. This is an expected result, since `minikube` is not running in a cloud environment, where it would interact with a cloud provider such as AWS or Google Cloud Platform.

7. List the running processes to check the node components:

    ```
    pgrep -a kubelet && pgrep -a kube-proxy
    ```

```
$ pgrep -a kubelet && pgrep -a kube-proxy
3000 /usr/bin/kubelet --kubeconfig=/etc/kubernetes/kubelet.conf --hostname-override=minikube --cluster-domain=cluster.local --authori
zation-mode=Webhook --client-ca-file=/var/lib/minikube/certs/ca.crt --fail-swap-on=false --pod-manifest-path=/etc/kubernetes/manifest
s --allow-privileged=true --cluster-dns=10.96.0.10 --cgroup-driver=cgroupfs --container-runtime=docker --bootstrap-kubeconfig=/etc/ku
bernetes/bootstrap-kubelet.conf
4316 /usr/local/bin/kube-proxy --config=/var/lib/kube-proxy/config.conf --hostname-override=minikube
$
```

Figure 3.8: Running node components

Since we have already interacted with Docker, it is evident that a container runtime will be found in the system. In addition, it is shown that **kubelet** and **kube-proxy** are running on the node, which shows that all required master and node components are running in our one-node local cluster.

8. Exit from the Terminal accessed in *Step 5* by pressing *Ctrl + C*.

> **Note**
>
> The code files for the exercises of this chapter can be found at https://github.com/TrainingByPackt/Introduction-to-DevOps-with-Kubernetes/tree/master/Lesson03

In this exercise, you were shown how to start a one-node local Kubernetes cluster. In addition, we checked all master and node components, so they are expected to be working flawlessly. In the next section, we will look at accessing a Kubernetes cluster to check its status and send workloads to the cluster.

Accessing Kubernetes Clusters

Accessing the Kubernetes clusters is a crucial step for installing and operating the cloud-native applications. In this section, we will look at the two primary ways of reaching Kubernetes clusters. The first method will cover the **Kubernetes Dashboard**, which is a web-based Kubernetes user interface. The second method will use the **Kubernetes CLI**, namely `kubectl`, to access the Kubernetes API. Kubernetes provide a rich API that enables us to install and operate complex cloud-native applications. It is designed as a **RESTful** API and can be consumed programmatically using client libraries as well as tools such as `kubectl`, **Terraform**, or **Ansible**.

Kubernetes Dashboard is the official user interface, which also runs as a containerized web application in the cluster. It is possible to deploy applications, troubleshoot running applications, and check the status of Kubernetes resources. The Dashboard enables basic cluster management and operational tasks, such as scaling applications up or down, or restarting instances. It is a very friendly tool for checking the status of applications and the overall cluster easily. In the following exercise, we'll learn to access the Dashboard and monitor the status of an application.

Exercise 9: Checking Application Status in Kubernetes Dashboard

In this exercise, we aim to access the Kubernetes dashboard and check the status of a running application. To complete the exercise, we need to ensure that the following steps are executed:

1. Run the following command in Terminal to access the Kubernetes dashboard of the cluster running in `minikube`:

    ```
    minikube dashboard
    ```

```
/devops $ minikube dashboard
  Enabling dashboard ...
● Verifying dashboard health ...
  Launching proxy ...
● Verifying proxy health ...
  Opening http://127.0.0.1:51267/api/v1/namespaces/kube-system/services/http:kubernetes-dashboard:/proxy/ in your default browser.
```

Figure 3.9: minikube dashboard command

This output indicates that the dashboard is enabled, and a local proxy is started.

2. Open the address from *Step 1*, if it is not automatically opened, in a browser:

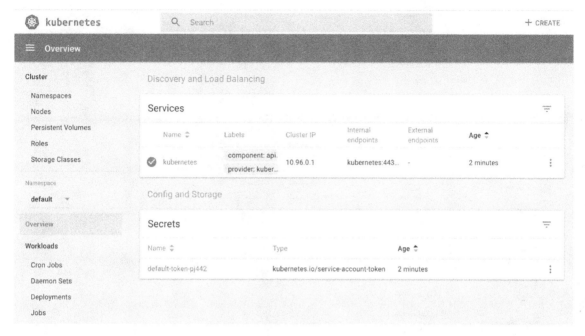

Figure 3.10: Kubernetes dashboard

3. Click **default** and select the **kube-system** namespace from the dropdown:

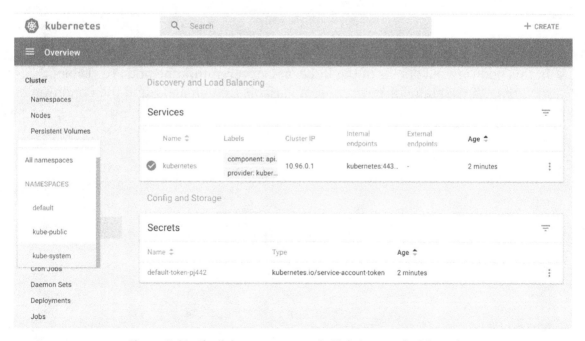

Figure 3.11: Changing namespace in Kubernetes dashboard

4. Scroll down to the **Pods** section and click on **kube-apiserver-minikube**:

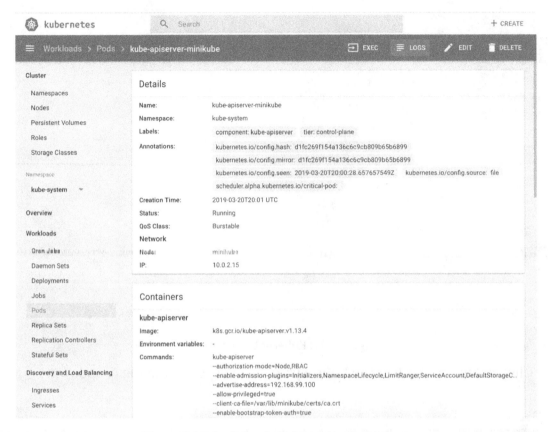

Figure 3.12: Pod view in Kubernetes dashboard

In this pod view, all details of the **kube-apiserver-minikube** pod are visible, including the containers, environment variables, commands, and the condition of the pod.

5. Click **Logs** in the header menu inside the pod view:

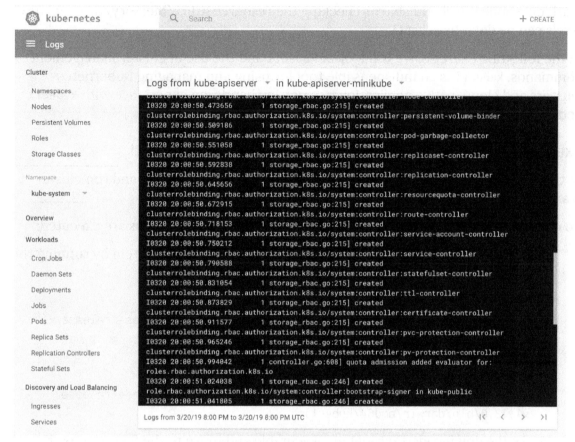

Figure 3.13: Logs of a pod in Kubernetes dashboard

On this screen, the stream of logs from the pod is presented in real time, as if the application were running locally. This is a straightforward way of checking the status of an application and troubleshooting the errors.

6. Stop the proxy started in *Step 1* by pressing *Ctrl + C*.

This exercise walks you through the steps to access the Kubernetes dashboard and check the logs of a running application. Although the dashboard is a handy and human-friendly tool, it is always required to access the Kubernetes API programmatically. Kubernetes provides an open source official CLI tool, namely **kubectl**, to interact with Kubernetes API. It is a CLI tool that can be installed on the local system and it can connect to any cluster with the required credentials. **kubectl** is a powerful tool that can handle not only basic operations, such as getting, deleting, or editing resources, but also cluster management and troubleshooting operations.

For instance, it is possible to deploy an application, check the logs, and create a proxy to the local system to access ports by using **kubectl**. Also, operational tasks, such as marking a node unschedulable or checking the resource (CPU/Memory/Storage) usage levels can be done by **kubectl**.

In the following exercise, we will look at **kubectl** and the use of cluster management commands. **kubectl** is an indispensable tool for using and managing Kubernetes clusters and cloud-native applications, so getting hands-on experience with **kubectl** and incorporating it into your daily workload is crucial.

Exercise 10: Carrying Out Cluster Management Using kubectl

In this exercise, we aim to access the Kubernetes API using **kubectl** and run cluster management commands.

To complete the exercise, we need to ensure that the following steps are executed:

1. Download the **kubectl** executable based on your operating system by running the commands in your local Terminal:

   ```
   # Linux
   curl -LO https://storage.googleapis.com/kubernetes-release/release/
   v1.13.0/bin/linux/amd64/kubectl

   # MacOS
   curl -LO https://storage.googleapis.com/kubernetes-release/release/
   v1.13.0/bin/darwin/amd64/kubectl
   ```

2. Make the downloaded **kubectl** an executable and move to the following path:

   ```
   chmod +x kubectl
   sudo mv kubectl /usr/local/bin
   ```

3. Check **kubectl config** with the following command:

   ```
   kubectl config current-context
   ```

```
/devops $ kubectl config current-context
minikube
/devops $ ▮
```

Figure 3.14: Output of kubectl config current-context

The result of **minikube** indicates that the **kubectl** context is correctly configured to the **minikube** cluster.

4. Check **cluster-info** with the following command:

```
kubectl cluster-info
```

```
/devops $ kubectl cluster-info
Kubernetes master is running at https://192.168.99.100:8443
KubeDNS is running at https://192.168.99.100:8443/api/v1/namespaces/kube-system/services/kube-dns:dns/proxy

To further debug and diagnose cluster problems, use 'kubectl cluster-info dump'.
/devops $
```

Figure 3.15: Output of kubectl cluster-info

This output lists the critical cluster components and their IP addresses. This is helpful output to find out whether there are any broken cluster components.

5. Get the client and server version with the following command:

```
kubectl version
```

```
/devops $ kubectl version
Client Version: version.Info{Major:"1", Minor:"13", GitVersion:"v1.13.0", GitCommit:"ddf47ac13c1a9483ea035a79cd7c10005ff21
a6d", GitTreeState:"clean", BuildDate:"2018-12-03T21:04:45Z", GoVersion:"go1.11.2", Compiler:"gc", Platform:"darwin/amd64"
}
Server Version: version.Info{Major:"1", Minor:"13", GitVersion:"v1.13.4", GitCommit:"c27b913fddd1a6c480c229191a087698aa92f
0b1", GitTreeState:"clean", BuildDate:"2019-02-28T13:30:26Z", GoVersion:"go1.11.5", Compiler:"gc", Platform:"linux/amd64"}
/devops $
```

Figure 3.16: Output of kubectl version

This command lists the versions of the Kubernetes API server and the **kubectl** client, and it is essential to check whether you found any inconsistencies between API requests and responses.

Get the supported API resources by using the following command:

```
kubectl api-resources -o name
```

```
/devops $ kubectl api-resources -o name
bindings
componentstatuses
configmaps
endpoints
events
limitranges
namespaces
nodes
persistentvolumeclaims
persistentvolumes
pods
podtemplates
replicationcontrollers
resourcequotas
secrets
serviceaccounts
services
mutatingwebhookconfigurations.admissionregistration.k8s.io
validatingwebhookconfigurations.admissionregistration.k8s.io
customresourcedefinitions.apiextensions.k8s.io
apiservices.apiregistration.k8s.io
controllerrevisions.apps
daemonsets.apps
deployments.apps
replicasets.apps
statefulsets.apps
tokenreviews.authentication.k8s.io
localsubjectaccessreviews.authorization.k8s.io
selfsubjectaccessreviews.authorization.k8s.io
selfsubjectrulesreviews.authorization.k8s.io
subjectaccessreviews.authorization.k8s.io
horizontalpodautoscalers.autoscaling
cronjobs.batch
jobs.batch
certificatesigningrequests.certificates.k8s.io
leases.coordination.k8s.io
events.events.k8s.io
daemonsets.extensions
deployments.extensions
ingresses.extensions
networkpolicies.extensions
podsecuritypolicies.extensions
replicasets.extensions
networkpolicies.networking.k8s.io
poddisruptionbudgets.policy
podsecuritypolicies.policy
clusterrolebindings.rbac.authorization.k8s.io
clusterroles.rbac.authorization.k8s.io
rolebindings.rbac.authorization.k8s.io
roles.rbac.authorization.k8s.io
priorityclasses.scheduling.k8s.io
storageclasses.storage.k8s.io
volumeattachments.storage.k8s.io
/devops $
```

Figure 3.17: Output of kubectl api-resources

This long list shows all the resources supported by the `minikube` Kubernetes cluster that is running. In the following section, the core building block resources from this list will be presented. Furthermore, throughout this book, most of these resources will be explicitly or implicitly used and discussed.

In this exercise, we've seen how to configure and use `kubectl` to interact with the Kubernetes API. Both the dashboard and `kubectl` are essential parts of the DevOps toolset to make daily life more comfortable, and automate operations. Therefore, it is suggested that you play around with `kubectl` and create aliases and shortcuts to incorporate this tool into your environment. In the following section, Kubernetes will be used to manage workloads, and the very first Kubernetes resources will be presented as the building block of complex cloud-native applications.

Fundamental Kubernetes Resources

Kubernetes creates a powerful abstraction to provide life cycle management of scalable and robust cloud-native applications. Master and node components, as discussed in the previous chapters, work continuously to fulfill the desired state of workloads defined by the users using the Kubernetes API and client tools. In this section, different Kubernetes concepts and resources are explained with their essentials and real-life practices.

The Pod

The pod is the building block of Kubernetes computation objects. A pod consists of containers that are tightly coupled and should be treated as a single application. These containers in the same pod are always scheduled on the same node since they share volume and networking interfaces. Therefore, the pod can be imagined as an encapsulated set of containers that should work together and share the same life cycle, such as scaling up or down together.

Pods can be defined with just one container and its associated metadata and runtime environments. In the following pod definition, a pod with the name **my-first-pod** is presented. There is only one container with the Docker image of **busybox** and the **command** for the **Hello DevOps!** output:

```
apiVersion: v1
kind: Pod
metadata:
  name: my-first-pod
spec:
  containers:
  - name: main
    image: busybox
    command: ['sh', '-c', 'echo Hello DevOps! && sleep 3600']
```

When this pod definition is submitted, Kubernetes schedules this pod to a node in the cluster. The **kubelet** service running in the respective node creates the container with the requirements defined and checks the status continuously by interacting the container runtime. Furthermore, a pod can have more than one containers that should work together and share resources.

In the following pod definition, two containers are defined to share a volume. Furthermore, the following pod follows a pattern of having one **main** container, **nginx**, to serve the files, and has a **sidecar** container, **debian**, to prepare and manage the served files:

```yaml
apiVersion: v1
kind: Pod
metadata:
  name: multiple-containers
spec:
  volumes:
  - name: shared
    emptyDir: {}
  containers:
  - name: main
    image: nginx
    volumeMounts:
    - name: shared
      mountPath: /usr/share/nginx/html
  - name: sidecar
    image: debian
    volumeMounts:
    - name: shared
      mountPath: /shared
    command: ["/bin/sh"]
    args: ["-c", "echo Hello from the sidecar container > /shared/index.html && sleep 3600"]
```

In this pod definition, an empty volume is defined with the name **shared** and mounted into two containers with different paths. The **debian** container writes `Hello from the sidecar container` to `index.html` in this volume, whereas the **nginx** container uses this volume to serve its contents, as illustrated in *Figure 3.18*:

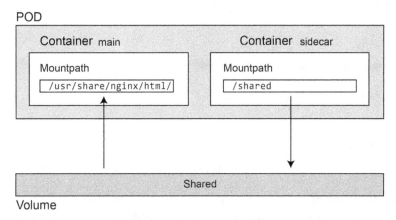

Figure 3.18: Shared volume between containers

Pods are the primary and fundamental building blocks of Kubernetes resources, so they are generally managed by higher levels of resources, such as replication sets, deployments, and stateful sets. In the following sections, we'll examine these higher-level resources and how they fulfill sophisticated scaling and life cycle management requirements.

Replication Sets

Replication sets (`ReplicaSet`) are the Kubernetes resources that maintain a set of replica pods running in the cluster. Kubernetes is designed to enable and support high availability. Therefore, it is expected to have the same pod instances running in the cluster as those defined in the replication sets. Similar to pods, replication sets are building blocks of life cycle management resources, such as deployments. They are used with other high-level resources to scale up or down or roll out new versions of the applications. A replication set definition looks similar to a pod definition, because it encapsulates a pod specification:

```
apiVersion: apps/v1
kind: ReplicaSet
metadata:
  name: high-available-hello
spec:
  replicas: 3
  selector:
```

```
    matchLabels:
      app: hello
  template:
    metadata:
      labels:
        app: hello
    spec:
      containers:
      - name: main
        image: busybox
        command: ['sh', '-c', 'echo Hello DevOps! && sleep 3600']
```

In this replication set definition, the same pod specification from `my-first-pod` is used. There are two critical points to check in this definition; `replicas` and `matchLabels`.

The `replicas` field defines the desired number of the pods that should be running in the cluster. Kubernetes controllers inside `kube-controller-manager` create and manage the pods to fulfill this request.

The `matchLabels` field defines a set of labels to match with the pods that should be replicated. Labels in Kubernetes are semantic tags attached to Kubernetes resources to group them. Controllers use these labels to target a group of resources and manage them. For instance, in this example, replication set controllers will check for the number of pods with the label `app:hello`, since they are mentioned in `matchLabels`.

Replication sets are the fundamental resources that make Kubernetes applications highly available and resilient to failures in the cluster. In our discussion of the next resource, replication sets will be used to achieve higher life cycle requirements.

Deployment

Deployments are one of the most potent Kubernetes resources that makes it easier to manage containerized applications at large scales. A deployment specification looks similar to a replication set with an encapsulated pod definition:

```
apiVersion: apps/v1
kind: Deployment
metadata:
  name: my-first-deployment
  labels:
    app: nginx
spec:
  replicas: 3
  selector:
    matchLabels:
      app: nginx
  template:
    metadata:
      labels:
        app: nginx
    spec:
      containers:
      - name: nginx
        image: nginx:1.7.9
        ports:
        - containerPort: 80
```

Although it looks similar to a replication set definition, the power of the deployments comes from the capabilities of the deployment controllers. By creating a deployment or changing the fields in a deployment specification, it is possible to manage these life cycle operations:

- **Rolling out a new application:** When the deployment is sent to the Kubernetes API, replication sets are defined, and the application is rolled to the cluster.

- **Rolling out an update to running application:** When a change is made to deployment specification, these changes are propagated by deleting old replication sets and creating new ones. This rollout of new versions is managed at a controlled rate so that there is no downtime when you add another environment variable to your pod specification.

- **Rollback to an older version:** If any problems occur while rolling out new releases, it is always possible to roll back the changes, since deployment controllers store history.

- **Scaling up or down a running application:** It is possible to change the number of replicas to scale down or up manually.

Deployments are high-level Kubernetes resources that enable complex life cycle operations. They are essential and among the most commonly used Kubernetes resources for deploying scalable, reliable, and highly available ephemeral workloads. In the next resource, we will discuss how to handle stateful applications, such as databases in Kubernetes with stateful sets.

Stateful Sets

Kubernetes enables both stateless ephemeral and stateful applications to be run with the same level of scalability and robustness, thanks to stateful sets (**StatefulSet**). Stateful sets fulfill the enhanced requirements of data-oriented applications, such as databases, with the help of persistent volumes. The stateful set definition looks similar to deployment and includes volume claim parts to create persistent volumes, as follows:

```
apiVersion: apps/v1beta2
kind: StatefulSet
metadata:
  name: my-first-statefulset
spec:
  selector:
    matchLabels:
      app: nginx
```

```
serviceName: "nginx"
replicas: 3
template:
  metadata:
    labels:
      app: nginx
  spec:
    containers:
    - name: nginx
      image: nginx:1.7.9
      ports:
      - containerPort: 80
      volumeMounts:
      - name: www
        mountPath: /usr/share/nginx/html
volumeClaimTemplates:
- metadata:
    name: www
  spec:
    accessModes: [ "ReadWriteOnce" ]
    resources:
      requests:
        storage: 1Gi
```

In **my-first-statefulset**, a persistent volume, **www**, is created for every pod instance and mounted to the **/usr/share/nginx/html** path inside containers.

When a stateful set is sent to the Kubernetes API, the controllers create ordered pods with the defined volumes. Special care of the stateful set pods prevents data loss when the pods are rescheduled to another node. This is because the same ordered volumes are bound to the same ordered pods, as illustrated in *Figure* 3.19. In addition, volumes attached to these pods stay in the system when the stateful set is scaled down or deleted:

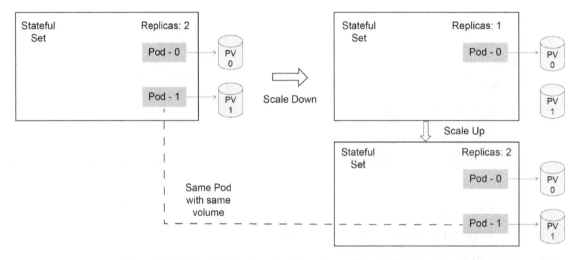

Figure 3.19: Stateful set and volume handling in Kubernetes

The stateful set controller and ordered execution of pods and volumes make stateful applications run in Kubernetes in a scalable and reliable way. With all of the fundamental resources of pods, replication sets, deployments, and stateful sets, it is possible to deploy any complex cloud-native application in Kubernetes. With the rich functionality of the Kubernetes API and toolsets, it is also possible to operate these applications in the cloud. In the following activity, a blog application and its database are installed in Kubernetes by using primary resources and the **kubectl** tool.

Activity 3: Installing a WordPress Blog and Database on Kubernetes

The aim of this activity to install and manage a **MySQL** database and a **WordPress** blog in Kubernetes in a cloud-native way. WordPress is based on **PHP** and is a free and open source content management system. It needs a **MySQL** database as the data source for user and content management. In this activity, database and blog containers should be stateful to persist their data, as expected in a production system.

Using the stateful set examples and previous **kubectl** exercises, it is expected that you will have a stateful set with two containers running and communicating with each other. Since the blog will be running inside Kubernetes, you need to access this by using the port-forward capabilities of **kubectl**. With the successful initialization of the WordPress container, it is expected that you will see the following setup screens:

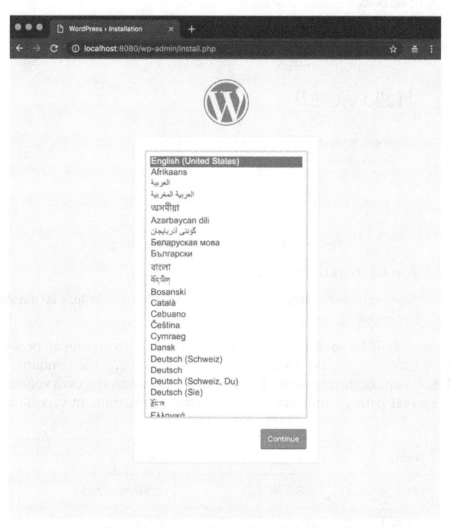

Figure 3.20: Setup Steps – WordPress Install

After the setup, the new blog should be up and running:

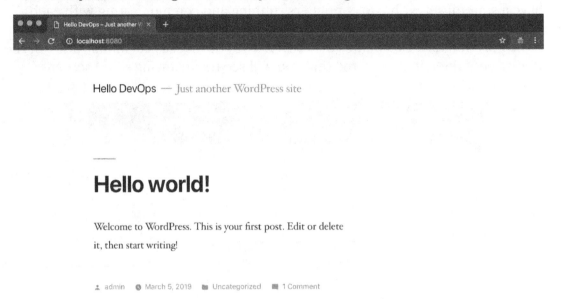

Figure 3.21: Home page – WordPress blog

Execute the following steps to complete this activity:

1. Create a two-container stateful set definition inside the **wordpress-database.yaml** file with the following specifications:

   The name should be **wordpress-database** and the replica count can be set to **1**. The database container should have the name of **database** and the container image of **mysql:5.7**. Publish the container to port **3306** and mount the **data** volume to the **/var/lib/mysql** path. In addition, set the following environment variables:

Name	Value
MYSQL_ROOT_PASSWORD	rootPassword
MYSQL_DATABASE	database
MYSQL_USER	user
MYSQL_PASSWORD	password

Figure 3.22: Environment variables

Create a blog container with the name **blog** using the **latest** WordPress container image and publish the container to port **80**. In addition, set the following environment variables:

Name	Value
WORDPRESS_DB_HOST	127.0.0.1:3306
WORDPRESS_DB_NAME	database
WORDPRESS_DB_USER	user
WORDPRESS_DB_PASSWORD	password

Figure 3.23: Environment variables

Include a volume claim with the name data and 1GB of storage.

Deploy the **wordpress-database** stateful set into the Kubernetes cluster.

2. Check the status of the **wordpress-database-0** pod and wait until it is ready.

3. Create a proxy to the local system from the blog container using the **port-forward** command of **kubectl**.

4. Open the forwarded address in the browser and fill in the WordPress setup form.

5. Open the forwarded address in the browser and check that your new blog is running in containers.

6. Stop the port forwarding started in step 4 and remove the stateful set.

> **Note**
>
> The solution to this activity can be found on Page 309.

Through this activity, we have operated a WordPress blog and its database in a Kubernetes cluster. For the blog and the database, only a stateful set is defined and sent to the cluster. Scheduling, networking, and storage operations were handled by Kubernetes in a couple of seconds, and the blog was ready. In addition, Kubernetes is always checking for node failures, and could reschedule the blog and database to another node without any data loss. Even for a single blog instance, it shows how powerful the Kubernetes resources and controllers are in creating scalable and reliable cloud-native applications.

Summary

In this chapter, we first described the characteristics of Kubernetes and the essential solutions it offers for running cloud-native microservice applications. Following that, we then presented Kubernetes architecture with the details of master and node components. Furthermore, a local Kubernetes solution was installed and run to show the components of the Kubernetes architecture in action. Then, we discussed how to access Kubernetes clusters to send workloads, and troubleshoot running applications with the help of the Kubernetes dashboard and the Kubernetes CLI tool.

Finally, the fundamental set of Kubernetes resources are presented, including pods, replication sets, deployments, and stateful sets. Also, the importance of labels was mentioned in explaining how Kubernetes handles these resources. At the end of the chapter, the popular blog application, WordPress, was installed in Kubernetes with its database as a stateful set.

With the fundamental basis of Kubernetes covered in this chapter, creating production-ready Kubernetes clusters and managing sophisticated applications on these clusters will be covered in the following chapters.

Creating a Kubernetes Cluster

Learning Objectives

By the end of this chapter, you will be able to:

- Analyze the requirements and concerns for a reliable Kubernetes cluster.
- Describe the various Kubernetes platform options.
- Create a minimum-viable Kubernetes cluster.
- Create and manage a production-ready Kubernetes cluster in the cloud.

In this chapter, we will create out first Kubernetes cluster and take a look at Kubernetes platform options.

Introduction

Kubernetes is a flexible platform that can work on a developer laptop, on-premise bare metal servers, or the virtual machines of a cloud provider. The knowledge and effort required to set up and maintain Kubernetes on different platforms varies tremendously, and is profoundly affected by the business requirements. Therefore, it is crucial to learn the basics of Kubernetes cluster setup and management to be successful in DevOps with Kubernetes. In the previous chapter, we looked at the Kubernetes architecture and the building blocks of Kubernetes. In addition, we looked at installing and accessing a cluster in order to create a basis for a deep-dive into Kubernetes clusters and platform options. In this section, we will first create a Kubernetes cluster using **kubeadm** to show the details of the manual in-house process. Following that, we will look at the evaluation criteria for choosing a Kubernetes platform. Then, we will look at different platforms and explore their favorable and unfavorable aspects with hands-on exercises. Finally, we will undertake a production-ready cluster management activity to illustrate the real-life complexities faced by Kubernetes operators.

Manual Kubernetes Cluster Setup

Kubernetes is a fairly elaborate system; however, it relies on developer experience to make it easier to set up and manage the clusters. **kubeadm** is the official Kubernetes toolkit for quickly and easily creating a minimal, viable, and certified cluster. This installs all required master and node components; however, cloud-specific or nice-to-have add-ons, such as the dashboard, are left out. **kubeadm** is used in many complex Kubernetes provider solutions as a building block; however, it should be mentioned that it cannot provision any infrastructure. On the other hand, it has a huge advantage of running on every platform, from high-end servers to Raspberry Pi nodes.

To create a Kubernetes cluster, the main approach is to initialize a master first, and join all the nodes afterward. Let's look at the following flowchart to understand this:

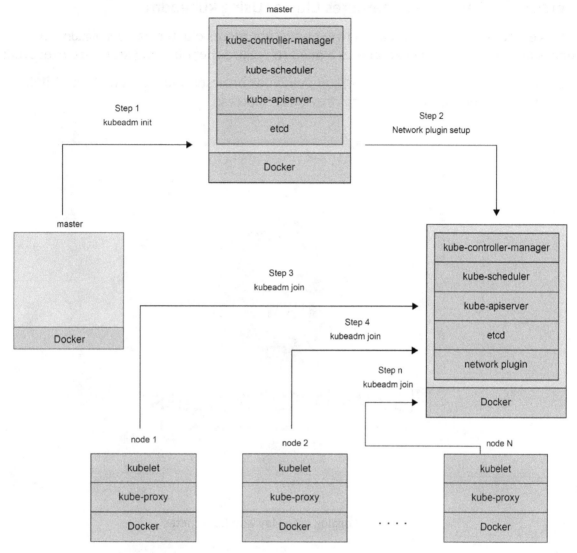

Figure 4.1: Flow of cluster creating with kubeadm

It is expected that you will have a complete and running control plane in the master, as shown in **Step 1** of *Figure 4.1*. In **Step 2**, network plugins are installed if required. Finally, the nodes are installed, and they register themselves to the master with **join** commands in **Step 3** and **Step 4** and so on, as illustrated in *Figure 4.1*. In the following exercise, we will show you how to create a manual Kubernetes cluster using **kubeadm**. It is essential to know how this is done without any automation and additional service to evaluate managed and turnkey solutions in the following sections.

Exercise 11: Creating a Kubernetes Cluster Using kubeadm

In this exercise, we aim to create a five-node Kubernetes cluster using **kubeadm.** To successfully complete the exercise, we need to ensure the following steps are executed:

1. Open https://labs.play-with-k8s.com in your browser and log in with the GitHub or Docker credentials from the previous chapters:

Figure 4.2: Logging in to Play with Kubernetes

> **Note**
>
> labs.play-with-k8s.com is a free playground service supported by Docker to create Kubernetes clusters.

2. Enable pop-ups and redirections in browser settings for the labs.play-with-k8s. com address by completing the following steps:

Click the lock icon in the address bar and select **Site settings**:

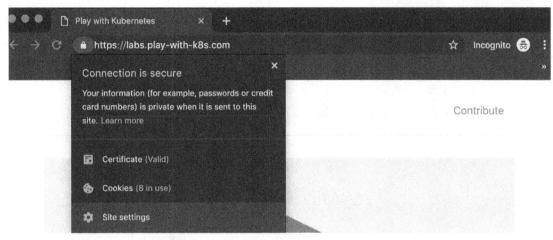

Figure 4.3: Website settings menu in Chrome

Choose **Allow** for **Pop-ups and redirects**:

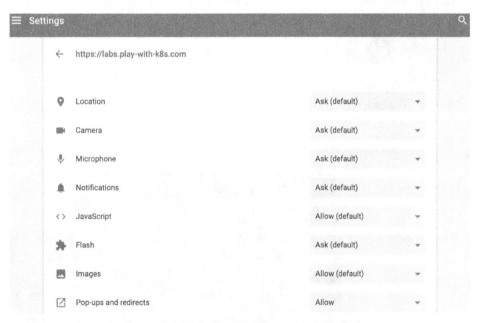

Figure 4.4: Website settings menu in Safari

Note

For the Safari browser, right-click the address bar and select **Settings for this Website** and then choose **Allow for Pop-up Windows**.

Click **Start** to create a session:

Figure 4.5: Starting a session in Play with Kubernetes

3. Click **Add New Instance** and wait until the Terminal is loaded:

Figure 4.6: Creating the first instance in Play with Kubernetes

4. Initialize **node1** as master with the following command in the Terminal loaded in step 3:

```
kubeadm init --apiserver-advertise-address $(hostname -i)
```

In a couple of minutes, **kubeadm** downloads and installs all the master node components:

Figure 4.7: kubeadm init output

5. Copy the **kubeadm join** command from the output to use in the further steps:

The output of the **kubeadm init** command can be tracked from the Terminal for **node1**:

Figure 4.8: kubeadm join token

6. Initialize cluster networking with the following command:

```
kubectl apply -n kube-system -f \
"https://cloud.weave.works/k8s/net?k8s-version=$(kubectl version | base64
|tr -d '\n')"
```

7. The result of the networking installation can be tracked from the Terminal for **node1**:

Figure 4.9: Cluster networking setup

With this command, a networking plugin is installed to manage the networking between the master and the nodes of the Kubernetes cluster.

8. Click **Add New Instance** and wait until the Terminal is loaded for **node2**:

Figure 4.10: Creating the second instance in Play with Kubernetes

9. Join **node2** to the cluster with the `kubeadm join` command copied in step 6:

> **Note**
>
> The following command includes the token as an example – do not forget the use your own token from step 6.

```
kubeadm join 172.27.0.2:6443 --token nhoc2x.
w9etr3ml7s9557x0 --discovery-token-ca-cert-hash
sha256:e56208fb4009baec6a49522890f50efa81f49895e7a3318c27bd23659cdeec80
```

The output of the **kubeadm join** command can be tracked from the Terminal for **node2**:

Figure 4.11: Joining node2 to the cluster

With this command, the worker node is initialized and has registered itself to the API server running in the master node.

10. Repeat steps 8 and 9 for **node3**, **node4**, and **node5**:

Figure 4.12: Five instances in Play with Kubernetes

11. Run the following command in **node1**:

```
kubectl get nodes
```

The output of the **kubeadm get nodes** command can be tracked from the Terminal for **node1**:

Figure 4.13: Ready nodes in the cluster

This output shows that five nodes are successfully initialized and connected to the cluster.

It takes 10 to 15 minutes to create a Kubernetes cluster with **kubeadm**, as long as the infrastructure provides the nodes with requirements, as in this playground.

12. Click **Close Session** to remove all nodes in the playground.

In this exercise, we have shown how we can manually create a certified and minimum-viable Kubernetes cluster. Although it is convenient to create Kubernetes clusters with **kubeadm**, there are additional concerns and issues to be resolved before creating a production-ready cluster. In the following section, these issues will be discussed and then the Kubernetes solution types will be presented.

Kubernetes Cluster Considerations

Kubernetes could run on various platforms to meet business and operational requirements. However, some critical questions and concerns should be clarified before choosing a platform. Some of these concerns overlap across multiple topics. Therefore, creating a workflow to choose the most appropriate product is no simple matter. It is recommended that you evaluate solution types and off-the-shelf products according to business requirements and limitations. Consider the following issues when analyzing and evaluating your requirements.

Development or Production-Ready Setup

The Kubernetes platform is ready to handle production-ready workloads; however, it also requires the use of disposable clusters in development and testing. CI/CD systems require a Kubernetes cluster to be ready in a couple of seconds, and could make sacrifices from some features, such as security, node resiliency, or high availability. Therefore, it is vital to select a Kubernetes solution based on development or production usage. It is possible to use single-node local solutions for development and testing environments, whereas more complicated and managed installations are required for production-ready environments.

In-House or Managed Services

The Kubernetes platform is self-healing, robust, and resilient; however, it needs human operators for installation, upgrading, and management. There are Kubernetes providers that not only install and give the credentials of Kubernetes clusters; but also manage them with their dedicated teams. On the other hand, it is also possible to have Kubernetes clusters installed on-premise or on the cloud, and managed by the in-house teams of organizations. It is a critical business decision to determine how Kubernetes clusters need to be managed in your organization. There are two dimensions of this issue that should be analyzed in depth: core value and budget. If managing Kubernetes clusters in-house will increase the core value of your products and services, then it is a valuable asset to have. On the other hand, if your organization considers itself as only being an end user of Kubernetes, it will create an additional burden. The second dimension of the budget applies to both in-house and managed services, since both will cost money. The organization should have a high level of investment in training and teams for in-house services, whereas managed services will require ongoing subscriptions with vendor lock-in.

On-Premises or Cloud Infrastructure

Kubernetes can run on cloud providers or on-premise systems; however, this is a decision to make upfront, since hybrid solutions are not mature enough yet. There are two important aspects that affect the decision between cloud-providers and on-premise systems. The first one is choosing between an in-house team or outsourced service for the cluster operations. The second one is the current and expected workload level to run on the clusters. For instance, if you have only a couple of services running on Kubernetes and do not expect high-scale usage soon, it seems reasonable to have a small setup in cloud providers, such as Amazon Web Services (AWS), the Google Cloud Platform (GCP), or Azure. However, if you are planning to have your security-critical data to operate in Kubernetes and have a dedicated team, then having on-premise systems is a feasible solution. Although it is possible to move Kubernetes workloads between clusters, it will need additional effort and investment to switch from on-premise to cloud infrastructure or vice versa.

Vanilla Kubernetes or Custom Solutions

Kubernetes itself is an application that can be customized based on your requirements. It is an extensible environment where you can plug in your schedulers, custom resource controllers, or security handlers. On the other hand, it is also possible to use only upstream, latest official releases, namely the vanilla Kubernetes. This decision affects the selection of custom providers, since some of them create their APIs, new dashboards, and controllers to manage the Kubernetes API and provide this as a service. On the other hand, if you expect to have active development on Kubernetes itself, it is advisable to have vanilla Kubernetes and add your custom flavors.

These three considerations are essential for choosing a Kubernetes platform solution and should be analyzed and clarified beforehand. Kubernetes platform solutions and their response to these considerations are discussed in the following section.

Kubernetes Platform Options

Kubernetes can run on practically every kind of infrastructure, from a commercial laptop to the high-end servers of cloud providers. It is possible to have fully-managed Kubernetes as a service or create a self-managed cluster on the bare-metal servers in your data center. Choosing which option to use to manage Kubernetes cluster depends on your budget, team, and required flexibility. In this section, Kubernetes platform options are grouped into three as local machine, hosted, and turnkey solutions. Each platform option is discussed in light of the considerations of the previous section and some example products.

Local Machine Solutions

Creating a local cluster is the simplest way of getting started with Kubernetes. The primary approach of these solutions is to install master and node components on the same computer. This leads to having a Kubernetes API and a worker running on the same node, which is suitable for development and testing, but is not suggested for production-grade workloads. Also, these solutions do not need operation teams, since they are not designed to have complex setups and requirements. These solutions focus on having vanilla Kubernetes with the minimum overhead and are therefore beneficial for testing new versions of Kubernetes.

The leading community-maintained and off-the-shelf local Kubernetes solutions are as follows:

Minikube: Minikube implements a local Kubernetes cluster to enable fast local development and high coverage of Kubernetes features. It is the official method for running Kubernetes locally and is maintained in the **kubernetes/minikube** (https://github.com/kubernetes/minikube) repository. Minikube uses the official stable releases of Kubernetes and supports all locally available Kubernetes features. Usage of Minikube was already covered in Exercise 8, and it is reasonably simple to create a cluster in a couple of seconds.

Docker Desktop: Docker Desktop is the toolbox installation of Docker for local development environments. It is a product developed and maintained by Docker, Inc, and can be downloaded from https://www.docker.com/products/docker-desktop. With Docker Desktop, it is possible to create a single-node Kubernetes cluster. All master and worker components run in Docker containers, so creating and starting a complete Kubernetes cluster is very fast and lightweight.

MicroK8s: MicroK8s is a Linux package that can be installed in various Linux flavors as a package. It makes running a local Kubernetes cluster as easy as installing a Linux application. Also, it supports upstream Kubernetes features and plugins for custom requirements. Installation documentation can be checked on its official website, https://microk8s.io. MicroK8s uses native Linux services to install and run Kubernetes master and node components, so a preliminary Linux experience is required in the long run.

Hosted Solutions

Hosted Kubernetes solutions are managed clusters that are running under the control of cloud providers. An end user is only expected to connect to the cluster and run the Kubernetes workload. There are two essential advantages of using hosted solutions: management effort and scalability. Creating and operating Kubernetes clusters requires effort and experience for a production-ready scalable and reliable setup. Therefore, if you do not have, or do not plan to have, a dedicated operations team, it is appropriate to have managed clusters. In addition, for a scalable cluster, there is a need to add and flexibly remove worker nodes. Cloud infrastructure providers support elastically starting and terminating servers, so it is suitable for managing Kubernetes clusters.

The leading hosted Kubernetes solutions are the ones created by the leading cloud infrastructure providers, such as GCP, AWS, and Microsoft Azure. They aim to provide Kubernetes solutions integrated with the cloud services they already offer, such as object stores, cloud identity services, or container registries. Significant differences and prominent features of these services can be listed as follows:

- **Google Kubernetes Engine** (GKE): GKE is the oldest Kubernetes service, was started in 2014, since Google is the original creator of container management systems. Therefore, GKE always provides the most advanced features with upstream Kubernetes versions. It is also one of the most intuitive Kubernetes solutions to set up and operate a managed cluster.

  Note

  Integration between other GCP applications and further documentation can be checked from the GKE official website, https://cloud.google.com/kubernetes-engine/.

- **Azure Kubernetes Service** (AKS): AKS is the Kubernetes solution provided by Microsoft on the Azure platform. It started in 2017 and provides managed Kubernetes clusters, which are well integrated into other Azure services, such as Azure Identity. However, AKS lacks some essential features, such as a highly available control plane and auto-repair of the cluster.

  Note

  The AKS documentation can be checked on its official website, https://azure.microsoft.com/en-us/services/kubernetes-service/.

- **Amazon Elastic Container Service for Kubernetes** (EKS): EKS is the newest service provided by AWS, and was made public in 2018. Compared to other solutions, it offers reasonably complex cluster creation, and is also missing worker-node management and auto-repair. In other words, EKS provides a managed control plane; however, EKS still lacks features to operate nodes.

> **Note**
>
> The EKS documentation can be checked on its official website, https://aws.amazon.com/eks/.

Turnkey Solutions

Turnkey solutions provide Kubernetes clusters deployed on the cloud or on-premise systems with a couple of commands. As an end user, with a couple of clicks or command-line executions, you will have Kubernetes clusters running on your favorite cloud provider or your data center. Compared to hosted solutions, they provide more flexibility with custom features and infrastructure options. Installation and management of control plane components and nodes are handled with the turnkey solution application. In other words, these solutions are the ready-to-use packaged knowledge of the Kubernetes operations experience.

Turnkey solutions are mostly provided by companies that have unique experience in the development and management of cloud systems, such as **CoreOS** or **Heptio**. Popular turnkey solutions with these prominent features will now be discussed.

Heptio

Heptio was founded by two of the original Kubernetes creators, and it provides a set of tools to install and manage Kubernetes clusters. Their services include diagnostic tools, reverse proxy implementations, and disaster recovery tools. The turnkey Kubernetes solution, namely **Heptio Kubernetes Subscription** (HKS), is the combination of their services and tools for installing upstream Kubernetes in production.

CoreOS Tectonic

Tectonic is the turnkey solution provided by CoreOS, and it enables hybrid clusters running on multiple cloud providers and on-premise systems. Tectonic supports upstream Kubernetes and all additional features are designed using Kubernetes primitives, such as custom resource controller managers similar to `kube-controller-manager`. The essential element of Tectonic is the support of hybrid clusters and the removal of vendor lock-in.

> **Note**
>
> Vendor lock-in means dependency on the services provided by a given vendor, so that switching to another vendor is complicated. In cloud development, it is achieved by making the users develop platform-dependent solutions that only work in the corresponding cloud provider. In other words, if you design a solution that uses proprietary services from AWS, you will need to redesign your architecture should you want to move to GCP.

Red Hat OpenShift

Red Hat, as a company, is the second-largest contributor to the Kubernetes project. OpenShift is the turnkey solution provided by Red Hat that is capable of multi-tenancy, improved networking, and high-level automation. OpenShift encapsulates upstream Kubernetes and provides an opinionated version with extra security and enterprise features. It is possible to have OpenShift in Red Hat Cloud, as well as installed on on-premise systems.

Kubernetes solution providers and their products are following the latest trends in the cloud-native world, along with microservices trends. However, the characteristics of the solution types stay roughly the same. Therefore, a comparison to help you in choosing an appropriate solution type is provided in *Figure* 4.14:

	Local machine solutions	Hosted solutions	Turnkey solutions
Appropriate for	• Local development and testing • Evaluating and to start learning Kubernetes	• Fully-managed environment • Not focusing on infrastructure setup and monitoring • No dedicated site reliability engineering (SRE) teams	• Taking more responsibility and flexibility on the systems • Private cloud networks or on-premise systems • Focusing on monitoring infrastructure • Dedicated site reliability engineering (SRE) teams

Figure 4.14: Kubernetes Platform Options

In the following exercise, we will create a hosted Kubernetes cluster in GKE, since this provides the most advanced developer experience among managed services.

Exercise 12 – Creating Managed Kubernetes Clusters on GCP

In this exercise, we will create a cluster in GKE and check the details of the new cluster. Before attempting this exercise, you will need to register on the GCP.

> **Note**
>
> If you are using GCP for the first time, you can activate a credit to explore GCP products. This requires a billing address and payment data, to be used after the credit is consumed.

Perform the following steps to complete the exercise:

1. Log into Google Cloud Console with your Google account at https://console.cloud.google.com:

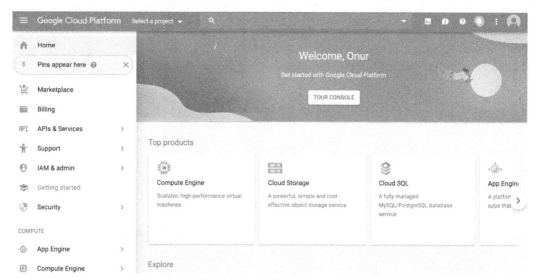

Figure 4.15: Google Cloud Console

2. Click on **Select a project** on the header menu, and then click **New Project** in the pop-up window:

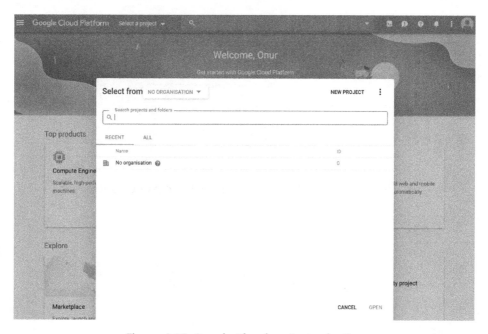

Figure 4.16: Google Cloud project selection

3. Fill **Project Name** with **devops** and select whether you are part of an organization, such as a company or school:

Figure 4.17: Google Cloud project creation

4. Open the Kubernetes cluster view under the **Compute – Kubernetes Engine** menu and wait until Kubernetes Engine is ready:

The Kubernetes Engine status is visible in the main section of the **Clusters**:

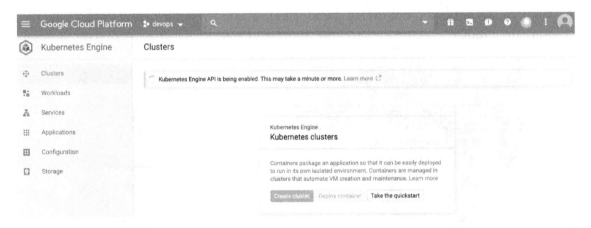

Figure 4.18: Google Cloud – Kubernetes Engine: Getting Ready

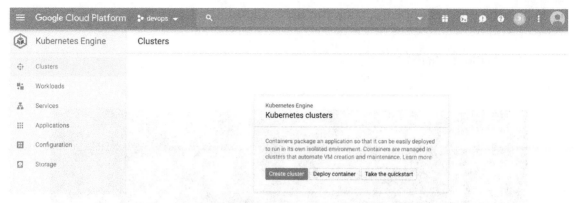

Figure 4.19: Google Cloud – Kubernetes Engine: Ready

> **Note**
>
> If this is your first usage of GCP, it could take a couple of minutes to set up the Google user permissions and enable the Kubernetes API. It will be indicated in the Kubernetes cluster view as **Kubernetes Engine API is being enabled. This may take a minute or more**.

5. Click **Activate Cloud Shell** in the header menu as follows:

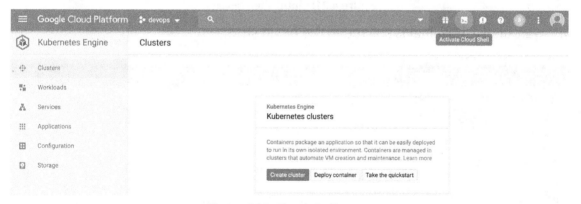

Figure 4.20: Cloud shell menu

6. When the pop-up appears, click the **Start Cloud Shell**, as follows:

Figure 4.21: Cloud shell details

7. Wait until a Terminal is started in the cloud shell:

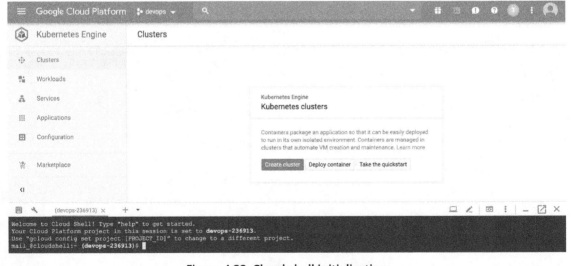

Figure 4.22: Cloud shell initialization

8. Set a default compute zone with the following command in the cloud shell:

```
gcloud config set compute/zone us-west1-a
```

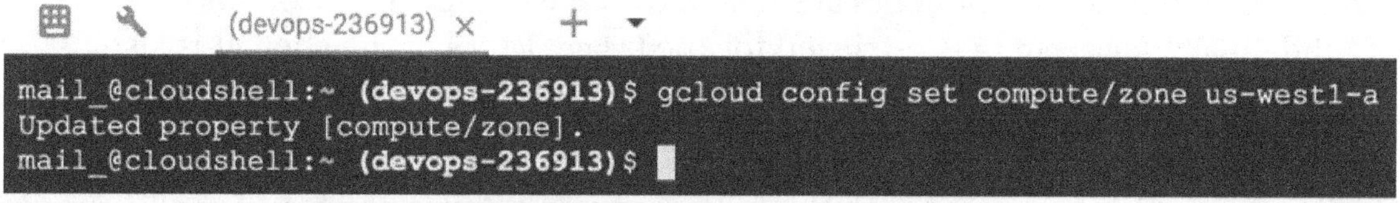

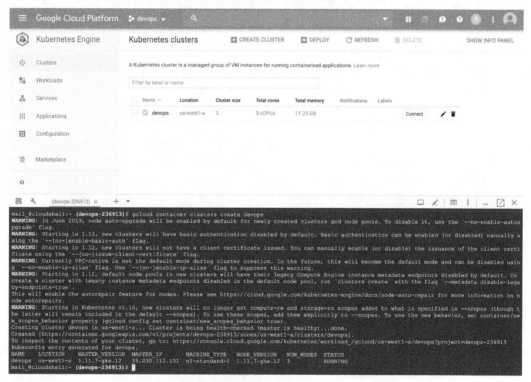

Figure 4.23: Default compute zone setting in gcloud

9. Create a GKE cluster with the following command in the cloud shell:

```
gcloud container clusters create devops
```

The output of the new cluster creation can be tracked from the cloud shell:

Figure 4.24: Creating the DevOps Kubernetes cluster

With that command, a control plane is created and started as a managed service on GCP. Following this, three Kubernetes nodes are provisioned as virtual machines in our project, and the node components are installed by default. All master and node components are tested to see whether they work as expected, and, finally, **kubeconfig** is retrieved for the **kubectl** tool in the shell. It is also possible to see the details of the cluster in the Kubernetes cluster table in the upper-side of this view.

10. Get the node information with the following command in the cloud shell:

```
kubectl get nodes
```

```
mail_@cloudshell:~ (devops-236913)$ kubectl get nodes
NAME                                      STATUS   ROLES    AGE   VERSION
gke-devops-default-pool-c42afc38-1hkz     Ready    <none>   3m    v1.11.7-gke.12
gke-devops-default-pool-c42afc38-d3hs     Ready    <none>   3m    v1.11.7-gke.12
gke-devops-default-pool-c42afc38-sdd7     Ready    <none>   3m    v1.11.7-gke.12
mail_@cloudshell:~ (devops-236913)$ █
```

Figure 4.25: Node information of the devops Kubernetes cluster

As expected, the three nodes are registered, and their status is **Ready**. This indicates that we have successfully created a three-worker node-managed Kubernetes cluster in GKE.

Through this exercise, we have shown how easy it is to create a managed Kubernetes cluster hosted in the cloud. If you need a fully-managed environment and if you do not want to focus on infrastructure setup and monitoring, creating such a managed Kubernetes cluster is appropriate for you. In the following activity, you will perform some operational tasks on this managed cluster.

Activity 4: Migrating a Running Application in Kubernetes Cluster

This activity aims to perform operational activities in a Kubernetes cluster installed in GKE. You will be required to use both Kubernetes and GCP primitives to upgrade cluster nodes without downtime.

You will start by installing a sample application that has more replicas than the number of nodes in the cluster. Then, you will be assigned to solve the "out-of-memory" issues of this application by creating a new set of worker nodes with higher memory limits. However, you need to handle this migration without this application undergoing any downtime.

Using the Kubernetes cluster from Exercise 12, you will first have three nodes of the **n1-standard-1** type:

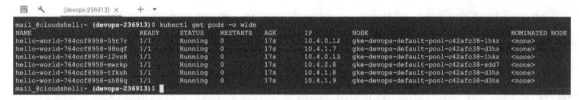

Figure 4.26: Node pool of the devops cluster before migration

In addition, the sample application will be running on these nodes:

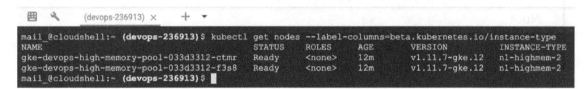

Figure 4.27: Sample application running before migration

With the migration, you will have two nodes of the **n1-highmem-2** type:

Figure 4.28: Node pool of the devops cluster after migration

As expected, the sample application will be running on the new nodes after migration:

Figure 4.29: Sample application running after migration

Perform the following steps to complete this activity:

1. Run a sample web application with six replicas in the cluster.

2. Check the status of pods of the sample web application and their nodes.

3. Create a node pool in GCP with a larger memory.

4. Wait until all nodes are **Ready** in the cluster.

5. Mark the nodes in the default node pool as unschedulable and make Kubernetes move the workloads from the default node pool.

6. Check the status of the nodes.

7. Ensure that the pods of the sample application are moved to new nodes.

8. Remove the default node pool.

9. Verify that the nodes from the default node pool are removed from the cluster

10. If you do not plan to use this Kubernetes cluster in the following chapters or the future, remove the Kubernetes cluster.

> **Note**
>
> The solution to this activity can be found on Page 314.

Through this activity, we have shown how we can perform operational activities in a Kubernetes cluster using Kubernetes and cloud provider tools. Kubernetes makes it possible to migrate an application to higher-performance workers with its tools and architecture, since it is designed to be cloud-native and microservice-oriented. The benefits of using a managed environment are also demonstrated by the fact that you do not have to buy the hardware, install the operating systems, and connect the cables of the new servers joined to the cluster. The elasticity of cloud providers makes it easier to scale vertically and horizontally based on your usage level, as in the sample application in this activity.

Summary

In this chapter, we started by creating a Kubernetes cluster manually using the official Kubernetes tools. We saw that it is convenient to create a minimum-viable verified cluster, as long as the underlying infrastructure is working. We then discussed Kubernetes cluster considerations as a guideline to decide which Kubernetes platform options are suitable. Kubernetes platform options were then discussed in detail with open source and off-the-shelf examples. Finally, we looked at how to create a managed cluster in the cloud without considering the monitoring and management of the infrastructure. At the end of the chapter, the managed cluster environment was used to illustrate operational activities undertaken in a Kubernetes cluster.

The Kubernetes cluster considerations, platform types, and on-hands exercises covered throughout the chapter will be revisited in the following chapters, since the installation and management of a Kubernetes cluster is a must-have tool in your DevOps toolset.

5

Deploy an Application to Kubernetes

Learning Objectives

By the end of this chapter, you will be able to:

- Perform object management using different techniques in Kubernetes

- Create and define Kubernetes services to connect applications

- Install and use Helm as the package manager for Kubernetes

- Use official Helm charts to configure and install applications on the clusters

In this chapter, we will explore object management in Kubernetes and deploy a WordPress blog to Kubernetes using object management techniques.

Introduction

Kubernetes is designed for managing cloud-native, reliable, and scalable applications in a microservice architecture. As a platform, Kubernetes provides all the resources, API endpoints, and tools that are required for deploying and managing applications. In the previous chapter, we analyzed the requirements for a reliable Kubernetes cluster and discussed various options for choosing a Kubernetes platform. Additionally, we learned how to manage a Kubernetes cluster from an operational perspective. In this chapter, we will focus on deploying and managing our applications on the Kubernetes cluster. First, we will explore object management in Kubernetes and discuss options for deploying applications to Kubernetes. Following that, we will explore how services are an essential Kubernetes resource for connecting microservice applications. In fact, with services, it is possible to install multiple applications that can connect and interact with each other. Finally, we will discuss Helm, which is used to deploy and manage applications as the official package manager of Kubernetes. Finally, an activity will be undertaken to deploy a WordPress blog to Kubernetes using object management techniques and Helm package management.

Object Management in Kubernetes

Kubernetes resources such as pods or deployments are maintained in **etcd** by **kube-apiserver**. Controller managers and schedulers interact with **kube-apiserver** to create pods for scaling up or for assigning nodes for scheduling. Additionally, every API request made by client tools such as **kubectl** is reflected on the cluster state maintained in **etcd**. While creating, updating, and deleting resources appears to be straightforward, there are multiple approaches that you can use to manage Kubernetes resources. In this section, the following three techniques for object management in Kubernetes will be discussed:

- **Imperative commands:** These are used for running **kubectl** commands directly on live Kubernetes resources.

- **Imperative configuration:** This is used for running **kubectl** commands with a specific command and configuration file.

- **Declarative configuration:** This is used for running **kubectl** commands with a configuration file and making **kubectl** automatically detect the required actions.

Imperative Commands

The easiest and the most straightforward way of interacting with Kubernetes is to provide an imperative command and some arguments. It is possible to create, update, and delete resources without any configuration file by using **kubectl** commands.

The following **kubectl** commands are used imperatively for creating, updating, or deleting resources:

- **kubectl run**: This creates a new deployment using one or multiple containers with specific container images, environment variables, and arguments. For instance, the following command will create a 5-replica deployment with the name and container image of **nginx**:

  ```
  kubectl run nginx --image=nginx --replicas=5
  ```

- **kubectl expose**: This creates a new service for exposing the deployments or pods specified in the command. For instance, the following command will create a service to expose the **80** port **nginx** deployment on **8080** port:

  ```
  kubectl expose deployment nginx --port=8080 --target-port=80
  ```

- **kubectl scale**: This changes the replica count of a deployment, replication set, or job. For instance, it is possible to increase the replica count of the **nginx** deployment to 10, as follows:

  ```
  kubectl scale --replicas=10 deployment/nginx
  ```

- **kubectl annotate**: This adds or removes annotations from a Kubernetes resource. For instance, it is possible to add a new annotation, **owner**, and value, **devops**, using the following command to the **nginx** deployment:

  ```
  kubectl annotate deployment nginx owner="devops"
  ```

- **kubectl get**: This retrieves the basic data of the Kubernetes resource in a human-readable YAML or JSON output. For instance, it is possible to get the running pods with the following command:

  ```
  kubectl get pods
  ```

- **kubectl delete**: This can be used with the type and name of a resource to delete from Kubernetes. For instance, it is possible to delete the **nginx deployment** and **service** as follows:

  ```
  kubectl delete deployment/nginx service/nginx
  ```

Imperative commands are a straightforward way of creating, updating, or deleting resources because they are easy to learn and remember. However, they are not suitable for production environments because they do not provide any history of previous states. For instance, it is not possible to roll back to an earlier version of the deployment using imperative commands. In addition to this, these commands are not suitable for complex configurations as they are limited to the command-line arguments provided by **kubectl**. Although they are as powerful as other methods, imperative commands should be used for testing, developing, or troubleshooting on Kubernetes clusters.

Imperative Configuration

Kubernetes resources can be managed with the help of **kubectl** commands and configuration files. It is possible to use a configuration file and imperatively specify commands such as **create**, **replace**, or **delete**.

The following **kubectl** commands are used imperatively for creating, updating, or deleting resources using configuration files:

- **kubectl create -f <FILE or URL>**: This creates the defined resource in the configuration file. For instance, the resource specified in https://raw. githubusercontent.com/TrainingByPackt/Introduction-to-DevOps-with-Kubernetes/master/Lesson05/nginx-deployment-5-replicas.yaml will be created in the cluster using the following command:

  ```
  kubectl create -f https://raw.githubusercontent.com/TrainingByPackt/
  Introduction-to-DevOps-with-Kubernetes/master/Lesson05/nginx-deployment-5-
  replicas.yaml
  ```

- **kubectl replace -f <FILE or URL>**: This updates the live Kubernetes resource with the one defined in the configuration file. Using the following command, the **nginx** deployment will be replaced with the one specified in the new file:

  ```
  kubectl replace -f https://raw.githubusercontent.com/TrainingByPackt/
  Introduction-to-DevOps-with-Kubernetes/master/Lesson05/nginx-deployment-
  10-replicas.yaml
  ```

- **kubectl delete -f <FILE or URL>**:This deletes the Kubernetes resources defined in the configuration file. For instance, the deployment defined in the file as **nginx** will be removed from the cluster, using the following command:

  ```
  kubectl delete -f https://raw.githubusercontent.com/TrainingByPackt/
  Introduction-to-DevOps-with-Kubernetes/master/Lesson05/nginx-deployment-
  10-replicas.yaml
  ```

With the imperative configuration, **kubectl** takes specified actions on the resources defined as YAML or JSON in the configuration files. These files are expected to be stored in the source code repositories. Additionally, configuration files make it possible to have more complex Kubernetes resources with a high level of configuration options. Therefore, using imperative configuration is suitable for production environments. However, it is critical to keep configuration files up-to-date if any other imperative commands are executed, such as **annotate** or **scale**.

For instance, let's imagine that you defined a deployment with 5 replicas in a configuration file created by **kubectl create -f**. Then, you needed to scale up the deployment to 10 replicas and run the imperative command of **kubectl scale**. From that moment, the configuration file does not have the latest replica number of 10. If you do not reflect the imperative changes to the file, you will have a 5-replica deployment in the next installation, as illustrated in *Figure* 5.1. Therefore, imperative commands with configuration files should be used with care:

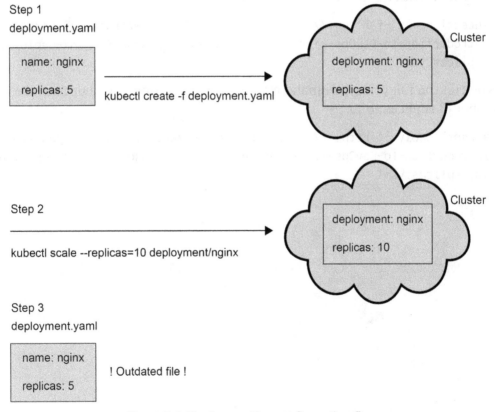

Figure 5.1: The imperative configuration flow

Declarative Configuration

Kubernetes resources can be defined as desired states in configuration files and can be managed with the help of **kubectl** automation capabilities. In other words, it is possible to use configuration files and let **kubectl** decide and take necessary actions.

The following **kubectl** commands are used for managing the resource with declarative configuration:

- **kubectl apply -f <FILE or URL>**: This creates or updates the resources defined in the configuration file. **kubectl** automatically checks the live resources in the cluster and compares this with the configuration provided in the files. It can create new resources if they do not exist in the cluster or update the live ones according to the new resource definitions. An update of the resources includes adding, removing, or changing the values of fields such as container images, labels, or annotations. For instance, the following command will create a **nginx** deployment with 5 replicas:

  ```
  kubectl apply -f https://raw.githubusercontent.com/TrainingByPackt/
  Introduction-to-DevOps-with-Kubernetes/master/Lesson05/nginx-deployment-5-
  replicas.yaml
  ```

  If you run the following command after the previous one, it will update the number of replicas to 10:

  ```
  kubectl apply -f https://raw.githubusercontent.com/TrainingByPackt/
  Introduction-to-DevOps-with-Kubernetes/master/Lesson05/nginx-deployment-
  10-replicas.yaml
  ```

The flow of **kubectl apply** commands is illustrated in *Figure* 5.2:

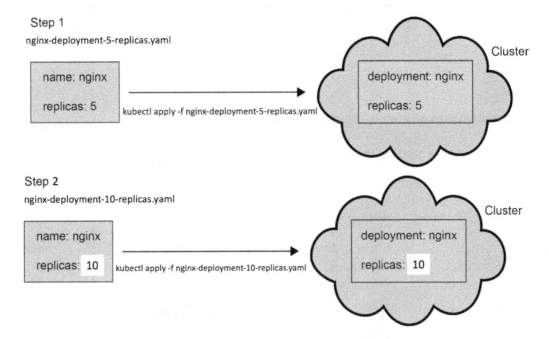

Figure 5.2: The declarative configuration flow

- **kubectl delete -f <FILE or URL>:** This deletes the Kubernetes resources defined in the configuration file in the same way as the imperative command. It is the recommended way of removing resources that are declaratively configured and maintained.

With declarative configuration, the main focus is on maintaining configuration files. Creating or updating resources in the cluster are left to the operational logic implemented in Kubernetes' tools and APIs. Since it does not rely on humans, it is appropriate for a production environment with distributed teams and **Continuous Integration/Continuous Delivery** systems. Additionally, declarative configuration can safely work on folders to apply multiple resources defined in various files. Inside a folder, **kubectl** will evaluate each resource separately to determine and perform the required actions. In other words, declarative configuration could be considered as maintaining a local *desired state* defined in configuration files and using Kubernetes' client tools to reflect this state in a Kubernetes cluster.

Each object management technique in Kubernetes has its advantages and disadvantages; therefore, choosing the most appropriate method for development, testing, and troubleshooting is essential. In the following exercise, these three techniques are illustrated with real-life examples.

> **Note**
>
> You will require a Kubernetes cluster to complete the following exercise. It is possible to use a **minikube** cluster from *Chapter 3, Introduction to Kubernetes* or a **Google Kubernetes Engine** cluster from *Chapter 4, Creating a Kubernetes Cluster*.

Exercise 13: Deploying Applications Using kubectl

In this exercise, we aim to create a deployment with imperative commands and manage it with declarative methods of **kubectl**. To successfully complete the exercise, perform the following steps:

1. Run the following command in Terminal to create an **nginx** deployment:

   ```
   kubectl run nginx --image=nginx --replicas=5
   ```

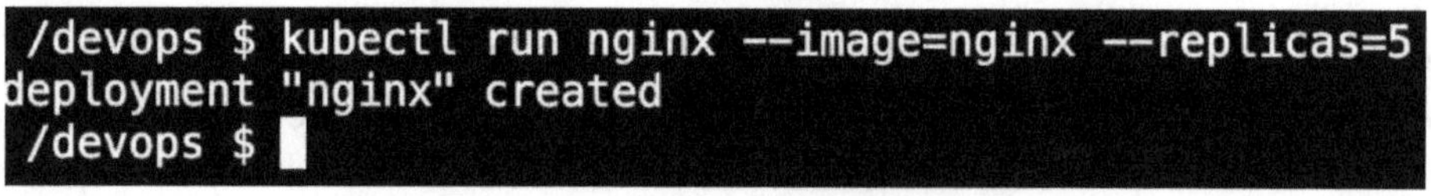

   ```
   /devops $ kubectl run nginx --image=nginx --replicas=5
   deployment "nginx" created
   /devops $
   ```

   Figure 5.3: Creating the nginx deployment

   The output indicates that the **nginx** deployment is created.

2. Check the status of the pods with the following command:

   ```
   kubectl get pods
   ```

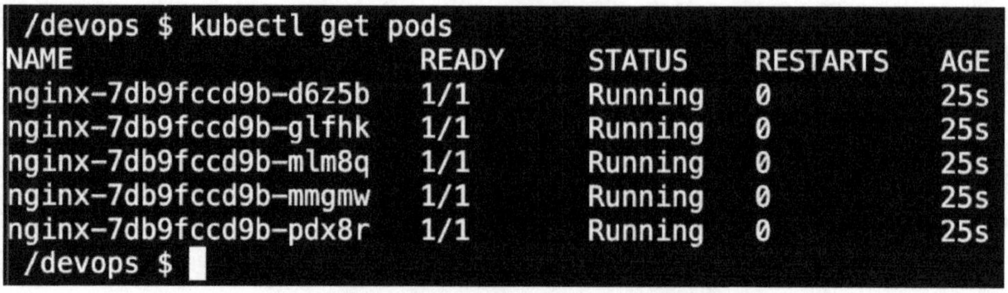

   ```
   /devops $ kubectl get pods
   NAME                      READY     STATUS     RESTARTS     AGE
   nginx-7db9fccd9b-d6z5b    1/1       Running    0            25s
   nginx-7db9fccd9b-glfhk    1/1       Running    0            25s
   nginx-7db9fccd9b-mlm8q    1/1       Running    0            25s
   nginx-7db9fccd9b-mmgmw    1/1       Running    0            25s
   nginx-7db9fccd9b-pdx8r    1/1       Running    0            25s
   /devops $
   ```

   Figure 5.4: The pods of the nginx deployment

This output shows that the deployment with 5 replicas is running in the cluster as expected.

3. Export the **nginx** deployment with the following command:

```
kubectl get deployment nginx -o yaml --export > deployment.yaml
```

With this command, deployment specification is written into the local file named **deployment**.

4. Open the **deployment.yaml** file with a text editor and change the **replicas** field to **10**, as follows:

```
/devops $ cat deployment.yaml
apiVersion: extensions/v1beta1
kind: Deployment
metadata:
  annotations:
    deployment.kubernetes.io/revision: "1"
  creationTimestamp: null
  generation: 1
  labels:
    run: nginx
  name: nginx
  selfLink: /apis/extensions/v1beta1/namespaces/default/deployments/nginx
spec:
  progressDeadlineSeconds: 2147483647
  replicas: 10
  revisionHistoryLimit: 2147483647
  selector:
    matchLabels:
      run: nginx
  strategy:
    rollingUpdate:
      maxSurge: 1
      maxUnavailable: 1
    type: RollingUpdate
  template:
    metadata:
      creationTimestamp: null
      labels:
        run: nginx
    spec:
      containers:
      - image: nginx
        imagePullPolicy: Always
        name: nginx
        resources: {}
        terminationMessagePath: /dev/termination-log
        terminationMessagePolicy: File
      dnsPolicy: ClusterFirst
      restartPolicy: Always
      schedulerName: default-scheduler
      securityContext: {}
      terminationGracePeriodSeconds: 30
status: {}
/devops $ 
```

Figure 5.5: The deployment specification

5. Deploy the changes using the **kubectl apply** command:

```
kubectl apply -f deployment.yaml
```

```
/devops $ kubectl apply -f deployment.yaml
deployment.extensions/nginx configured
/devops $
```

Figure 5.6: Applying deployment changes

6. Check the status of pods using the following command:

```
kubectl get pods
```

```
/devops $ kubectl get pods
NAME                      READY   STATUS    RESTARTS   AGE
nginx-7db9fccd9b-2vpd9    1/1     Running   0          43s
nginx-7db9fccd9b-8sjsr    1/1     Running   0          4m39s
nginx-7db9fccd9b-c6bkp    1/1     Running   0          4m39s
nginx-7db9fccd9b-j97z7    1/1     Running   0          43s
nginx-7db9fccd9b-jzglp    1/1     Running   0          43s
nginx-7db9fccd9b-k2fcd    1/1     Running   0          4m39s
nginx-7db9fccd9b-sf9gv    1/1     Running   0          4m39s
nginx-7db9fccd9b-vs56f    1/1     Running   0          4m39s
nginx-7db9fccd9b-w8vqn    1/1     Running   0          43s
nginx-7db9fccd9b-xgltr    1/1     Running   0          43s
/devops $
```

Figure 5.7: The pods of the nginx deployment

This output shows that the deployment with 10 replicas is running in the cluster as expected.

7. Run the following command to delete the **nginx** deployment:

```
kubectl delete -f deployment.yaml
```

```
/devops $ kubectl delete -f deployment.yaml
deployment.extensions "nginx" deleted
/devops $
```

Figure 5.8: Deleting the nginx deployment

In this exercise, we demonstrated how to imperatively create a Kubernetes resource and then convert it into a file and manage it with declarative configuration. All these three object management methods are useful for daily tasks while working with Kubernetes. In the following section, a new Kubernetes resource will be presented to enable interaction between multiple applications in the cluster.

Service Discovery in Kubernetes

Kubernetes manages containerized microservice applications by creating pods. Pods are the building blocks of Kubernetes, where multiple containers are grouped together and share the same network interface. For every pod, Kubernetes assigns an IP that is reachable within the Kubernetes cluster; however, the pods are ephemeral in their nature. In other words, pods and their IPs could change when they are assigned to different nodes. In order to reliably access pods, Kubernetes provides an abstraction layer known as **service**. Kubernetes services group a logical set of pods that can run on the different nodes inside the cluster and enable other pods to reach them over the service.

Let's imagine having a **backend** deployment in Kubernetes with two replicas and a **frontend** deployment with three replicas. To reach the **backend** pods from the **frontend** pods, the IPs of the **backends** should be made available to the **frontends**, as shown in *Figure* 5.9. Additionally, a health status check is required since some of the backend instances can break and their IPs should be removed from the **frontend** configuration. Kubernetes creates an abstraction layer in front of the **backend** instances and decouples the **backend** and **frontend** instances, as illustrated in *Figure* 5.10. With the help of services, the **frontend** instances only need to know how to connect the service:

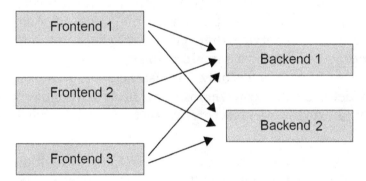

Figure 5.9: Frontend instances connecting to backend instances

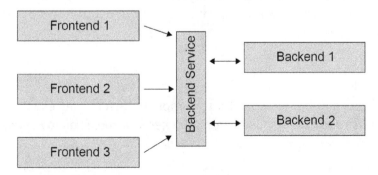

Figure 5.10: Frontend instances connecting to the backend service

Kubernetes services are defined by grouping pods with their labels. For instance, using the following service description, port **80** of each pod with the **app = nginx** label will be reachable from port **8080**:

```
kind: Service

apiVersion: v1

metadata:

  namespace: default

  name: nginx-service

spec:

  selector:

    app: nginx

  ports:

  - protocol: TCP

    port: 8080

    targetPort: 80
```

When this service is created, Kubernetes will assign an IP for this service and it will be reachable by all pods inside the cluster. If other pods want to connect to the **nginx** pods abstracted by this service, they only need to know the service IP address. Furthermore, Kubernetes provides a **domain name system (DNS)** inside the cluster to connect services with their names only. For instance, it is possible to connect the service previously defined with **http://nginx-service:8080** from the pods in the same namespace; and **http://nginx-service.default:8080** from all the namespaces in the cluster.

With the **service** Kubernetes resource, it is possible to deploy multiple decoupled applications in a scalable and reliable way. This is a powerful way of connecting scalable applications with an essential abstraction layer. In the following exercise, we will demonstrate how to create a deployment with its service and how to access the service from other pods.

> **Note**
>
> You will require a Kubernetes cluster to complete the following exercise. It is possible to use a **minikube** cluster from *Chapter 3, Introduction to Kubernetes* or a GKE cluster from *Chapter 4, Creating a Kubernetes Cluster*.

Exercise 14: Access Applications Using Services

In this exercise, we aim to create a deployment and service accessible from other pods in the cluster. To successfully complete the exercise, perform the following steps:

1. Run the following command in Terminal to create an **nginx** deployment:

   ```
   kubectl run nginx --image=nginx --replicas=5
   ```

   ```
   /devops $ kubectl run nginx --image=nginx --replicas=5
   deployment.apps/nginx created
   /devops $
   ```

   Figure 5.11: Creating the nginx deployment

   The output indicates that the **nginx** deployment is created.

2. Create a service for the **nginx** deployment using the following command:

   ```
   kubectl expose deployment/nginx --target-port=80 --port=8080
   ```

   ```
   /devops $ kubectl expose deployment/nginx --target-port=80 --port=8080
   service/nginx exposed
   /devops $
   ```

   Figure 5.12: Exposing the nginx deployment

   This output shows that the service with the name **nginx** is created.

3. Create a **curl** instance and an open connection into the pod using the following command:

   ```
   kubectl run curl --rm --image=radial/busyboxplus:curl -i --tty
   ```

   ```
   /devops $ kubectl run curl --rm --image=radial/busyboxplus:curl -i --tty
   kubectl run --generator=deployment/apps.v1 is DEPRECATED and will be removed in a future version. Use kubectl
   ator=run-pod/v1 or kubectl create instead.
   If you don't see a command prompt, try pressing enter.
   [ root@curl-66bdcf564-226qb:/ ]$
   ```

   Figure 5.13: Terminal access in the pod

   With command prompt, you are executing commands interactively in a pod created from the **radial/busyboxplus:curl** image.

4. Connect to the **nginx** instances using the following command:

```
curl nginx:8080
```

```
root@curl-66bdcf564-226qb:/ $ curl nginx:8080
<!DOCTYPE html>
<html>
<head>
<title>Welcome to nginx!</title>
<style>
    body {
        width: 35em;
        margin: 0 auto;
        font-family: Tahoma, Verdana, Arial, sans-serif;
    }
</style>
</head>
<body>
<h1>Welcome to nginx!</h1>
<p>If you see this page, the nginx web server is successfully installed and
working. Further configuration is required.</p>

<p>For online documentation and support please refer to
<a href="http://nginx.org/">nginx.org</a>.<br/>
Commercial support is available at
<a href="http://nginx.com/">nginx.com</a>.</p>

<p><em>Thank you for using nginx.</em></p>
</body>
</html>
root@curl-66bdcf564-226qb:/ $
```

Figure 5.14: The nginx output

Here, you can see **Welcome to nginx!**, which indicates that the default **nginx** welcome page is retrieved as expected. It also shows that the service abstraction works from the curl pod to reach the **nginx** pods.

5. Exit the pod created in step 3 using the **exit** command:

```
root@curl-66bdcf564-226qb:/ $ exit
Session ended, resume using 'kubectl attach curl-66bdcf564-226qb -c curl -i -t' command when the pod is running
deployment.apps "curl" deleted
/devops $
```

Figure 5.15: Exiting the curl pod

6. Delete the **nginx** deployment and service using the following command:

```
kubectl delete deployment/nginx service/nginx
```

```
/devops $ kubectl delete deployment/nginx service/nginx
deployment.extensions "nginx" deleted
service "nginx" deleted
/devops $
```

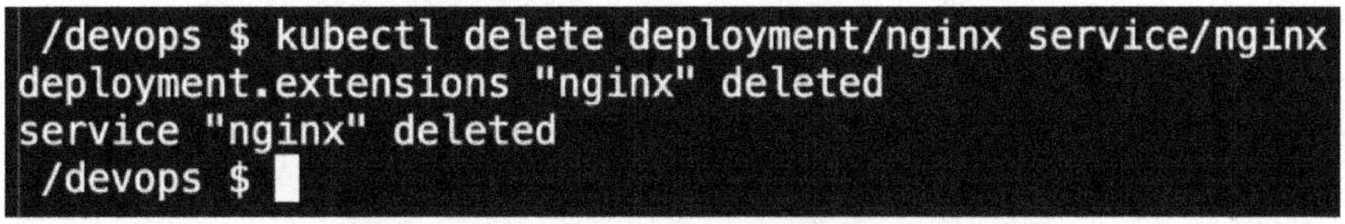

Figure 5.16: Deleting multiple resources

In this exercise, we demonstrated how to reach the pods of a deployment with service abstraction. With Kubernetes services, it is possible to deploy applications that interact with each other in a scalable and reliable way. However, as applications become more complex, it becomes more complicated to manage configuration files and **kubectl** commands. Therefore, in the following section, we will explore how the official package manager of Kubernetes can be used to solve this problem.

Kubernetes Package Manager: Helm

Cloud-native applications with multiple microservices require the writing of complex configuration files with interdependent resources such as volumes, configuration maps, secrets, pods with multiple containers, and services to expose pods. Writing YAML or JSON configuration files for each resource, along with the maintenance of these files, is exhausting and is also prone to errors. Helm is the official Kubernetes package manager that is used to solve this issue by managing resource definitions with templates. It works by separating resource definition and configuration values. Additionally, it makes it easier to deploy complex applications for users.

Helm consists of a server-side backend (**tiller**) running in the cluster and a command-line client tool (**helm**). Applications are packaged as charts in Helm, where all required Kubernetes resource templates and value files are packaged. Helm has an active chart repository where popular and stable open source Helm charts are maintained (https:// github.com/helm/charts/tree/master/stable). Stable charts include numerous popular applications from various fields, such as databases (such as MySQL, MongoDB, and PostgreSQL), CI/CD tools (such as Concourse, Jenkins, and Gitlab), content management systems (such as Joomla and WordPress), and even machine learning applications (such as TensorFlow).

All **helm** charts have templates for Kubernetes resources as well as the required configuration values. It is essential to check which values are required prior to using a Helm chart. For instance, WordPress' **helm** chart has listed all the configuration parameters with their descriptions and default values under the **README** file of the **helm** chart repository (https://github.com/helm/charts/tree/master/stable/wordpress#configuration):

Configuration

The following table lists the configurable parameters of the WordPress chart and their default values.

Parameter	Description	Default
global.imageRegistry	Global Docker image registry	nil
global.imagePullSecrets	Global Docker registry secret names as an array	[] (does not add image pull secrets to deployed pods)
image.registry	WordPress image registry	docker.io
image.repository	WordPress image name	bitnami/wordpress
image.tag	WordPress image tag	{VERSION}
image.pullPolicy	Image pull policy	Always if imageTag is latest, else IfNotPresent
image.pullSecrets	Specify docker-registry secret names as an array	[] (does not add image pull secrets to deployed pods)
wordpressUsername	User of the application	user
wordpressPassword	Application password	*random 10 character long alphanumeric string*
wordpressEmail	Admin email	user@example.com
wordpressFirstName	First name	FirstName
wordpressLastName	Last name	LastName
wordpressBlogName	Blog name	User's Blog!
wordpressTablePrefix	Table prefix	wp_
allowEmptyPassword	Allow DB blank passwords	true
allowOverrideNone	Set Apache AllowOverride directive to None	no

Figure 5.17: The configuration for the WordPress Helm chart

The configuration section of the WordPress chart has a very long list of parameters, which shows it is a highly configurable Helm chart. It is a very good opportunity to reuse these templates and configuration parameters without writing YAML files from scratch thanks to the **helm** package manager and open source community. Helm is a powerful package manager officially supported by Kubernetes and it is essential to the learn basics of Helm to deploy complex microservice applications into clusters. In the following exercise, we will install **helm** in the Kubernetes cluster and check its health status.

> **Note**
>
> You will require a Kubernetes cluster to complete the following exercise. It is possible to use a **minikube** cluster from *Chapter 3, Introduction to Kubernetes* or a GKE cluster from *Chapter 4, Creating a Kubernetes Cluster*.

Exercise 15: Installing Helm in the Kubernetes Cluster

In this exercise, we will install the official package manager of Kubernetes in a cluster. To successfully complete the exercise, perform the following steps:

1. Install the Helm client on your local computer by running the following official script on Terminal:

   ```
   curl https://raw.githubusercontent.com/helm/helm/master/scripts/get | bash
   ```

```
/devops $ curl https://raw.githubusercontent.com/helm/helm/master/scripts/get | bash
  % Total    % Received % Xferd  Average Speed   Time    Time     Time  Current
                                 Dload  Upload   Total   Spent    Left  Speed
100  7028  100  7028    0     0  50947      0 --:--:-- --:--:-- --:--:-- 50927
Helm v2.13.1 is available. Changing from version v2.12.0.
Downloading https://kubernetes-helm.storage.googleapis.com/helm-v2.13.1-darwin-amd64.tar.gz
Preparing to install helm and tiller into /usr/local/bin
Password:
helm installed into /usr/local/bin/helm
tiller installed into /usr/local/bin/tiller
Run 'helm init' to configure helm.
/devops $ 
```

Figure 5.18: The download and installation of Helm

This downloads the **helm** executable and installs this on the local computer.

2. Install the server side of Helm to the Kubernetes cluster, namely **tiller**:

```
helm init
```

```
/devops $ helm init
$HELM_HOME has been configured at /Users/i313226/.helm.

Tiller (the Helm server-side component) has been installed into your Kubernetes Cluster.

Please note: by default, Tiller is deployed with an insecure 'allow unauthenticated users' policy.
To prevent this, run `helm init` with the --tiller-tls-verify flag.
For more information on securing your installation see: https://docs.helm.sh/using_helm/#securing-your-helm-installation
Happy Helming!
/devops $
```

Figure 5.19: Installation of Tiller

Happy Helming! indicates that the server side of Helm is installed to the cluster.

3. Check the available number of **tiller-deploy** deployment instances in the **kube-system** namespace with the following command:

```
kubectl get deployment tiller-deploy -n kube-system
```

```
/devops $ kubectl get deployment tiller-deploy -n kube-system
NAME            READY   UP-TO-DATE   AVAILABLE   AGE
tiller-deploy   1/1     1            1           91s
/devops $
```

Figure 5.20: Tiller deployment status

Wait a couple of minutes until there is 1 of 1 instance available for **tiller-deploy** deployment, which indicates that the backend for **helm** is running successfully.

4. Check the version of the **helm** installation:

```
helm version
```

```
/devops $ helm version
Client: &version.Version{SemVer:"v2.12.0", GitCommit:"d325d2a9c179b33af1a024cdb5a4472b6288016a", GitTreeState:"clean"}
Server: &version.Version{SemVer:"v2.12.0", GitCommit:"d325d2a9c179b33af1a024cdb5a4472b6288016a", GitTreeState:"clean"}
/devops $
```

Figure 5.21: Helm version information

The same client and server versions indicate that there are no expected API mismatches.

5. Search for WordPress Helm charts using the following command:

```
helm search wordpress
```

```
/devops $ helm search wordpress
NAME                    CHART VERSION    APP VERSION    DESCRIPTION
stable/wordpress        5.8.2            5.1.1          Web publishing platform for building blogs and websites.
/devops $
```

Figure 5.22: The WordPress Helm chart

Here, we can see that chart version **5.8.2** is available and it installs WordPress version **5.1.1**.

In this exercise, the official Kubernetes package manager, **helm**, is installed in a cluster and the installation status is validated. It is essential to learn **helm** with hands-on experience to deploy complex microservice applications into clusters. In the following activity, you will be asked to install the popular WordPress application with its official **helm** chart.

Activity 5: Installing and Scaling a WordPress Blog in Kubernetes Using Helm

Note

You will require a Kubernetes cluster to complete the activity. It is possible to use a **minikube** cluster from *Chapter 3, Introduction to Kubernetes* or GKE cluster from *Chapter 4, Creating a Kubernetes Cluster*.

This activity aims to install and manage a WordPress blog and its database in a Kubernetes cluster by using the official **helm** chart. You will be required to use both the Helm and **kubectl** tools to install and access the blog for initial setup.

You need to install WordPress into the Kubernetes cluster by using the official Helm chart and validate that it is running. Then, you are required to complete the setup procedure of WordPress. With the successful setup, you need to scale the number of WordPress instances to three in order to reach the expected popularity.

With the successful start of WordPress, the new blog should be up and running as follows:

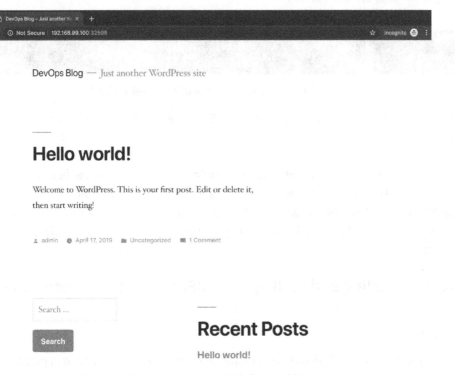

Figure 5.23: Home page - WordPress blog

Additionally, there should be three instances of WordPress pods with the successful scale-up:

```
/devops $ kubectl get pods
NAME                                      READY   STATUS    RESTARTS   AGE
devops-blog-mariadb-0                     1/1     Running   0          13m
devops-blog-wordpress-66488fc656-b5s8k    1/1     Running   0          8m38s
devops-blog-wordpress-66488fc656-sddd8    1/1     Running   0          69s
devops-blog-wordpress-66488fc656-wt79x    1/1     Running   0          69s
/devops $
```

Figure 5.24: WordPress pods

Perform the following steps to complete this activity:

1. Install the WordPress **helm** chart. The release name should be **devops-blog** and the username should be **admin**. Use **devops** as your password and **DevOps Blog** as the blog name.

2. Wait until all the pods are running and are ready.

3. Open the home page of WordPress and check that it is installed successfully.

4. Scale the WordPress instances to three.

5. Check the status of the pods with three instances.

6. Check that the home page is still accessible in the browser.

7. Delete the WordPress installation.

> **Note**
>
> The solution to this activity can be found on Page 318.

In this activity, we have installed and operated a production-ready, scalable WordPress blog and its database in a Kubernetes cluster. For the blog and its database, various Kubernetes resources were created, such as secrets, volumes, deployments, and ingress. With the help of Helm, it is possible to install complex microservice applications using a couple of commands and configuration values. Therefore, it is essential to learn the basics of Helm and to deploy and manage production-ready microservice applications.

Summary

In this chapter, we first started exploring object management methods in Kubernetes. We learned about imperative commands using kubectl, how to combine imperative commands using configuration files, and, finally, we demonstrated some declarative configuration approaches using examples. Following this, we discussed how services are a crucial Kubernetes resource, which are used to connect microservices in clusters. We used hands-on exercises to show how microservice applications should be configured in order to discover other applications. Since it is now possible to create more complex applications by interacting with each other, their resource files will be more complex to manage. Therefore, we presented the official Kubernetes package manager, Helm. Helm separates the resource definition and configuration values to install applications using a couple of commands. At the end of the chapter, Helm was utilized to install and scale up a blog application. Deploying applications to Kubernetes is one of the essential points, since Kubernetes is designed for managing cloud-native, reliable, and scalable applications. The tools, commands, and approaches shown in this chapter will be used in the following chapters and will be useful for your daily Kubernetes operations. In the next chapter, we will examine how to configure applications in Kubernetes using configuration maps, secrets, and volumes.

Configuration and Storage Management in Kubernetes

Learning Objectives

By the end of this chapter, you will be able to:

- Implement configuration management in Kubernetes
- List some of the secret management best practices
- Implement methods for handling secrets in Kubernetes
- Configure and deploy a sample application with persistent storage

In this chapter, you will learn about configuration and storage management in Kubernetes.

Configuration Management

Configuration management takes care of the life cycle of the configurations of a system or application. These settings help to make configuring computer programs benefit optimally from the environment they run on. You can also use these settings to make them behave differently in some cases. Configuration management includes, but is not limited to, creating, tracking, storing, and updating the individual configuration items.

Configuration management also refers to the handling of the infrastructure configuration. From this aspect, it can boost the efficiency of an automated process instead of a manual configuration process. Configuration management systems such as **Puppet**, **Chef**, and **Ansible** bring plenty of benefits to the table. Some of which ease automation, providing consistency throughout the system, and matching the system to the desired state. However, as Kubernetes increasingly touches upon this area and solves these problems in its own way, these tools are losing their popularity.

In the following section, we explain two types of configurations that configuration management for modern cloud-native applications takes care of: infrastructure configurations and application runtime configurations. Then, we will show how application runtime configurations can be managed by using the native Kubernetes resources.

Infrastructure Configurations

Infrastructure configurations include all the resource definitions and configurations needed for managing the infrastructure. It is also called **Infrastructure as Code** (IaC). IaC is a way to automate the deployment of a system without manual work, which decreases the possibility of human error and increases the deployment speed significantly. It is a must to make many DevOps practices possible. Keeping the infrastructure configurations in version control is also very important, especially for tracking configuration changes, supporting automation, and the assurance of peer review. Handling infrastructure in version control just like code also allows us to test and deploy continuously using CI/CD tools. This topic is extensive with its building blocks, but we won't go into too much detail in this book. Instead, we will focus on application runtime configurations, which are explained in the next section.

Runtime Configurations

An application's configuration includes everything that may differ from one deployment to another. Environment-related information, URLs to the external services, and database credentials are just a few examples. If the configuration values include any sensitive information, such as database credentials, they are categorized as secrets and treated with more care in terms of any security issues. You'll learn about secrets in more detail in the next section.

Every application usually has at least three sets of configurations for development, test, and production environments.

One of the principles of the twelve-factor app methodology is the separation of the configuration from the code. The twelve-factor app methodology suggests using config values from the environment as an environment variable. This is a useful technique to handle configurations easily in a language and operating system agnostic way. It also makes it easy to find the configuration value rather than scanning the source code to see where to change it for anyone who wants to change a configuration value.

> **Note**
>
> The twelve-factor app is a set of principles constructed to provide ideal patterns for developing modern applications. For more information, you can visit https://12factor.net/.

Storing configuration files should be stored in version control. This allows you to track the changes and roll back a configuration change if necessary.

Configuration Management in Kubernetes

Kubernetes provides centralized management of application configurations and makes it possible to update the configurations on the fly without needing to recompile or reboot your application. It propagates the changes to all the containers that have the configs as mounted volumes so that you don't have to change every instance's configurations manually one by one.

Kubernetes provides a built-in resource called **ConfigMap** to ease the management of application configurations. This encourages the decoupling of the configurations from the source code and managing them independently.

Data inside a ConfigMap consists of key-value pairs, where the key is the name of the provided file or the key provided in the command and the value is file content or the value provided in the command. The following table shows the API reference for the ConfigMap object. You can see in the following table which fields correspond to what type of an object in a ConfigMap definition:

Field	Description	Type	Required
apiVersion	API version represents the version of the Kubernetes API where this object definition resides.	String	No
Kind	Kind is the Kubernetes resource type of this object.	String	No
metadata	Metadata includes the information that distinguishes this object from the others, such as name and namespace.	ObjectMeta	No
data	Data includes the configuration value, which consists of key-value pairs. Keys must be unique to prevent conflicts.	Object	No
binaryData	Different to the data field, binary data is used to keep the non-UTF-8 configuration values.	Object	No

Figure 6.1: Kubernetes ConfigMap API reference

The configurations residing in ConfigMaps can be consumed from the Pods either as environment variables or as files on a mounted volume.

A sample ConfigMap definition is as follows:

```
apiVersion: v1

kind: ConfigMap

metadata:

  name: test-config

  namespace: default

data:

  environment: test
```

Creating a ConfigMap

There are a few different ways to create a ConfigMap object in Kubernetes. One way is to create the ConfigMap file manually either in **JSON** or **YAML** and deploy it to the cluster using **kubectl apply/create**. Using this option, you can also commit the definition file you created to a version control system like Git.

Let's create a file named **app-config.yaml** with the following ConfigMap definition. Create a file using **vi** and copy-paste the following definition:

```
$ vi app-config.yaml


apiVersion: v1

kind: ConfigMap


metadata:

  name: app-config

data:

  environment: test
```

Now, deploy it using:

```
$ kubectl apply -f app-config.yaml

$ kubectl get configmap app-config -o yaml
```

Here is the outcome of **kubectl get** showing the **app-config** ConfigMap object created by the previous **kubectl apply** command:

```
apiVersion: v1
data:
  environment: test
kind: ConfigMap
metadata:
  annotations:
    kubectl.kubernetes.io/last-applied-configuration: |  {"apiVersion":"v1","
data":{"environment":"test"},"kind":"ConfigMap","metadata":{"annotations":{},
"name":"app-config","namespace":"default"}}
  creationTimestamp: 2019-02-23T20:28:31Z
  name: app-config
  namespace: default
  resourceVersion: "4067078"
  selfLink: /api/v1/namespaces/default/configmaps/app-config
  uid: 95e6d30e-37a9-11e9-b54c-42010a840235
```

Alternatively, the **kubectl create configmap** command can be used to create a ConfigMap. This creates ConfigMaps directly from literals, files, or even directories.

Let's try creating a ConfigMap from two literals:

```
$ kubectl create configmap test-config --from-literal=test-config-1=test1
--from-literal=test-config-2=test2
$ kubectl get configmap test-config -o yaml
```

Here is the outcome of **kubectl get**, showing the **test-config** ConfigMap object created by the previous **kubectl create configmap** command:

```
apiVersion: v1
data:
  test-config-1: test1
  test-config-2: test2
kind: ConfigMap
metadata:
  creationTimestamp: 2019-02-22T19:14:38Z
  name: test-config
```

```
  namespace: default

  resourceVersion: "406620"

  selfLink: /api/v1/namespaces/default/configmaps/test-config

  uid: d820c9fd-37a8-11e9-b54c-42010a840235
```

You can also create a ConfigMap from files or directories by using the **--from-file** option instead of **--from-literal**. The only constraint is that the files must contain plaintext (unencrypted) key-value pairs:

```
$ echo "test-config=test" > configs.txt


$ kubectl create configmap test-config-2 --from-file=configs.txt
$ kubectl get configmap test-config-2 -o yaml
```

Here is the outcome of **kubectl get**, showing the **test-config-2** ConfigMap object created by the previous **kubectl create configmap** command:

```
apiVersion: v1

data:

  configs.txt: |

    test-config=test

kind: ConfigMap

metadata:

  creationTimestamp: 2019-02-25T14:19:18Z

  name: test-config-2

  namespace: default

  resourceVersion: "473070"

  selfLink: /api/v1/namespaces/default/configmaps/test-config

  uid: 56a79682-3908-11e9-bd9a-82d3ccfe1531
```

In this section, we explored different ways of creating ConfigMaps. We created a ConfigMap definition file manually and deployed it using **kubectl apply**. Also, we used **kubectl create configmap** to conveniently create a ConfigMap from literals or files, eliminating the need to create a definition file manually.

Updating a ConfigMap

ConfigMaps can be updated like any other built-in Kubernetes resources using **kubectl apply** as follows:

```
$ kubectl apply -f app-config.yaml
```

If you created the ConfigMap without a file using **kubectl create**, you can simply use the following command to update the ConfigMap. This will utilize the YAML file automatically created with **kubectl create configmap**:

```
$ kubectl create configmap test-config --from-literal=test-config-1=updated-
test1 --from-literal=test-config-2=updated-test2 -o yaml --dry-run | kubectl
replace -f -
```

Alternatively, you can also use **kubectl edit** or **kubectl patch** the same way as any other Kubernetes resource:

```
$ kubectl patch configmap test-config -p='{"data":{"test-config-1": "updated-
test1"}}'
```

Consuming ConfigMaps from a Pod

ConfigMaps can be consumed from a Pod in two ways. These are by injecting the configurations inside the ConfigMap as environment variables to the application container and by mounting volumes with the configurations residing on separate files. Pods can consume ConfigMaps only from the same namespace.

Here is an example pod definition where the ConfigMap is injected as an environment variable:

```
apiVersion: v1
kind: Pod
metadata:
  name: test-config-pod
spec:
  containers:
  - name: test
    image: busybox
    env:
      - name: LOG_LEVEL
        valueFrom:
          configMapKeyRef:
```

```
        name: app-config
        key: log-level
```

Here is another example where the ConfigMap is mounted as a volume:

```
apiVersion: v1
kind: Pod


metadata:
  name: test-config-pod-2
spec:
  containers:
  - name: test
    image: busybox
    volumeMounts:
    - name: config-volume
      mountPath: "/configurations"
  volumes:
  - name: config-volume
    configMap:
      name: app-config
```

When you mount ConfigMap as a volume to a Pod, each data item in the ConfigMap becomes a separate file in the volume.

Note that consuming the ConfigMaps from the mounted volume has the advantage of making updates possible. Therefore, when you update the ConfigMap after the first creation, this change will be propagated to the containers that consume this ConfigMap. You need to keep in mind that the current value is cached, so it takes a couple of minutes for the updates to be propagated.

Be aware that ConfigMaps must be created before the Pods that use them. Otherwise, Pods won't start until ConfigMaps exist.

Exercise 16: Create ConfigMaps from a Literal and a File

In this exercise, we aim to create ConfigMaps from a literal and a configuration file:

1. Create a file with sample configuration values:

    ```
    $ cat > config.txt <<EOF
    environment: "test"
    max-limit: 999
    log-level: "debug"
    EOF
    ```

2. Create the **lesson-6** namespace and create a ConfigMap from this file:

    ```
    $ kubectl create ns lesson-6
    $ kubectl create configmap app-config-file --from-file=config.txt -n lesson-6
    $ kubectl get configmap app-config-file -o yaml -n lesson-6
    ```

```
/devops $ kubectl create configmap app-config-file --from-file=configs.txt -n lesson-6
configmap/app-config-file created
/devops $
/devops $ kubectl get configmap app-config-file -o yaml -n lesson-6
apiVersion: v1
data:
  configs.txt: |
    environment: "test"
    max-limit: 999
    log-level: "debug"
kind: ConfigMap
metadata:
  creationTimestamp: 2019-02-23T21:35:44Z
  name: app-config-file
  namespace: lesson-6
  resourceVersion: "4077099"
  selfLink: /api/v1/namespaces/lesson-6/configmaps/app-config-file
  uid: fa01e783-37b2-11e9-b54c-42010a840235
/devops $
```

Figure 6.2: Creating an app-config-file ConfigMap

3. Create a ConfigMap from literal:

    ```
    $ kubectl create configmap app-config --from-literal=environment=test -n lesson-6
    $ kubectl get configmap app-config -o yaml -n lesson-6
    ```

```
/devops $ kubectl create configmap app-config --from-literal=environment=test -n lesson-6
configmap/app-config created
/devops $
/devops $ kubectl get configmap app-config -o yaml -n lesson-6
apiVersion: v1
data:
  environment: test
kind: ConfigMap
metadata:
  creationTimestamp: 2019-02-23T21:33:35Z
  name: app-config
  namespace: lesson-6
  resourceVersion: "4076778"
  selfLink: /api/v1/namespaces/lesson-6/configmaps/app-config
  uid: ace55ef9-37b2-11e9-b54c-42010a840235
/devops $
```

Figure 6.3: Creating an app-config ConfigMap

4. Create a file named **ConfigPod.yaml** with the following content, which consumes these ConfigMaps from a Pod. Then, deploy this Pod:

```
$ kubectl apply -f ConfigPod.yaml -n lesson-6
apiVersion: v1
kind: Pod
metadata:
  name: test-config-pod
spec:
  containers:
  - name: test
    image: busybox
    command:
      - sleep
      - "99999"
    env:
      - name: ENVIRONMENT
        valueFrom:
          configMapKeyRef:
            name: app-config
            key: environment
    volumeMounts:
    - name: config-volume
      mountPath: "/configurations"
  volumes:
  - name: config-volume
    configMap:
      name: app-config-file
```

```
/devops $ kubectl apply -f ConfigPod.yaml -n lesson-6
pod/test-config-pod created
/devops $
/devops $ kubectl get pods -n lesson-6
NAME              READY     STATUS    RESTARTS    AGE
test-config-pod   1/1       Running   0           13s
/devops $
```

Figure 6.4: Deploying test-config-pod to the cluster

5. Get into the container and check the content of **/configurations**:

```
$ kubectl exec -it test-config-pod -n lesson-6 sh
$ cat configurations/config.txt
$ echo $ENVIRONMENT
```

```
/devops $ kubectl exec -it test-config-pod -n lesson-6 sh
/ # ls configurations/
configs.txt
/ # cat configurations/configs.txt
environment: "test"
max-limit: 999
log-level: "debug"
/ #
/ # echo $ENVIRONMENT
test
/ #
```

Figure 6.5: Creating an SH into the container and checking the content of configs.txt

6. Create another file with sample configuration values:

```
$ cat > config-2.txt <<EOF
environment: "dev"
max-limit: 111
log-level: "info"
EOF
```

7. Update the existing ConfigMap using the **config-2.txt** file:

```
$ kubectl create configmap app-config-file --from-file=config-2.txt -o yaml -n
lesson-6 --dry-run | kubectl replace -f -
```

```
/devops $ kubectl create configmap app-config-file --from-file=config-2.txt -o yaml -n lesson-6 --dry-run | kubectl replace
-f -
configmap/app-config-file replaced
/devops $
```

Figure 6.6: Replacing app-config-file using the file

8. Get into the container and check the content of **/configurations**:

```
$ kubectl exec -it test-config-pod -n lesson-6 sh
$ cat configurations/config-2.txt
```

```
/devops $ kubectl exec -it test-config-pod -n lesson-6 sh
/ # cat configurations/config-2.txt
environment: "dev"
max-limit: 111
log-level: "info"
/ #
```

Figure 6.7: Creating an SH into the container and checking the content of config-2.txt

> **Note**
>
> You might need to wait a couple of minutes (until configmap is synced) before seeing expected results. Immediate run of this steps fails.

Kubernetes provides a ConfigMap built-in resource as a way to decouple the

configurations from your application's source code and manage them from a centralized system in the best way possible. That's why it is important to make use of them for runtime configurations. In this section, we learned configuration management in general and how we can manage our configurations in Kubernetes. In the next section, we will take a look at a special type of configurations called secrets. We will learn secret management best practices and how we can manage our secrets in Kubernetes.

Secret Management

Security is usually a cumbersome topic for developers, but if it is not taken care of, it can result in severe consequences. Secret management is one of the building blocks for achieving a completely secure system in DevOps. It usually refers to techniques and tools for handling sensitive information (secrets) in a digital system. Any sensitive information could be treated as a secret. For example, these are some of the most commonly used secrets in DevOps:

- API keys
- Database passwords
- TLS certificates

Secret management implies managing the life cycle of secrets, which includes creating, storing, consuming, and even disposing of them safely. Secrets can be managed using a secret management software, such as Hashicorp's Vault (https://www.vaultproject.io/) or Square's Keywhiz (https://square.github.io/keywhiz/). Although they can be helpful with some secret management practices, they can also bring unnecessary complexity to your system. So, they should be evaluated very carefully for the needs of your system, and full manual management should be considered as well before blindly going for a secret management tool. Regardless of the chosen method for managing secrets, some best practices should be taken into consideration. These are presented in the next section.

Secret Management Best Practices

In this section, we'll go through some secret management best practices. These points are essential to understand in order to manage secrets in a DevOps environment. The following figure shows secret management best practices, which are valuable practices for securing sensitive information:

Figure 6.8: Secret management best practices

Identifying Secrets

The very first step for secret management is to identify all kinds of secrets. They include, but are not limited to, passwords, SSH keys, and certificates for communication (for example, TLS). It is very important that this should be a continuous process. That is, all new configuration values should be evaluated and treated as secret if they include any sensitive information. Also, secrets should be constrained to have enough complexity to make them difficult to solve. For example, when you integrate your application with another one, you'd usually need a kind of credential to authenticate with, and also some configuration values to customize the other application. You should go through all these configuration values, including the credentials, decide which ones could be sensitive information, and categorize them as secrets. Only by identifying them can you consider more measures to secure them.

Decoupling Secrets from the Source Code

It is, unfortunately, a common practice, especially for a quick start, to keep secrets such as credentials or connection tokens hardcoded in the source code or in a shared folder; this could easily result in a security breach that could even lead to the bankruptcy of companies.

We already talked about why configurations should be decoupled from the source code in the previous topic. This practice is even more critical when it comes to secrets. It is a DevOps best practice to keep the source code clear of any secrets and inject secrets into applications either as an environment variable or in a file. This not only decreases the possibility of a compromise, but also makes managing all the secrets under centralized management possible. Imagine that you keep a customer's database credentials in the source code. A hacker could reverse engineer the application to see the source code if they can get access to the application. In such cases, the hacker could obtain the credentials for the customer's database. How catastrophic would that be for your business with the customer and for your overall reputation?

Rotating Secrets

Rotating secrets means regularly changing secrets. It is an integral part of secret management. It is crucial to mitigate security vulnerabilities that could arise when an employee leaves the company or if a secret is exposed in another way at some point. For instance, a system could be hacked because of a security breach that happened a year ago if there is no secret rotation policy embraced for that system.

Principle of Least Privilege

A typical DevOps environment makes use of many different technologies and tools in which secret management is indispensable. The secrets used in various tools could have quite high privileges for the tool to operate without any problem. In such cases, the compromise of these secrets could be catastrophic. A hacker could take control of and destroy the whole system by exploiting highly privileged credentials. That's why all secrets must have the least possible privileges to achieve their job.

Preventing Printing Out Secrets on Application Logs

You need to make sure that secrets are never printed out in logs. This may sound rather obvious, but this is also a widespread mistake, especially when printing the whole object in case of an error. This should be kept in mind while writing code. For example, you might have a system where the logs are available to the public. If you merge code printing sensitive information to the logs by mistake, this information could easily be exploited by someone with bad intentions.

Encryption at Rest

Secrets should be handled with great care, not only during transit, but also at rest. They shouldn't be stored as plain text but encrypted. This way, even if secrets are compromised at some point, they'd be useless without the encryption key. Google Cloud provides a service called Cloud Key Management Service (KMS) to tackle this problem (https://cloud.google.com/kms/). It can be used for encrypting and decrypting secrets so that they can be stored more securely. KMS has integration with Google Kubernetes Engine, so it can be used to encrypt the secrets residing on Kubernetes etcd. A malicious person or a piece of code can grant access to the storage at some point, but they can't do anything if the secrets there are encrypted. This brings us to the next topic, where we will go through secret management in Kubernetes.

Secret Management in Kubernetes

Kubernetes provides a built-in resource called secret to ease the management of secrets. Each secret object is used to store a small amount of sensitive information.

Data that is kept in the secret resource is in the form of key-value pairs.

The following table shows the API reference for the secret object. You can see which fields correspond to what type of an object in a secret definition:

Field	Description	Type	Required
apiVersion	API version represents the version of the Kubernetes API where this object definition resides.	String	No
kind	Kind is the Kubernetes resource type of this object.	String	No
metadata	Metadata includes the information that distinguishes this object from the others, such as name and namespace.	ObjectMeta	No
type	The type field is used to distinguish user-generated secret objects from programmatically-generated ones such as service account secrets.	Object	No
data	Data includes the secret value, which consists of key-value pairs. Keys must be unique to prevent conflicts. The value provided in the data field must be encoded first.	Object	No
stringData	Different than the data field, string data is used to directly set plain text values instead of encoded ones.	String	No

Figure 6.9: Kubernetes Secret API reference

(https://kubernetes.io/docs/reference/generated/kubernetes-api/v1.13/#secret-v1-core)

A sample **Secret** definition is as follows:

```
apiVersion: v1
kind: Secret
metadata:
  name: credentials
type: Opaque
data:
  username: dXNlcgo=
  password: dGVzdC10b    2tlbg==
```

Secrets can be referenced in pods either as an environment variable or in a volume.

Creating a Secret

There are several ways to create a secret object in Kubernetes. One way is to create the secret file manually either in JSON or YAML and deploy it to the cluster using **kubectl apply/create**. With this option, you may need to encode the secret by yourself and use it in the secret definition file based on your choice between using the **data** or **stringData** fields. Let's go on to learn how to create a secret.

You can simply encode your credential using **base64**:

```
$ echo -n 'test-token' | base64
$ dGVzdC10b2tlbg==
```

Then, create a secret file named **test-secret.yaml** using the encoded credential from the previous step within the **data** field:

```
apiVersion: v1
kind: Secret
metadata:
  name: test-secret
type: Opaque
data:
  token: dGVzdC10b2tlbg==
```

Deploy it using:

```
$ kubectl create -f test-secret.yaml
```

Additionally, to decode the existing secrets in the cluster, you can make use of the **kubectl get secret** command:

```
$ kubectl get secret test-secret -o yaml
```

Here is the output of **kubectl get**, showing the test-secret secret object created by the previous **kubectl create** command:

```
apiVersion: v1
data:
  token: dGVzdC10b2tlbg==

kind: Secret
metadata:
  creationTimestamp: 2019-02-20T20:09:51Z
  name: test-secret
  namespace: default
  resourceVersion: "7138986"
  selfLink: /api/v1/namespaces/default/secrets/test-secret
  uid: 7b1b57d5-354b-11e9-bd98-42010a9c01eb
type: Opaque
```

Now, we can utilize **base64** again to decode the secret:

```
$ echo 'dGVzdC10b2tlbg==' | base64 -D
test-token
```

> **Note**
>
> The **-D** option is only valid on macOS. For Linux, please use **-d** instead.

Alternatively, you can provide the credentials in open text as **stringData** instead of **data**. That way, the text will be encoded for you:

```
apiVersion: v1

kind: Secret

metadata:

  name: test-secret

type: Opaque

stringData:

  token: test-token
```

Deploy this using:

```
$ kubectl apply -f test-secret.yaml
```

Now, when you take a look at the secret content, you will see that it is the same as we encoded in the previous example:

```
$ kubectl get secret test-secret -o yaml
```

Here is the output of **kubectl get**, showing the test-secret secret object created by the previous **kubectl apply** command:

```
apiVersion: v1

data:

  token: dGVzdC10b2tlbg==

kind: Secret

metadata:

  creationTimestamp: 2019-02-20T20:24:14Z

  name: test-secret

  namespace: default

  resourceVersion: "473531"

  selfLink: /api/v1/namespaces/default/secrets/test-secret

  uid: 06e67b21-3909-11e9-bd9a-82d3ccfe1531

type: Opaque
```

Another way of creating a secret is to make use of **kubectl create secret**, which will generate the secret from either a file or a literal, and then deploy it onto the cluster.

The previous secret you created, **test-secret**, could also be created running
following command:

```
$ kubectl create secret generic test-secret-2 --from-literal=token=test-
token
```

Alternatively, you can put the token into a file and create the secret directly from the
file:

```
$ echo test-token > token.txt
```

```
$ kubectl create secret generic test-secret-3 --from-file=token=token.txt
```

Updating a Secret

Secrets can also be updated like any other built-in Kubernetes resources using **kubectl
apply**:

```
$ kubectl apply -f test-secret.yaml
```

If you created the secret without a file using **kubectl create**, you can use the following
command to update the secret easily. This will utilize the YAML file automatically
created by **kubectl create secret**:

```
$ kubectl create secret generic test-secret --from-literal=token=new-test-
token -o yaml --dry-run | kubectl replace -f -
```

Alternatively, you can also use **kubectl edit** or **kubectl patch** the same way as any other
Kubernetes resource:

```
$ kubectl patch secret test-secret -p='{"stringData":{"token": "new-test-
token"}}'
```

Consuming Secrets from a Pod

Secrets can be used in a pod in two ways. These are by injecting them as an
environment variable to the application container and by mounting volumes with the
secrets residing on a file. Pods can only consume secrets from the same namespace.

Here is an example od definition where the secret is injected as an environment
variable:

```
apiVersion: v1
kind: Pod
metadata:
  name: test-secret-pod
spec:
```

```
containers:
- name: test
  image: busybox
  env:
    - name: TOKEN
      valueFrom:
        secretKeyRef:
          name: test-secret
          key: token
```

Here is another example where the secret is mounted as a volume:

```
apiVersion: v1
kind: Pod
metadata:
  name: test-secret-pod-2
spec:
  containers:
  - name: test
    image: busybox
    volumeMounts:
    - name: token-volume
      mountPath: "/secrets"
  volumes:
  - name: token-volume
    secret:
      secretName: test-secret
```

When multiple containers need to consume a secret, the volume must be referenced only once, but for each container, you must add a separate **volumeMount**.

Consuming secrets from the mounted volume has the advantage of making updates possible. Therefore, when you update secrets after their initial creation, this change will be propagated to the containers that consume this secret. You need to keep in mind that the current value is cached and that's why it takes some time for the updates to be propagated.

Be aware that secrets must be created before the pods that use them. Otherwise, pods won't start until secrets exist.

Exercise 17: Create and Update a Secret

In this exercise, we aim to create a secret, decode it and update the existing secret. Perform the following steps to complete the exercis:

1. Create a random token:

```
$ openssl rand -hex 8
```

```
/devops $ openssl rand -hex 8
b83f7d3cc64efc58
/devops $
```

Figure 6.10: Creating a random token

2. Create a secret using the **kubectl create secret** command:

```
$ kubectl create secret generic token -n lesson-6 --from-
literal=token=b83f7d3cc64efc58
```

```
/devops $ kubectl create secret generic token -n lesson-6 --from-literal=token=b83f7d3cc64efc58
secret/token created
/devops $
```

Figure 6.11: Creating a token secret from a literal

3. View the secret and decode it:

```
$ kubectl get secret token -n lesson-6 -o yaml
$ echo "YjgzZjdkM2NjNjRlZmM1OA==" | base64 -D
```

```
/devops $ kubectl get secret token -n lesson-6 -o yaml
apiVersion: v1
data:
  token: YjgzZjdkM2NjNjRlZmM1OA==
kind: Secret
metadata:
  creationTimestamp: 2019-02-18T21:03:36Z
  name: token
  namespace: lesson-6
  resourceVersion: "6822125"
  selfLink: /api/v1/namespaces/lesson-6/secrets/token
  uid: a8a3e7b6-33c0-11e9-bd98-42010a9c01eb
type: Opaque
/devops $
/devops $ echo "YjgzZjdkM2NjNjRlZmM1OA==" | base64 -D
b83f7d3cc64efc58
```

Figure 6.12: Checking the content of the secret and decoding the token

4. Create a new random token using the **openssl** command from step 1 and replace the existing secret:

```
$ kubectl create secret generic token --from-
literal=token=0c796ab82c385dd2 -n lesson-6 -o yaml --dry-run | kubectl
replace -f -
```

```
/devops $ openssl rand -hex 8
69573f31bcde6e3b
/devops $
/devops $ kubectl create secret generic token --from-literal=token=69573f31bcde6e3b -n lesson-6 -o yaml --dry-run | kubectl replace -f -
secret/token replaced
/devops $
/devops $ kubectl get secret token -n lesson-6 -o yaml
apiVersion: v1
data:
  token: NjklNzNmMzFiY2RlNmUzYg==
kind: Secret
metadata:
  creationTimestamp: 2019-02-18T21:03:36Z
  name: token
  namespace: lesson-6
  selfLink: /api/v1/namespaces/lesson-6/secrets/token
  uid: a8a3e7b6-33c0-11e9-bd98-42010a9c01eb
type: Opaque
/devops $
```

Figure 6.13: Replacing the existing token in the secret with a new one

As a separate resource type, secrets are treated with more care on Kubernetes. For example, unlike other resources, Kubernetes does not reveal the contents of secrets when you run **kubectl get** or **kubectl describe**. By making use of this type, you can manage all your secrets from a centralized system and decoupled from the application. That's why this abstraction would be the best way to manage secrets for your applications running on Kubernetes.

In this chapter, we covered secret management in general and learned how we can manage secrets in Kubernetes. In the next section, we will learn how to handle storage in Kubernetes.

Activity 6: Updating Configurations on the Fly

Imagine that you are running an application on Kubernetes and it is ready for production use. Your boss asks you to finally deploy the application on the production environment. You get very excited, deploy the application on the production cluster, and make it available to customers. You check the logs and you realize that the application is deployed with the test configurations. You immediately update the configurations that are being used by the application. Then, a security team member passing by checks the logs and realizes that the application is using 8-byte tokens and asks you to improve it to 32-byte. While changing the configurations, the application must not be down. Your task is first to deploy the application that uses the ConfigMap and secret you created during the chapter. Then, update the configuration and secrets according to the scenario.

> **Note**
>
> To complete this activity, all previous exercises in the chapter will need to have been completed. You can either use a real cluster or Minikube for this activity.

Execute the following steps to complete this activity:

1. We created a ConfigMap named **app-config** and a secret named **token** earlier in the chapter; include them in your solution. Create a pod definition file that consumes this ConfigMap and the secret.

2. Deploy the pod.

3. Make sure that the pod is running and check the logs to see the current environment coming from ConfigMap and the token coming from the secret.

4. Replace the current environment variable set by the **app-config** ConfigMap.

5. Check the logs to see the updated environment information.

> **Note**
>
> It may take a few minutes for the pod to get the changes.

6. Generate and encode a 32-byte token.

7. Replace the current token set by the secret.

8. Recheck the logs to see the updated token.

> **Note**
>
> The solution to this activity can be found on page 323.

Storage Management

Storage management tries to provide an answer to all the problems regarding the storage aspect of DevOps. This is especially important because, for DevOps environments to run smoothly, storage needs to be provisioned quickly and efficiently.

Automation is a keyword for DevOps, which aims to reduce the human error factor as much as possible and provide a stable environment to improve development and release processes. By adding highly needed scalability and availability to the recipe, dynamic storage provisioning is a must to match all the demands capably. It simplifies the workflows required for a DevOps environment.

Developers not only rely on tools and technologies, but also densely utilize storage for development purposes. That's why organizations need to provide the right tools to enable people to do their jobs in a practical way and add more value to the organization.

Luckily, with the rise of cloud and modern storage management solutions, storage provisioning times have reduced from months to seconds.

DevOps processes make heavy use of the container ecosystem, which also results in the necessity for a storage platform that supports containers. That's where Kubernetes comes into play, as the platform abstracts away the underlying storage provisioning infrastructure and provides a unified interface for users to manage storage. In the next section, we will look at methods for managing storage for your applications using the native resources provided by Kubernetes.

Storage Management in Kubernetes

Kubernetes provides a couple of built-in resources, such as Volumes, to manage storage needed for an application running on the cloud. As Kubernetes is highly adopted in the industry, there are many plugins available out of the box to make use of dynamic storage provisioning on the cloud or on-premise installations. This provides the required speed and efficiency for automation in DevOps. In the next section, we will demonstrate these native Kubernetes resources and show how to utilize them.

Volume

Kubernetes aims to address two problems with Volume abstraction. One is containers having only ephemeral storage, which is gone when the container crashes, and the other one is the need to share a common volume between the containers inside a pod.

Kubernetes provides a wide range of volume types to utilize all the cloud offerings as well as supporting on-premise solutions.

Here, you can find the full list of the volume types supported by Kubernetes: https://kubernetes.io/docs/concepts/storage/#types-of-volumes

In this book, we'll cover a few of the most used volume types, which are **emptyDir**, **gcePersistentDisk**, and **glusterfs**.

emptyDir

emptyDir is a type of volume that takes advantage of the underlying storage system on a node. It provides an empty volume mounted to the pod so that every container can access it through the same or different paths, depending on the configuration. The lifetime of a Volume is determined by the pod that uses it, so pod restart does not clean the volume, but killing the pod deletes the volume as well.

Here is a sample pod definition using **emptyDir**:

```
apiVersion: v1
kind: Pod
metadata:
  name: emptydir-pod
spec:
  containers:
  - image: busybox
    name: test
    volumeMounts:
```

```
    - mountPath: /test-folder
      name: emptydir-volume
  volumes:
  - name: emptydir-volume
    emptyDir: {}
```

gcePersistentDisk

gcePersistentDisk is a volume type specific to Google Cloud for handling persistent disks. This can be used to obtain a persistent disk required for an application running on Google Compute Engine (GCE), in which data is not erased when the pod is killed. As another advantage, you can also create the volume beforehand and populate it with data, which will be served to your application once the pod is running.

This command can be used to create a persistent disk on GCE:

```
$ gcloud compute disks create --size=20GB --zone=europe-west3-a test-disk
```

Here is a sample pod definition using the test-disk created by the previous command:

```
apiVersion: v1
kind: Pod
metadata:
  name: gce-pod
spec:
  containers:
  - image: busybox
    name: test
    volumeMounts:
    - mountPath: /test-folder
      name: gce-volume
  volumes:
  - name: gce-volume
    gcePersistentDisk:
      pdName: test-disk
      fsType: ext4
```

glusterfs

glusterfs is a volume type specific to **GlusterFS**, which is a free and open source network file system. Just like persistent disks on GCE, volumes created by GlusterFS are not cleaned when the pod is removed. It also has the same advantage of providing pre-populated volume to your application. However, as an open source product, you need to maintain it, as opposed to the managed storage solution from GCE.

> **Note**
>
> You can head here to learn more about GlusterFS: https://docs.gluster.org/en/ latest/Administrator%20Guide/GlusterFS%20Introduction

Here is a sample pod definition using a volume created on GlusterFS:

```
apiVersion: v1
kind: Pod
metadata:
  name: glusterfs-pod
spec:
  containers:
  - image: busybox
    name: test
    volumeMounts:
    - mountPath: /test-folder
      name: glusterfs-volume
  volumes:
  - name: glusterfs-volume
    glusterfs:
      endpoints: glusterfs-cluster
      path: test-volume
```

Exercise 18: Use emptyDir Volume to Share Content Between Containers

In this exercise, we aim to use **emptyDir** as a volume type to create and share a volume between two containers in the same pod:

1. Here is the pod definition to achieve this:

```
apiVersion: v1
kind: Pod
metadata:
  name: emptydir-pod
spec:
  containers:
  - image: busybox
    command:
    - sleep
    - "99999"
    name: test-container-1
    volumeMounts:
    - mountPath: /test-folder
      name: emptydir-volume
  - image: busybox
    command:
    - sleep
    - "99999"
    name: test-container-2
    volumeMounts:
    - mountPath: /test-folder
      name: emptydir-volume
  volumes:
  - name: emptydir-volume
    emptyDir: {}
```

2. Deploy the pod and check whether it is running using:

```
$ kubectl apply -f emptyDir-pod.yaml -n lesson-6
$ kubectl get pods -n lesson-6
```

```
/devops $ kubectl apply -f emptyDir-pod.yaml -n lesson-6
pod/emptydir-pod created
/devops $
/devops $ kubectl get pods -n lesson-6
NAME            READY      STATUS      RESTARTS     AGE
emptydir-pod    2/2        Running     0            35s
/devops $
```

Figure 6.14: Deploying emptydir-pod to the cluster

3. Get into the first container, create a dummy file, and exit:

```
$ kubectl exec -it emptydir-pod -c test-container-1 -n lesson-6 sh
$ echo lesson-06 > test-folder/test-file
$ exit
```

```
/devops $ kubectl exec -it emptydir-pod -c test-container-1 -n lesson-6 sh
/ # ls test-folder/
/ # echo lesson-06 > test-folder/test-file
/ # exit
```

Figure 6.15: Creating an SH into one of the containers to create a shared folder

4. Get into the second container and check the content of the file:

```
$ kubectl exec -it emptydir-pod -c test-container-2 -n lesson-6 sh
$ cat test-folder/test-file
```

```
/devops $ kubectl exec -it emptydir-pod -c test-container-2 -n lesson-6 sh
/ # ls test-folder/
test-file
/ # cat test-folder/test-file
lesson-06
/ #
```

Figure 6.16: Creating an SH into the other container to see the content of the shared folder

We can see from the output that the second container has the same volume mounted, hence the containers in the same pod can share content between them in this way.

Now, we'll continue with the other Kubernetes built-in resources for managing storage efficiently, which are **Persistent Volume** (PV), **Persistent Volume Claim** (PVC), and **StorageClass**.

Persistent Volume (PV)

PV provides the abstraction for volumes that are provisioned on the cluster. They are similar to Volumes, which we went through in the last section, but as a separate resource, PV has an independent life cycle from the pods that use it. Therefore, it does not get affected by any change to the status of pods.

Although cluster administrators can manually provision the underlying physical storage and create PVs, they can also be provisioned dynamically if the cluster has support for dynamic storage.

Just like Volumes, there are many supported types for PVs. You can find the full list here: https://kubernetes.io/docs/concepts/storage/persistent-volumes/#types-of-persistent-volumes

Here is a sample PV, which utilizes the GlusterFS plugin:

```
kind: PersistentVolume
apiVersion: v1
metadata:
  name: glusterfs-volume
spec:
  capacity:
    storage: 10Gi
  accessModes:
    - ReadWriteOnce
  glusterfs:
    endpoints: glusterfs-cluster
    path: test-volume
```

You can create a file named **glusterfs-volume.yaml** using this sample PV, and deploy it to the cluster:

```
$ kubectl create -f glusterfs-volume.yaml
```

You can use generic **kubectl** commands to verify that it is deployed without any problem:

```
$ kubectl get pv glusterfs-volume
$ kubectl describe pv glusterfs-volume
```

Persistent Volume Claim (PVC)

A PVC is a Kubernetes resource type, which is used to request PV for the pod they are used in. They can be directly referenced as Volume in pods.

Kubernetes handles the matching of suitable PV with a PVC. On platforms with dynamic storage support, such as GKE, PV is automatically created to match the needs of the PVC. Once a suitable match is found or created, they are bound to each other. Then, Kubernetes mounts the volume to the Pod.

With a PVC, the user can determine the size and the access mode that the application needs, and also the storage class, which can specify the disk types (this will be explained more in the next section).

Access Modes

There are the supported access modes that you can use on PVCs:

- ReadWriteOnce: A single node can read or write to the volume.

- ReadOnlyMany: Many nodes can read data from the volume but cannot write.

- ReadWriteMany: Many nodes can read or write to the volume.

Here is a sample PVC, which requests 50GB of storage:

```
apiVersion: v1
kind: PersistentVolumeClaim
metadata:
  name: test-pvc
spec:
  accessModes:
    - ReadWriteOnce
  resources:
    requests:
      storage: 50Gi
```

You can create a file named **test-pvc.yaml** using this sample PVC, and deploy it to the cluster:

```
$ kubectl create -f test-pvc.yaml
```

You can use generic **kubectl** commands to verify that it is deployed without any problem:

```
$ kubectl get pvc test-pvc
$ kubectl describe pvc test-pvc
```

Storage Class

Many cloud providers offer different types of storage for various needs, such as speed and redundancy. Kubernetes provides storage class as a way to choose between different storage types for the Volumes you want to mount to your application. You can also create a storage class to configure custom provisioning.

Usually, a default storage class is already provided by cloud providers, so you don't need to specify a storage class if you don't need to choose a different storage type explicitly. For example, when you create a managed Kubernetes cluster on GKE, it comes with a default storage class. This storage class only provisions standard persistent disks when requested by a PVC. If you want to use any other disk type for your application, you need to provide a new storage class.

When you create a PVC, Kubernetes automatically generates a PV according to the specifications coming from the storage classes.

Here is a sample storage class, which provisions standard disks on GCE:

```
kind: StorageClass

apiVersion: storage.k8s.io/v1

metadata:

  name: slow

provisioner: kubernetes.io/gce-pd

parameters:

  type: pd-standard

  replication-type: none
```

You can create a file named **slow.yaml** using this sample PVC, and deploy it to the cluster:

```
$ kubectl create -f slow.yaml
```

You can use generic **kubectl** commands to verify that it is deployed without any problem:

```
$ kubectl get storageclass slow
$ kubectl describe storageclass slow
```

The following diagram shows how each abstraction interacts with the others as a part of storage management in Kubernetes:

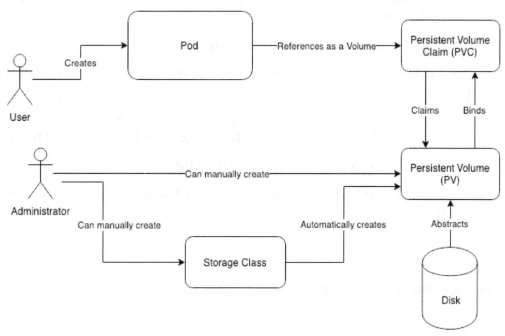

Figure 6.17: Storage management in Kubernetes

In this chapter, we have covered all the resources in Kubernetes that are used to manage storage in an effective and fast manner. In the following activity, we will deploy a relational database management system with backing persistent disks to store data by utilizing the resources provided by Kubernetes.

Activity 7: Running a Persistent Database on Kubernetes

Imagine that you work on a microservice that is responsible for the payments on an e-commerce website. You are required to deploy a database management system. The data kept in this database needs to stay secure for a long time, especially for legal and audit purposes. Data loss could mean catastrophe for the company. Your task is to deploy a MySQL relational database management system (because of the high number of transactions in this microservice) with a volume that won't be cleaned up if the pod crashes or is removed.

> **Note**
>
> To complete this activity, you can use Minikube or a managed Kubernetes cluster such as GKE.

Execute the following steps to complete this activity:

1. Create a **Deployment** definition file for MySQL, which uses a secret for the user password and a Volume using a PVC.

2. Create a service definition file for your deployment.

3. Generate a password and deploy a secret using the password as a literal to the cluster.

4. Create a PVC that requests 20GB of storage and deploy it to the cluster. Then, check whether a PV is automatically created by Kubernetes and bound to the PVC.

5. Deploy MySQL Deployment and Service to the cluster.

6. Check whether the Pod is running and verify that MySQL works properly by trying to access the server.

> **Note**
>
> The solution to this activity can be found on Page no 326.

So, we now have a running MySQL deployment with 20 GB disk space on our Kubernetes cluster, and we verified that we can access it without any problem using the password that we determined.

Summary

In this chapter, we first described the configuration management and mentioned different types of configurations that need to be considered under the umbrella of DevOps. With hands-on exercises, we showed how you can manage configurations for an application running on Kubernetes.

We then progressed to secret management, which is a particular type of configuration for handling sensitive information. We introduced some of the best practices that need to be taken into consideration when working with secrets. We also explained how secrets can be managed as an independent resource on Kubernetes. At the end of the chapter, we applied what we went through in the first two sections to a real-life scenario in an activity.

Storage management was the last topic of this chapter, in which we described why it is an essential concept for DevOps. We also explained the built-in Kubernetes resources for managing storage in a practical way. In the next chapter, we will be demonstrating two of the fundamental DevOps practices, upgrading and scaling an application.

Updating and Scaling an Application in Kubernetes

Learning Objectives

By the end of this chapter, you will be able to:

- List different ways of updating an application

- Update an application in Kubernetes using different techniques and also by using Helm

- Perform the scale up, scale out and scale operations on a application in Kubernetes

- Use autoscalers in Kubernetes

This chapter, explains how to update and scale an application on Kubernetes

Updating an Application

In the previous chapter, *Configuration and Storage Management in Kubernetes*, we saw how to manage configurations and secrets generally as well as in Kubernetes. We also went through the process of handling storage and explored how Kubernetes provides a number of abstractions in order to make this easy for users. After covering configuration and storage management as key practices in DevOps, in this chapter, we will see how we can update and scale an application, as they are equally important practices that we need to apply in DevOps.

Updating an application is an inevitable part of software management – especially DevOps. In continuous integration and delivery, applications can be updated a number of times a day or even an hour. These updates can be disruptive in cases where high availability is a very important function of the application. No user likes to land on a website where they see an error message saying that the service is currently not available. That's why it is critical to perform updates with great care, and as quickly as possible, without causing application downtime.

There are some advanced techniques that can be used in order to perform updates. Each technique introduces a different update process, with its own advantages and disadvantages. They also cover roll back scenarios, if needed. Of course, it is always possible to update an application by shutting it down and starting its new version, which is called simple or **reckless deployment**. However, as mentioned previously, this will lead to application downtime, causing customer frustration and impacting your company's reputation.

In the following section, we will explore four of these update techniques, namely **blue-green deployments**, **rolling updates**, **canary releases**, **dark launches**, and **feature toggles**, including their advantages and usage areas.

Blue-Green Deployments

In blue–green deployments, two independent production environments are configured in exactly the same way for updating an application. One environment (**Environment 1**) serves the software actively in production, while the other one (**Environment 2**) serves the software in the idle state. These two environments never become active at the same time. While updating the software from the old version (**v1**) to the new one (**v2**), the load balancer is simply switched between these environments. Hence, application downtime is either minimal or even eliminated.

For instance, for a monolithic application – where you can't avoid shutting down the application altogether and starting up a new one – you can use blue-green deployment for a seamless update process. You can prepare the application and run it in the new environment so that when you switch the traffic, it'll be ready to serve. The order of the blue-green deployment procedure is as follows:

1. The blue environment gets normal traffic, while the green one is disabled from the load balancer:

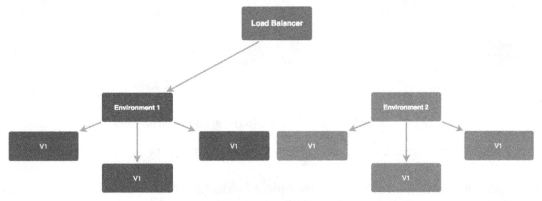

Figure 7.1: The initial phase of blue-green deployment

2. The application on the green environment is updated to the new version and tests are run in order to verify that the new version of the software behaves correctly:

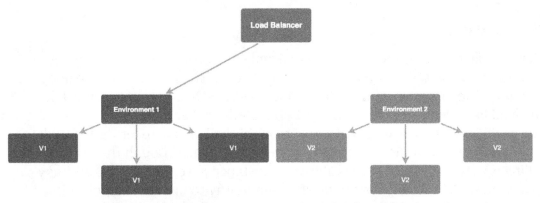

Figure 7.2: Preparing the green environment for the updated version

3. Once verified, the load balancer is switched to only serve the traffic to the green environment:

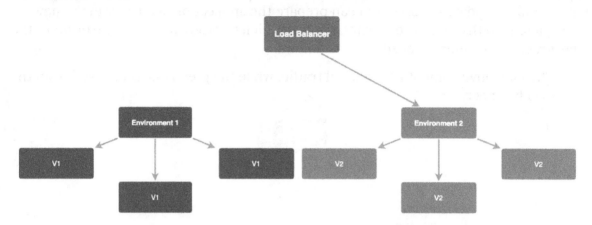

Figure 7.3: Switching the traffic to the green environment

4. The blue environment is deleted after ensuring that everything works well.

In this technique, rollbacks are also as simple as switching the load balancer back to the old environment. One big advantage of blue-green deployment is that it can be used for monolithic applications as well. The main disadvantage of this technique is having to maintain two independent environments, which must be robust and performant enough to serve production traffic.

Rolling Updates

With the rolling updates technique, there is only one production environment in which there are multiple instances of the application. These instances are updated one by one. The instance being updated does not receive any traffic as it is taken out of the load balancer. After the update is completed for that instance, it starts receiving traffic again, and another instance is taken out of the load balancer for the update. This continues until all the instances have been updated. Although the overall traffic handling is reduced, since there is always an instance alive, this update strategy causes zero downtime. That's why it's the most common way to update an application. For example, when you need to update the backend services for a website, you can use a rolling update so that users will keep using the website seamlessly without noticing any changes or facing any problems during your update process. To be able to use this technique, the application must support running with multiple instances, and even with multiple versions at the same time.

In the following diagram, each step of a rolling update is demonstrated:

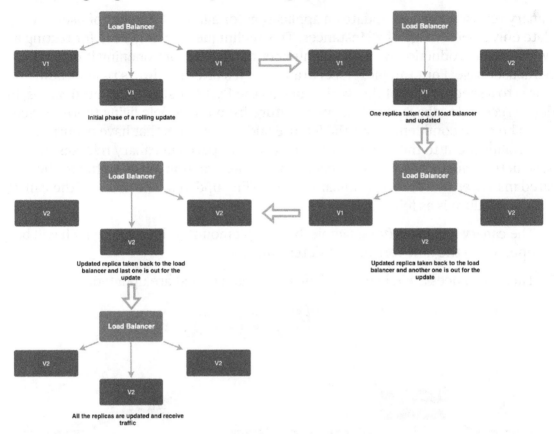

Figure 7.4: The steps of a rolling update

Using this technique, rollbacks happen in the same way, that is, instances are downgraded to the old version one by one. One disadvantage here is that, at the same time, multiple versions of the same application will be active, so this can cause unpredictable behavior. Therefore, the rolling update should be tested beforehand in a test environment.

Canary Releases

In canary releases, you can update an application for a limited number of users or update only a percentage of all instances. This technique is mostly used for testing a new feature in production with a small number of users before opening it up to the general user base. For example, global brands such as Netflix always roll out new features to a specific part of the world, such as the East Coast of the United States, in order to receive feedback about the new feature from the people living there. Hence, you can be more confident about the feature and fix any bugs that have occurred before rolling it out to the whole world. To be able to perform canary releases, the infrastructure must allow you to direct a determined fraction of the traffic to the desired instances. It works in a similar way to rolling updates. The order of the canary release procedure is as follows:

1. The canary instances (for example, based on amount or location), which will be updated to the new version, are determined.

2. These instances are taken out of the load balancer and are updated:

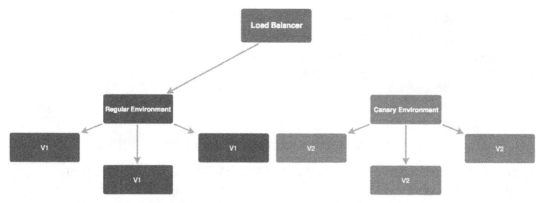

Figure 7.5: Preparing the canary environment for the updated version

3. They are then added to the load balancer with a predetermined amount of traffic after the update is completed:

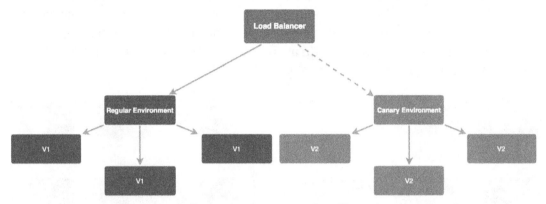

Figure 7.6: Switching a predetermined amount of traffic to the canary environment

4. If the results are satisfactory with the new feature, all the instances are updated to the latest version in the same way until there is no instance left with the old version:

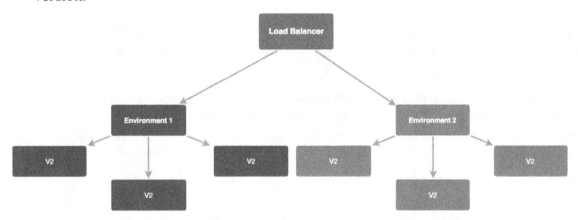

Figure 7.7: Updating the regular environment to the same version and distributing the traffic equally

This technique is particularly useful for getting feedback from some users before making it generally available. Just like rolling updates, in canary releases, there are multiple versions of the application that are active at the same time. This can cause unexpected behaviors and needs to be tested beforehand. To roll back an application, you can use the rolling update strategy; you only need to roll back the instances with the new version.

Dark Launches and Feature Toggles

Similar to canary releases, dark launches are also used to test new features in production environments. In comparison, in dark launches, you don't expose the new functionality to the users. Instead, you only deploy and test the backend and decide whether the feature is ready to be made available for the users. If so, you deploy the frontend as well and make it available to users:

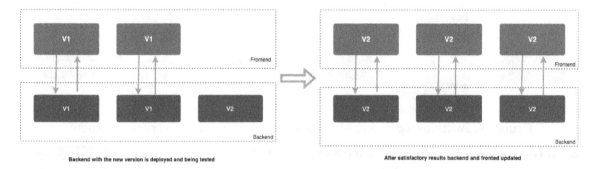

Figure 7.8: Phases of a dark launch

Another similar way of releasing a new feature is to release it as disabled by default. In this way, the new feature does not affect the behavior of the software until it is enabled. You can make the same version of the software available to everyone and toggle the feature only for the designated beta users.

The most significant advantage of this compared to canary releases is that you do not need to maintain multiple versions of the software in production at the same time. Instead, the same version is active with the toggle on or off based on how you want to test the new feature.

On the other hand, a significant disadvantage is that these techniques require the capability of feature toggling or dark launching at the source code level. This can be tricky – especially for an application with a large code base. Hence, from a development point of view, they involve much more work than canary releases.

Rolling back is pretty simple for these types of updates; the feature toggle should be disabled, or the dark launch feature should be made unavailable for the users.

Software Update versus Software Upgrade

Both terms are very commonly used in DevOps. Put simply, an upgrade is a particular type of update where the new version of the software comes with significant improvements over the current one. Companies usually make minor releases, also called patches, for fixing bugs or slightly improving the software, while they make major releases with new features and significant improvements. Patches are usually free of charge, but software upgrades usually cost money. In both cases, the same techniques can be used to update the software to the new version.

In the next section, we will go through how an application can be updated in Kubernetes.

Updating an Application in Kubernetes

Updates are handled differently for different resources in Kubernetes. Since deployments are used for stateless applications, they need to be managed differently from **StatefulSets**, which are used for stateful applications. In this section, we will explore how updates can be handled in StatefulSets and deployments.

StatefulSet Update Strategies

In StatefulSets, an update strategy can be configured using the **updateStrategy** field in the resource definition. It can be set to the two following values: **OnDelete** and **RollingUpdate**.

OnDelete

When the **OnDelete** option is used, the Kubernetes controller does not automatically update the StatefulSet's pods. You must first delete the pods in order for the update process to take place. This is particularly useful for performing checks to verify whether the new version works correctly. However, in this way, an update is entirely a manual process that takes a lot of time and cannot be used in automation scenarios.

Here is a sample **StatefulSet** definition using the **OnDelete** option:

```
apiVersion: apps/v1
kind: StatefulSet
metadata:
  name: test-statefulset
spec:
  serviceName: test-svc
  replicas: 2
```

```
updateStrategy:
  type: OnDelete
selector:
  matchLabels:
    app: test
template:
  metadata:
    labels:
      app: test
  spec:
    containers:
    - name: test
      image: busybox
```

RollingUpdate

Choosing **RollingUpdate** as the update strategy allows the Kubernetes controller to update pods by deleting and recreating them automatically. Using this strategy, pods are updated one by one in reverse ordinal order. The controller makes sure that the updated pods come to the ready state before continuing with the other pods – this is to prevent updating all the instances to a problematic version. Moreover, if an updated pod does not become healthy after a while, the controller rolls it back to the previous version.

Here is a sample **StatefulSet** definition using the **RollingUpdate** option:

```
apiVersion: apps/v1
kind: StatefulSet
metadata:
  name: test-statefulset
spec:
  serviceName: test-svc
  replicas: 2
  updateStrategy:
    type: RollingUpdate
  selector:
    matchLabels:
```

```
      app: test
  template:
    metadata:
      labels:
        app: test
    spec:
      containers:
      - name: test
        image: busybox
```

As you can see, the only difference with the previous definition is the **updateStrategy** field. Because of this, you can also modify an existing StatefulSet's update strategy type on the fly by using a **patch** command:

```
$ kubectl patch statefulset test-statefulset -p
'{"spec":{"updateStrategy":{"type":"RollingUpdate"}}}'
```

This will change the update strategy type to **RollingUpdate**. We will continue with the deployment update strategies in the following section.

Deployment Update Strategies

In deployments, the update strategy can be configured by using the strategy field in the resource definition. It can be set to the two following values: **Recreate** and **RollingUpdate**.

Recreate

When **Recreate** is chosen as the update strategy, the Kubernetes controller terminates all the pods and recreates them using the new version. This leads to application downtime, so this should not be used in production unless it is really needed for the application.

Here is a sample **Deployment** definition using the **Recreate** option:

```
apiVersion: apps/v1
kind: Deployment
metadata:
  name: test-deployment
spec:
  replicas: 2
```

```
strategy:
  type: Recreate
selector:
  matchLabels:
    app: test
template:
  metadata:
    labels:
      app: test
  spec:
    containers:
    - name: test
      image: busybox
```

RollingUpdate

Just like StatefulSets, the **RollingUpdate** strategy can be used for deployments as well. The Kubernetes controller then updates the pods one by one, by making sure that the updated pods become ready before it continues with the others.

Here is a sample Deployment definition using the **RollingUpdate** strategy:

```
apiVersion: apps/v1
kind: Deployment
metadata:
  name: test-deployment
spec:
  replicas: 2
  strategy:
    type: RollingUpdate
  selector:
    matchLabels:
      app: test
  template:
    metadata:
      labels:
```

```
        app: test
    spec:
      containers:
      - name: test
        image: busybox
```

You can switch between different update strategy types on an existing deployment by patching the deployment, as follows:

```
$ kubectl patch deployment test-deployment -p
'{"spec":{"strategy":{"type":"RollingUpdate"}}}'
```

Performing Blue-Green Deployment in Kubernetes

Apart from using the provided update strategies, you can also perform blue-green deployments manually on Kubernetes. For this, you need to set the **Service** selector to direct the traffic to the new deployment. However, this type of update should be avoided unless it is really necessary, as this is highly manual.

Let's say that you want to update your deployment using **nginx:1.14** to the one using **nginx:1.15** by performing blue-green deployment. You can do this by following these steps:

> **Note**
>
> NGINX is an open source HTTP web server. For more information on NGINX, you can take a look at https://www.nginx.com/resources/wiki.

1. Deploy the **deployment** using the **nginx:1.14** version, as follows:

```
apiVersion: apps/v1
kind: Deployment
metadata:
  name: nginx-deployment-114
spec:
  replicas: 2
  selector:
    matchLabels:
      app: nginx-114
  template:
    metadata:
      labels:
        app: nginx-114
```

```
    spec:
      containers:
      - name: nginx
        image: nginx:1.14
        ports:
        - containerPort: 80
```

2. Deploy the **<u>Service selector</u>** to route the traffic to the deployment using the **nginx:1.14** version, as follows:

```
apiVersion: v1
kind: Service
metadata:
  name: nginx-svc
  labels:
    app: nginx
spec:
  ports:
  - port: 80
    name: web
  clusterIP: None
  selector:
    app: nginx-114
```

3. Deploy the **deployment** using the **nginx:1.15** version, as follows:

```
apiVersion: apps/v1
kind: Deployment
metadata:
  name: nginx-deployment-115
spec:
  replicas: 2
  selector:
    matchLabels:
      app: nginx-115
  template:
    metadata:
      labels:
        app: nginx-115
    spec:
```

```
        containers:
        - name: nginx
          image: nginx:1.15
          ports:
          - containerPort: 80
```

4. After testing and verifying that this version works fine, switch the **Service selector** to route the traffic to the new deployment:

```
$ kubectl patch service nginx-svc -p
'{"spec":{"selector":{"app":"nginx-115"}}}'
```

5. If there are any problems, switch the **Service selector** to route the traffic to the old deployment in order to roll back the update:

```
$ kubectl patch service nginx-svc -p
'{"spec":{"selector":{"app":"nginx-114"}}}'
```

Performing Rolling Updates in Kubernetes

Rolling updates allow your application to be updated with zero downtime in Kubernetes. The controller updates the pods one by one so that there will be some pods available to receive traffic all the time. Moreover, when you use a rolling update as the update strategy for a deployment, you can determine the maximum number of new pods that can be created and the maximum number of pods that can be unavailable during an update by setting the `maxSurge` and `maxUnavailable` fields. Both options are set to one (1) by default.

maxSurge

This is an optional field that determines the maximum number of pods that can be created during an update. It can be set as a percentage value or as an absolute number. The percentage value is rounded up while converting to the absolute number. `maxSurge` cannot be set to zero (0) when `maxUnavailable` is also set to zero (0)

maxUnavailable

This is an optional filed that determines the maximum number of pods that can be unavailable during an update. Like `maxSurge`, this can also be set as a percentage value or as an absolute number. The percentage value is rounded down while converting to the absolute number. `maxUnavailable` cannot be set to zero (0) when `maxSurge` is also set to zero (0).

Take a look at the following sample deployment definition using the **maxSurge** and **maxUnavailable** sets:

```
apiVersion: apps/v1
kind: Deployment
metadata:
  name: test-deployment
spec:
  replicas: 10
  strategy:
    type: RollingUpdate
    rollingUpdate:
      maxUnavailable: 50%
      maxSurge: 10%
  selector:
    matchLabels:
      app: test
  template:
    metadata:
      labels:
        app: test
    spec:
      containers:
      - name: test
        image: busybox
```

In this example, if you update the deployment, then the controller can terminate half of the pods in order to update them based on the **maxUnavailable** value (50%). The controller also knows that it can increase the number of pods to a maximum of 11 based on the **maxSurge** value (10%).

Updating a Deployment Using a Rolling Update

Let's say that you want to update your deployment, which is using **nginx:1.14**, to one that is using **nginx:1.15** by performing a rolling update. You can do this by following these steps:

1. We assume that the **nginx** deployment using version 1.14 is already deployed on the cluster:

   ```
   $ kubectl apply -f nginx-deployment.yaml
   apiVersion: apps/v1
   kind: Deployment
   metadata:
     name: nginx-deployment
   spec:
     replicas: 4
     selector:
       matchLabels:
         app: nginx
     template:
       metadata:
         labels:
           app: nginx
       spec:
         containers:
         - name: nginx
           image: nginx:1.14
           ports:
           - containerPort: 80
   ```

2. We can change the image of the deployment to **nginx** version 1.15 in a number of ways, such as by using **kubectl set image** or **kubectl edit deployment**, or by changing the file and redeploying it using **kubectl apply**:

   ```
   $ kubectl set image deployment/nginx-deployment nginx=nginx:1.15 --record

   $ kubectl edit deployment nginx-deployment

   $ kubectl apply -f nginx-deployment.yaml
   ```

3. We can keep track of the rollout by checking the status using **kubectl rollout status**:

   ```
   $ kubectl rollout status deployment/nginx-deployment
   ```

4. If the update finishes successfully, we check whether the pods are running without any problem. We can also check the deployment's events by using **kubectl describe** to see whether the update was successful:

```
$ kubectl get pods
$ kubectl describe deployment nginx-deployment
```

5. If there is a problem, then we can check the rollout history to find a previous revision to roll back to by using **kubectl rollout history**:

```
$ kubectl rollout history deployment/nginx-deployment
```

6. Finally, if there is a problem, we can roll back to the previous revision or a specified revision using the **--to-revision** option:

```
$ kubectl rollout undo deployment/nginx-deployment --to-revision=1
```

Therefore, we have demonstrated how we can perform a rolling update in Kubernetes in order to update our application from one version to another without any downtime. We have also shown how we can roll back an update if something goes wrong using the new version of the application. In the next section, we will talk about how to utilize Helm in order to update our applications.

Updating an Application using Helm

In the previous chapter, we explored the Helm package manager for Kubernetes. As you will remember, Helm is used for packaging applications that are running on Kubernetes with all their resources such as ConfigMaps, deployments, and services. Each application package is called a chart. Using Helm, you can conveniently deploy, update, or roll back your applications.

You can update a chart using Helm as follows:

```
$ helm upgrade <release_name>
```

This will trigger an update for all the resources that the application has on the cluster. These resources will be updated based on their update strategies.

Similar to **kubectl**, you can also check the revision history and roll back to an older version:

```
$ helm history <release_name>
```

```
$ helm rollback <release_name> <revision>
```

Exercise 19: Updating a Deployment in Kubernetes Using a Rolling Update

In this exercise, we aim to demonstrate how to roll out a new version of a deployment using the rolling update strategy:

1. Create a new namespace called **lesson-7** and deploy **busybox** with version 1.29 to this namespace:

```
$ kubectl create ns lesson-7
$ kubectl apply -f busybox-deployment.yaml -n lesson-7
apiVersion: apps/v1
kind: Deployment
metadata:
  name: busybox-deployment
spec:
  replicas: 3
  strategy:
    type: RollingUpdate
  selector:
    matchLabels:
      app: busybox
  template:
    metadata:
      labels:
        app: busybox
    spec:
      containers:
      - name: busybox
        image: busybox:1.29
        command:
          - sleep
          - "99999"
```

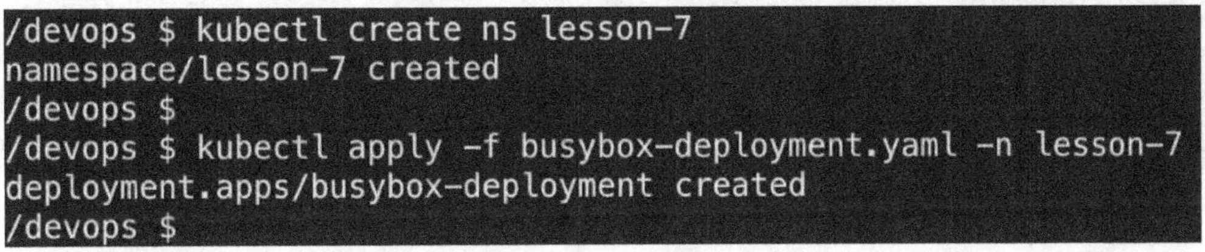

```
/devops $ kubectl create ns lesson-7
namespace/lesson-7 created
/devops $
/devops $ kubectl apply -f busybox-deployment.yaml -n lesson-7
deployment.apps/busybox-deployment created
/devops $
```

Figure 7.9: Creating the lesson-7 namespace and deploying the busybox-deployment

2. Check whether the pods are running, as follows:

```
$ kubectl get pods -n lesson-7
```

```
/devops $ kubectl get pods -n lesson-7
NAME                                 READY   STATUS    RESTARTS   AGE
busybox-deployment-555d4857b-sg7jw   1/1     Running   0          77s
busybox-deployment-555d4857b-tg5jx   1/1     Running   0          77s
busybox-deployment-555d4857b-ttz7k   1/1     Running   0          77s
/devops $
```

Figure 7.10: Checking whether the pods are running without any problems

3. Change the image of the **busybox** deployment to use version 1.30:

```
$ kubectl set image deployment/busybox-deployment busybox=busybox:1.30
--record -n lesson-7
```

```
/devops $ kubectl set image deployment/busybox-deployment busybox=busybox:1.30 --record -n lesson-7
deployment.extensions/busybox-deployment image updated
/devops $
```

Figure 7.11: Setting the deployment image to busybox version 1.30

4. Check the rollout status, as follows:

```
$ kubectl rollout status deployment/busybox-deployment -n lesson-7
```

```
/devops $ kubectl rollout status deployment/busybox-deployment -n lesson-7
deployment "busybox-deployment" successfully rolled out
/devops $
```

Figure 7.12: Checking the rollout status

5. Once successfully finished, check whether the new pods are running without any problems:

```
$ kubectl get pods -n lesson-7
```

```
/devops $ kubectl get pods -n lesson-7
NAME                                  READY   STATUS    RESTARTS   AGE
busybox-deployment-64b5bc44db-7vcn7   1/1     Running   0          104s
busybox-deployment-64b5bc44db-v5s4r   1/1     Running   0          101s
busybox-deployment-64b5bc44db-w7897   1/1     Running   0          110s
/devops $
```

Figure 7.13: Checking whether the pods are running without any problems

6. Clean up the environment by removing the deployment, as follows:

```
$ kubectl delete -f busybox-deployment.yaml -n lesson-7
```

In this exercise, we demonstrated how to update a deployment using the rolling update in Kubernetes. By doing it in this way, we can update the application without any downtime. We also saw how we can make use of the `kubectl set image` command by eliminating the need to modify the deployment file, which would be error-prone. In the next chapter, *Troubleshooting Applications in Kubernetes*, we will explore what scaling an application means and how to perform it in Kubernetes.

Scaling an Application

Scalability is a system's capability for handling the growing amount of work that is requested from it. As an application gets more users over time, it starts to receive many more requests than before. If the application cannot handle the number of new requests, then its performance will drop significantly, which reduces the usability of the application. It may even start to reject the requests and go down for some time. Of course, it is a pretty bad user experience when an application is down or does not work as expected.

At this point, it is essential to find out which resource is a bottleneck – only then can you work on a solution to mitigate the problem. The bottleneck is usually one of the following resources, though it could be something completely different:

- CPU

- Memory

- Disk

- I/O operations

Once the root cause of the problem is found, scaling options can be evaluated. Until then, trying to provide a solution will just be a blind guess.

Bear in mind the scalability when architecting an application; leveraging the twelve-factor app methodology helps a lot too when it comes to building a scalable application. Your application can benefit from utilizing the twelve-factor app principles, especially when you need to scale it over time, so that you won't need to worry much in the future.

> **Note**
>
> The twelve-factor app is a set of principles constructed to provide ideal patterns for developing modern applications. For more information, you can visit the website at https://12factor.net/.

Moreover, you should not try to scale an application without considering the consequences. Addressing scalability introduces a lot of complexity to the code. This will result in longer development times for new features, cause problems to be harder to debug and solve, and make testing the application painful. Therefore, it is very significant to understand the root cause first and then explore whether it can be addressed differently.

To figure out the root cause, or to find the resource that is being the bottleneck, you can use monitoring tools, which we will explore in *Chapter 9, Monitoring Applications in Kubernetes*.

Once you decide to scale your application, you need to make a choice between the different scaling methods – they all have different advantages and disadvantages. There are two particular ways in which to scale an application: horizontal and vertical scaling. We will explain them in the next section.

Horizontal versus Vertical Scaling

Horizontal scaling (scaling out) means the ability to scale by adding more resources, such as new nodes, computers, or containers to an overall system, such as a cluster, in order to distribute the load. It aims to make use of low-cost, off-the-shelf hardware, also called commodity hardware, instead of spending a lot of money on a single powerful machine. This method turns out to be the best for reaching the required computing power at its limits, which is not possible to achieve if using a single system. This is realized by accumulating the computing power that comes with all the systems added together. However, this comes at a price. Scaling out an application requires plenty of code changes and increases the overall complexity of the source code. It even affects the architecture of the application; that's why it is best to architect an application with scalability in mind. Also, with the introduction of new computers to the overall system, communication between these computers can become costly in terms of overall performance. This network will cause delays. Because of this, communication between these computers needs to be minimized. All these technical challenges need to be clearly evaluated when deciding to scale out a system or an application.

Vertical scaling (scaling up) means the ability to scale by increasing the capacity of the internal resources within a single computer or a node in order to enable it to handle more work. These improvements are usually carried out by mounting additional CPUs, memory, or disks. In this way, these improved systems can manage to serve more requests or can allow the virtualization of more resources, such as virtual machines (VMs). This method is much easier and faster to apply than scaling out. However, there is a hard limit to the number of resources that you can increase in a system. After some point, it is impossible to add more resources to a single unit as it cannot host that many resources:

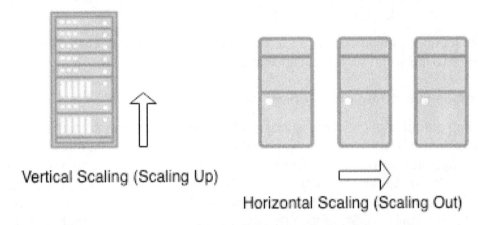

Figure 7.14: Horizontal versus vertical scaling

Horizontal Scaling	Vertical Scaling
Low-cost hardware	Expensive hardware
More computing power through the accumulation of many systems	Has the hard limits of a single system
Has more complexity in the code	Has less complexity in the code
Network delays	Single point of failure

Figure 7.15: Horizontal versus vertical scaling

In the end, you need to evaluate both methods and make a decision that is based on the advantages and disadvantages that they bring to your application. It's usually a trade-off between convenience and budget. However, hard limits on the hardware need to be taken into consideration as well.

If horizontal scaling is the way to go for your application, then autoscaling can be utilized to manage the workload efficiently. We will explore autoscaling in the following section.

Autoscaling

Autoscalers are tools that automatically scale an application out or in by monitoring the related resources that are needed to keep the cost down and performance stable. They can either increase or decrease the number of instances based on the load. Cluster admins determine an autoscaling policy such as minimum and maximum instance count or the resource type that will trigger the scaling – and autoscalers take care of the scaling by adhering to this policy. Thanks to autoscalers, unpredictable incoming traffic can be handled efficiently. They work 24*7 and make sure there are always enough instances to match the load. We will delve further into autoscalers in this chapter when we talk about autoscaling in Kubernetes.

In the next section, we will explain an important concept called eventual consistency, which comes to life when scaling an application to several replicas.

Strong versus Eventual Consistency

When scaling out an application, it is essential to think about how to manage the data. If the data is distributed as well, this can lead to inconsistencies when reading the data from different partitions. In order to prevent this from happening, you can lock the partitions for some time to let them sync, however, this will reduce the availability of the application. Instead, distributing systems can help to create a new consistency model called eventual consistency. In theory, this model guarantees that reading an updated value from all the partitions will give you the same result after some time. This might be perfectly fine for a personal notebook application, but it is not especially useful for financial applications. Applications where consistency of data is critical require strong consistency, which means that reading the data will always return the same value as its name implies.

For the same reason, transactions are not possible within the distributed system either. That's why modules with strong consistency needs must be together and reside on the same system. This is just another reason to keep scalability in mind while architecting a new application.

In the next section, we will explore how to scale an application in a Kubernetes cluster.

Scaling an Application in Kubernetes

There is a built-in way of scaling an application horizontally on a Kubernetes cluster. You can utilize the native Kubernetes resource deployment for scaling your application quickly. When you create a deployment object, you need to provide a value for the number of replicas. Once the deployment is applied to the cluster, it will generate a **Replication Controller**, which is responsible for controlling the number of replicas created by this deployment. Each replica represents a rod that includes the application containers. When you change this value for the number of replicas, it will be automatically reflected on the cluster, either by deleting the existing pods or by creating new ones. In this way, scalability is handled out of the box by Kubernetes.

While creating new pods, Kubernetes also ensures there are enough resources on nodes before scheduling a pod to them. In this way, a pod is only scheduled if there are enough resources for it to run without any problems.

Furthermore, in some cases – for example, when there is no incoming traffic at all – you might want to scale down to zero replicas, which means that there are no running pods on your application. Kubernetes natively supports this as well. You can just set the number of replicas field to zero, which will terminate all the pods created by this deployment.

When your application has more than one replica running, you will need a load balancer to distribute the traffic to all the replicas. To achieve this, as we learned in *Chapter 4, Creating a Kubernetes Cluster*, services have an integrated load balancer that checks the availability of the pods and distributes the traffic only to the available pods (which are running and have the **ready** status). Services achieve this by implementing a simple load balancing algorithm. As long as you don't need a more sophisticated way to distribute the traffic to your replicas, you can simply create a **Service** object to do this for you.

To scale an application, you can use generic **kubectl** commands to modify an object in Kubernetes, such as **kubectl patch** or **kubectl edit**. You can also use the **kubectl scale** command, which is only used for this particular need.

Here is a sample Deployment definition:

```
apiVersion: apps/v1
kind: Deployment
metadata:
  name: test-deployment
spec:
  replicas: 1
  selector:
```

```
    matchLabels:
      app: test
  template:
    metadata:
      labels:
        app: test
    spec:
      containers:
      - name: test
        image: busybox
        command:
          - sleep
          - "99999"
```

As you can see from the **Deployment** definition, the replicas field is set to 1. That's why there will be only one pod created for this deployment.

To scale this Deployment up or down, you can use **kubectl scale**, as follows:

```
$ kubectl scale deployment/test-deployment --replicas 3
```

Alternatively, you can modify the deployment object to change the replicas field either with **kubectl edit** or by using **patch**:

```
$ kubectl edit deployment test-deployment
$ kubectl patch deployment test-deployment -p '{"spec":{"replicas":3}}'
```

After running one of these commands, you can check the pods to see whether they are scaled accordingly. You can also check the event logs from the deployment object by using **kubectl describe**:

```
$ kubectl describe deployment test-deployment
```

Kubernetes also supports autoscaling through a native resource called Horizontal Pod Autoscalers (HAPs), which will be explained in the next section. Before that, let's demonstrate how to scale a deployment in Kubernetes up and down.

Exercise 20: Scaling a Deployment Up and Down in Kubernetes

In this exercise, we aim to demonstrate how to scale a deployment up and down manually using **kubectl** commands:

1. Deploy the **busybox** deployment with one replica to the **lesson-7** namespace:

```
$ kubectl apply -f deployment.yaml -n lesson-7
apiVersion: apps/v1
kind: Deployment
metadata:
  name: busybox
spec:
  replicas: 1
  selector:
    matchLabels:
      app: busybox
  template:
    metadata:
      labels:
        app: busybox
    spec:
      containers:
      - name: busybox
        image: busybox
        command:
          - sleep
          - "99999"
```

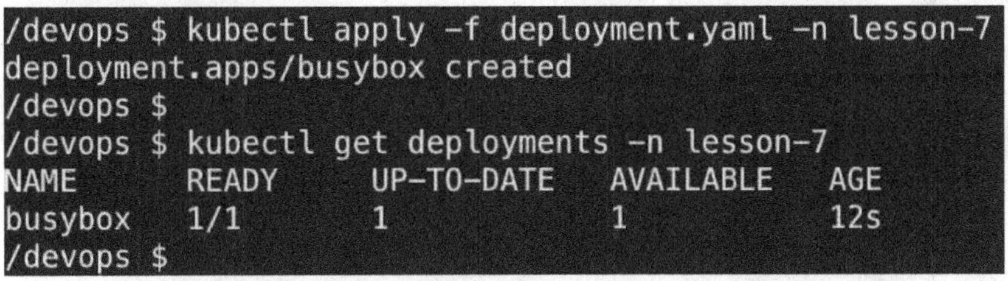

```
/devops $ kubectl apply -f deployment.yaml -n lesson-7
deployment.apps/busybox created
/devops $
/devops $ kubectl get deployments -n lesson-7
NAME       READY     UP-TO-DATE    AVAILABLE    AGE
busybox    1/1       1             1            12s
/devops $
```

Figure 7.16: Deploying the busybox deployment to the cluster

2. Scale up the deployment to three replicas, as follows:

```
$ kubectl scale deployment/busybox -n lesson-7 --replicas 3
```

```
/devops $ kubectl scale deployment/busybox -n lesson-7 --replicas 3
deployment.extensions/busybox scaled
/devops $
/devops $ kubectl get deployments -n lesson-7
NAME       READY     UP-TO-DATE   AVAILABLE   AGE
busybox    3/3       3            3           2m48s
/devops $
```

Figure 7.17: Scaling up the deployment to three replicas

3. Check the deployment object details to see the event logs:

```
$ kubectl describe deployment/busybox -n lesson-7
```

```
/devops $ kubectl describe deployment/busybox -n lesson-7
Name:                   busybox
Namespace:              lesson-7
CreationTimestamp:      Tue, 05 Mar 2019 22:47:59 +0100
Labels:                 <none>
Annotations:            deployment.kubernetes.io/revision=1
                        kubectl.kubernetes.io/last-applied-configuration={"apiVersion":"apps/v1","kind":"Deployment",
"metadata":{"annotations":{},"name":"busybox","namespace":"lesson-7"},"spec":{"replicas":1,"selector":{"mat...
Selector:               app=busybox
Replicas:               3 desired | 3 updated | 3 total | 3 available | 0 unavailable
StrategyType:           RollingUpdate
MinReadySeconds:        0
RollingUpdateStrategy:  25% max unavailable, 25% max surge
Pod Template:
  Labels:  app=busybox
  Containers:
   busybox:
    Image:      busybox
    Port:       <none>
    Host Port:  <none>
    Command:
      sleep
      99999
    Environment:  <none>
    Mounts:       <none>
  Volumes:        <none>
Conditions:
  Type         Status  Reason
  ----         ------  ------
  Progressing  True    NewReplicaSetAvailable
  Available    True    MinimumReplicasAvailable
OldReplicaSets:  <none>
NewReplicaSet:   busybox-66976d48b8 (3/3 replicas created)
Events:
  Type    Reason             Age  From                   Message
  ----    ------             ---  ----                   -------
  Normal  ScalingReplicaSet  5m   deployment-controller  Scaled up replica set busybox-66976d48b8 to 1
  Normal  ScalingReplicaSet  2m   deployment-controller  Scaled up replica set busybox-66976d48b8 to 3
/devops $
```

Figure 7.18: Checking the deployment details

Here, you can see from the event logs at the end of the page that the deployment was successfully scaled up to three replicas.

4. Scale down the application to zero replicas:

```
$ kubectl scale deployment/busybox -n lesson-7 --replicas 0
```

```
/devops $ kubectl scale deployment/busybox -n lesson-7 --replicas 0
deployment.extensions/busybox scaled
/devops $
/devops $ kubectl get deployments -n lesson-7
NAME       READY    UP-TO-DATE    AVAILABLE    AGE
busybox    0/0      0             0            9m10s
/devops $
```

Figure 7.19: Scaling down the deployment to zero replicas

5. Check the event logs of the deployment again:

```
$ kubectl describe deployment/busybox -n lesson-7
```

```
/devops $ kubectl get deployments -n lesson-7
NAME       READY    UP-TO-DATE    AVAILABLE    AGE
busybox    0/0      0             0            9m10s
/devops $
/devops $ kubectl describe deployment/busybox -n lesson-7
Name:                   busybox
Namespace:              lesson-7
CreationTimestamp:      Tue, 05 Mar 2019 22:47:59 +0100
Labels:                 <none>
Annotations:            deployment.kubernetes.io/revision=1
                        kubectl.kubernetes.io/last-applied-configuration={"apiVersion":"apps/v1","kind":"Deployment",
"metadata":{"annotations":{},"name":"busybox","namespace":"lesson-7"},"spec":{"replicas":1,"selector":{"mat...
Selector:               app=busybox
Replicas:               0 desired | 0 updated | 0 total | 0 available | 0 unavailable
StrategyType:           RollingUpdate
MinReadySeconds:        0
RollingUpdateStrategy:  25% max unavailable, 25% max surge
Pod Template:
  Labels:  app=busybox
  Containers:
   busybox:
    Image:       busybox
    Port:        <none>
    Host Port:   <none>
    Command:
      sleep
      99999
    Environment:  <none>
    Mounts:       <none>
  Volumes:        <none>
Conditions:
  Type          Status  Reason
  ----          ------  ------
  Progressing   True    NewReplicaSetAvailable
  Available     True    MinimumReplicasAvailable
OldReplicaSets:  <none>
NewReplicaSet:   busybox-66976d48b8 (0/0 replicas created)
Events:
  Type    Reason            Age  From                  Message
  ----    ------            ---  ----                  -------
  Normal  ScalingReplicaSet  10m  deployment-controller  Scaled up replica set busybox-66976d48b8 to 1
  Normal  ScalingReplicaSet  8m   deployment-controller  Scaled up replica set busybox-66976d48b8 to 3
  Normal  ScalingReplicaSet  1m   deployment-controller  Scaled down replica set busybox-66976d48b8 to 0
/devops $
```

Figure 7.20: Checking the deployment details

As you can see from the event logs, the deployment was successfully scaled down to zero replicas.

6. Clean up the environment by removing the deployment:

```
$ kubectl delete -f deployment.yaml -n lesson-7
```

Here, we demonstrated how to scale a deployment up and down in Kubernetes. We can see that it is even possible to scale down a deployment to zero replicas. In the next section, we will go through the autoscaling resource in Kubernetes, namely, HPA.

Horizontal Pod Auto-Scaler (HPA)

HPA is a built-in Kubernetes resource that automatically adjusts the number of replicas (or pods) to match the loads by periodically observing CPU utilization and by adhering to the rules provided by the user. It only supports autoscaling based on CPU utilization.

A HPA can be defined as a YAML file, just like any other Kubernetes resource, and can easily be set up by using kubectl commands.

Here is a sample HPA definition:

```
apiVersion: autoscaling/v1
kind: HorizontalPodAutoscaler
metadata:
  name: autoscaler
spec:
  maxReplicas: 8
  minReplicas: 3
  scaleTargetRef:
    apiVersion: apps/v1
    kind: Deployment
    name: test-deployment
  targetCPUUtilizationPercentage: 70
```

Once you deploy this to the cluster (for example, by using **kubectl apply -f**), it will start watching the CPU utilization of the pods created by the **test-deployment** deployment object. Based on the target CPU utilization (**70%**), it can increase the number of pods to a maximum of eight, or decrease them to a minimum of three pods.

You can also use the **kubectl autoscale** command, which will automatically create an HPA object:

```
$ kubectl autoscale deployment test-deployment --min=3 --max=8 --cpu-percent=70
```

You can check already-existing HPAs in the cluster by running **kubectl get** or examining the detailed description of the object with **kubectl describe**:

```
$ kubectl get hpa --all-namespaces
$ kubectl describe hpa <name>
```

You can use **kubectl edit** or **kubectl patch** to modify the object as follows:

```
$ kubectl edit hpa <name>
$ kubectl patch hpa <name> -p '{"spec":{"minReplicas":2}}'
```

Finally, you can delete the HPA by running the following command:

```
$ kubectl delete hpa <name>
```

Here, we have covered the HPA object in Kubernetes, and now we will move to an activity where we will practice what we explored in this chapter.

Activity 8: Enabling Autoscaling and Performing a Rolling Update

Imagine that you have built a very cool application and you can't wait to make it publicly available. You don't know how many people will start using it at the beginning – that's why you set an autoscaler so that, even if you are not available for any kind of manual operation, your application can handle the increasing amount of traffic. You deploy your application and set up the autoscaler to make sure that scaling works automatically. You check the pods and notice that there is a sudden increase in the number of pods, although you haven't informed anyone yet. Then, you realize that there is a bug in the application that exhausts the CPU, and the autoscaler is trying to adjust the replicas based on this unnecessary load. You immediately perform a rolling update to fix the problem. Then, you check again to see whether the autoscaler scales down the number of replicas, and whether everything works out smoothly.

> **Note**
>
> To complete this activity, you need to use a real cluster. You can create and use a managed cluster on Google Kubernetes Engine (GKE).

Execute the following steps to complete this activity:

1. Create a deployment definition file that uses the **suakbas/lesson07:v1** image and has the **RollingUpdate** strategy type set; this application does a CPU-intensive operation.

2. Deploy the deployment and check whether the pod is running.

3. Create a **HorizontalPodAutoscaler** for this deployment using the **suakbas/lesson07:v1** image, which has two as the minimum number of pods and five as the maximum. It should also have a CPU percentage target of 50%.

4. Check the **HorizontalPodAutoscaler** for the deployment using the **suakbas/lesson07:v1** image to see the current status.

5. Check the pods to see whether they are scaled up and are running without any problems.

6. Perform a rolling update by changing the used image to **suakbas/lesson07:v2**. This application just sleeps, which relieves the CPU; Then, check whether the rolling update has finished successfully.

7. Recheck the HorizontalPodAutoscaler that you created before to see the current status after the update. Watch the change in the number of pods and check the latest status after a few minutes.

8. Clean up the environment by removing the namespace.

> **Note**
>
> The solution to this activity can be found on page 330.

In this activity, we set an autoscaler in Kubernetes and examined how it scales a sample application up and down. We also performed a rolling update to update the deployment from a CPU-intensive application to a non-intensive one. In this way, we exercised the DevOps practices that we explored throughout this chapter and used them in a running Kubernetes cluster.

Summary

In this chapter, we first mentioned the importance of updating an application without causing any downtime. Then, we continued with different strategies to update an application, such as blue–green deployments and rolling updates. We also explored the terminological difference between updating and upgrading software.

In the section that followed, we explored how to update an application in Kubernetes. We studied the different object types in Kubernetes, such as StatefulSets, and explored the existing update strategies that we can use. Then, we performed the most common update strategies: blue–green deployment and rolling updates in Kubernetes. We continued with a hands-on exercise to update a deployment using the rolling update strategy in a Kubernetes cluster.

We then progressed to scaling. We explored its meaning and its importance, especially in DevOps. We introduced different scaling techniques, such as vertical and horizontal scaling. After this, we continued with autoscaling and explored an important concept, namely, eventual consistency. Then, we moved onto scaling an application in Kubernetes. We investigated methods to scale an application up and down using the native objects and existing kubectl commands. We performed an exercise to demonstrate scaling a deployment up and down in a Kubernetes cluster.

In the last section, we discussed HAP, which is a built-in Kubernetes object that is used to adjust the number of replicas of an application automatically based on CPU utilization. We then performed an activity where we set an autoscaler in Kubernetes and examined the behavior based on the resource consumption on a running cluster. In the next chapter, we will demonstrate ways in which to troubleshoot an application in Kubernetes. We will do practical exercises in order to gain an understanding of how we can perform these operations in a Kubernetes cluster.

8

Troubleshooting Applications in Kubernetes

Learning Objectives

By the end of this chapter, you will be able to:

- List troubleshooting practices
- List the different states of a Pod
- Set up liveness and readiness probes
- Use different kubectl commands to troubleshoot applications in Kubernetes

This chapter explains how to troubleshoot the problems encountered in applications running on Kubernetes.

Introduction

In the previous chapter, we went through many different ways to update and scale your application in Kubernetes. We also explored setting up an autoscaler so that we wouldn't worry about scaling our applications up and down manually to handle incoming traffic. Now we continue with another essential topic that we need to embrace as a part of DevOps, which is troubleshooting. It is important to know how to fix problems quickly. In the next section, we will go through the necessary information for better troubleshooting in general. Kubernetes provides us with all the necessary functionality to troubleshoot applications, which we will explore in the *Troubleshooting in Kubernetes* section.

Troubleshooting

As a term, troubleshooting refers to searching for the real cause of an issue and giving your best effort to tackle it as soon as possible to make a system or an application operational again. It is an important concept in DevOps. Troubleshooting can be done in a trial-and-error way where someone checks whatever occurs to them to check, but at the cost of a lot of time. Therefore, it should instead be done in a systematic way. In this chapter, we will see how we can systematically approach problems, and we will also present some practices for troubleshooting an application. Later, we'll dig deeper into the ways of troubleshooting an application in Kubernetes.

Troubleshooting can take place at various stages of development. For example, while network engineers try to solve a problem within a network, quality engineers dig into an issue to figure out what's not working for the end-to-end scenarios. That's why having good troubleshooting skills appeals to the people from a broad range of areas.

It is of great importance to have troubleshooting skills, especially when working on an application where availability is crucial. For instance, if you are running an e-commerce website, downtime would mean losing many customers, and, consequently, lots of money. For some tech giants such as Facebook or Twitter, downtime on their website would even result in being in the news and destroying their reputation. Good troubleshooting skills would play a significant role in solving problems as quickly as possible so that downtime is really short or can even be eliminated.

There are many aspects that could influence the effectiveness of troubleshooting. We present some of the key ones in the following sections. To have good troubleshooting skills, you should be highly competent with these concepts and should apply them appropriately in real-life situations.

Identifying the Problem

While identifying the problem, the first thing that you need to ensure is understand of how things work. Trying to fix a problem without prior knowledge could lead to more severe problems. In the end, an easy problem that could have been solved with prior knowledge could turn into a complex issue resulting in a disaster.

Another course of identifying the problem is to check what exactly changed in the system that led to this problem. Most of the time, problems occur right after making some changes. It's crucial to know what changed to understand the root cause. Sometimes, a change thought to be small and harmless could cause many issues, which is why they shouldn't be disregarded while troubleshooting a problem.

Communication is also an essential factor to identify a problem quickly. An immediate call or a chat with the relevant people would save much time as compared to sending an email and waiting for an answer. When people can collaborate effectively, solving a problem is easier and faster.

Improving Tests

Another aspect of troubleshooting is to ensure that already-solved problems will not occur again. That's why it is essential to identify problematic areas and invest in more tests to cover them. This way, these situations can be seen and handled in the test environment before they happen in production. Fixing a problem right away might save you in that instance alone, but covering it in a test that runs regularly can prevent it from occurring again.

We need to ensure that there are not only unit or integrations tests, but also sufficient number of **end-to-end** (E2E) tests covering end-to-end scenarios. These tests should run regularly in CI/CD so that we would be able to see the problems and fix them before going live.

Documentation

Just as with adding tests, we also need to ensure that the root cause of the problem and how we solved it are documented so if the same problem occurs again in the future, you or someone in the team would know the root cause right away instead of going through the same steps you went through the first time. This knowledge is precious as it would save the team a lot of time and effort if an issue recurs.

If possible, we should document the instance of the problem occurrence, its root cause, contextual information, and each step we took to solve the problem. This information log significantly reduces the time it will take to tackle the problem next time.

Tools

Using the right tools for logging, monitoring, and tracing would ease the way to figure out what's wrong. The infrastructure (for example, the health of the nodes) should especially be monitored all the time as it could be the root cause of many problems within the application. We will go through several tools and cover this aspect in the next chapter where we explain monitoring applications in Kubernetes.

Logging

Logs are one of the most critical assets for understanding what your code is doing in production. Logs are mostly the first thing you'll be checking during troubleshooting, which is why it is important to have as much information in them as possible to figure out the problem quickly. They should include time of the problem, any informational messages, and contextual information, helping to categorize each event and understand its behavior. However, logging too much information could easily consume too many resources and slow down your application and make it harder to find the actual problem. The application cannot afford to produce too many logs, but you need them to understand the behavior. This problem brings up the concept of **logging levels**.

Logging levels

The logging level determines the number of logs for different severity grades. Making this configurable helps you to receive more logs during troubleshooting and fewer logs when the application needs to be performant. There are several commonly used logging levels:

- **Debug**: In this level, every little detail of diagnostic information is being logged to help you understand a problem. This level is usually set when someone is troubleshooting an application.

- **Info**: In this level, informational logs are presented. For example, they include information such as the starting of an application or the successful connection to another service. These logs show the usual behavior of the application.

- **Warning**: In this level, there is unusual behavior that hasn't created a problem. For example, an external connection could be dropped and reestablished. These warning messages should be investigated to ensure that they will not lead to a severe issue later on.

- **Error**: In this level, there are failures that have occurred in the application. These need to be taken into serious consideration and should be fixed as soon as possible. For example, an external connection could be dropped and might not be able to be established for some time. This usually indicates that something is not working and needs attention.

Utilizing different log levels can help troubleshoot problems as well as enable an application to run faster. That's why it is important to make use of them and be able to configure them while the application is running. Various techniques to ensure effective troubleshooting are shown in *Figure 8.1*:

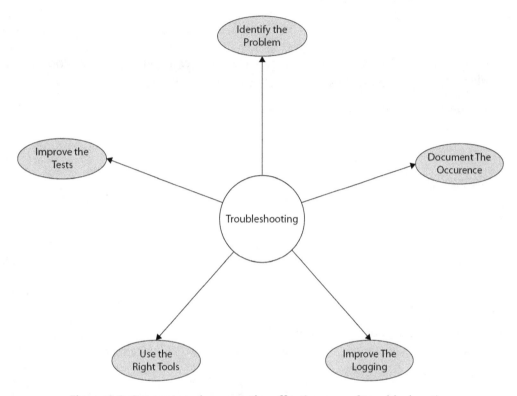

Figure 8.1: Concepts to improve the effectiveness of troubleshooting

All these concepts help you to understand the root cause of the problem and solve it efficiently. It is essential to understand that you need to fix the problem in a way that it will not easily occur again. It should have already been caught in the CI/CD process by the tests and solved before going to production. Even if it recurs, there should be documentation explaining the steps to be taken to solve it. Furthermore, by making use of different logging levels, the application should provide the capabilities to enable us to troubleshoot effectively. In this section, we covered the different aspects of troubleshooting applications in general. In the next one, we will present the fundamental concepts and tools to troubleshoot applications in Kubernetes.

Troubleshooting Applications in Kubernetes

To be able to troubleshoot applications efficiently, you need to understand some key concepts in Kubernetes. This will light up the way to ease the process of figuring out and solving issues. As one of these concepts, we explain the Pod life cycle in the next section.

Pod Life Cycle

In Kubernetes, a Pod goes through many different stages. They are controlled either by the creator of the Pod object or by the Kubernetes controller. In the lifetime of a Pod, it is never destroyed unless that is explicitly requested.

Pod Status

Every Pod object has a status field that shows the life cycle events of the Pod. It consists of many subfields for us to understand what the current health status of the Pod is.

Here's an example of what a Pod status includes:

```
status:

  conditions:

  - lastProbeTime: null


//[...]



Events:
    FirstSeen      LastSeen      Count  From
SubobjectPath      Type          Reason                    Message
    ---------      ---------     -----  ----               ----------
--- --------       ------                -------
    1m             48s                7     {default-scheduler }
          Warning          FailedScheduling    pod (nginx-deployment-
1370807587-fz9sd) failed to fit in any node
  fit failure on node (kubernetes-node-6ta5): Node didn't have enough
resource: CPU, requested: 1000, used: 1420, capacity: 2000
  fit failure on node (kubernetes-node-wul5): Node didn't have enough
resource: CPU, requested: 1000, used: 1100, capacity: 2000
```

> **Note**
>
> You can find the complete Pod status at https://github.com/TrainingByPackt/ Introduction-to-DevOps-with-Kubernetes/blob/master/Lesson08/podstatus.txt.

There is a lot of information there. The condition list, the container statuses, the restart count, and the phase are the most critical fields while troubleshooting a problem. We will go through each of them to clarify what they mean for you. Let's first start by explaining Pod conditions.

Pod Conditions

Pod conditions list all the different conditions a Pod goes through. It consists of six fields:

- **lastProbeTime**: This is a timestamp that shows the last time the condition was enquired.

- **lastTransitionTime**: This is a timestamp that shows the last time the Pod status changed.

- **Message**: This has the details of the condition changes.

- **Reason**: This provides the reason for the last condition change in a single word.

- **Status**: This shows the status of the related condition, which can be **True**, **False**, or **Unknown**.

- **Type**: This shows the type of condition, which will be explained further in the next section.

Condition Types

There are different conditions types that a Pod can have. They are explained one by one as follows:

- **Unschedulable**: This means that the Pod cannot be scheduled to a node, which can be because of resource constraints of the Pod or a lack of resources in the cluster.

- **PodScheduled**: This means that the Pod is successfully scheduled to a node.

- **Initialized**: This denotes that all the **init** containers started without any problem.

- **ContainersReady**: This shows that all the containers in the Pod are ready.

- **Ready**: This shows that the Pod can handle incoming requests now.

This list of conditions provides historical information to help diagnose a problem. Now we continue with the phase subfield.

Pod Phase

Phase is yet another subfield in the Pod status, and provides high-level information about the current status of the Pod. There are seven possible Pod phases, which are as follows:

- **Pending**: This phase specifies that the Pod is waiting for something to finish. This could be the phase where the container images are being downloaded or where the nodes are being evaluated to schedule the Pod.

- **Failed**: This phase specifies that at least one of the containers finished with failure.

- **CrashLoopBackOff**: This phase shows that at least one of the containers finished with failure. This phase appears after a few restart trials, which can be set by **restartPolicy**, which will be defined later.

- **Running**: This phase indicates that the Pod is successfully scheduled to a node, and all the related containers started. However, it does not give any guarantees for the health of the containers.

- **Succeeded**: This phase shows that the containers in the Pod have successfully concluded.

- **Completed**: This phase states that the Pod has reached completion and is no longer running. This can be observed in the Pods created by a Job.

- **Unknown**: This phase informs that Kubernetes does not know the current state of the Pod. This usually happens when Kubernertes API Server can no longer access the node where the Pod is running.

The following figure shows the phases of a Pod and the transitions between them:

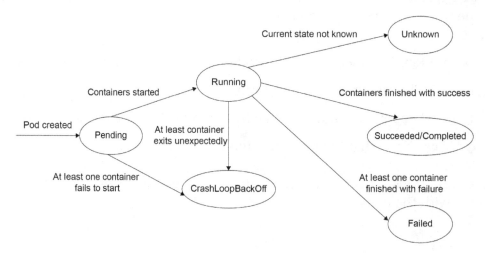

Figure 8.2: Different Phases of a Pod

Understanding what each phase means helps with quickly identifying whether something is wrong. However, only checking this field does not help. You should combine all the information you get from these fields to understand the problem.

You can use this command to see the current phase of any Pod:

```
$ kubectl get pod <pod-name> -o jsonpath={.status.phase}
```

Restart Policy

Restart policy is a subfield of Pod spec. It can take one of these three values: **Always**, **Never**, and **OnFailure**, and **Always** is the default choice. This field specifies when Kubernetes should restart the Pod if there is a problem. Whenever a Pod is restarted, the restart count on the Pod status is incremented to show the number of restarts.

> **Note**
>
> Kubernetes restarts the Pod without changing the node. Once a Pod is scheduled to a node successfully, it is guaranteed that it won't be rescheduled to another one.

Container States

Container state is a subfield of container status, which is a part of the Pod status. This field shows the current state of the containers inside the Pod. They can be in three different states:

- **Waiting**: This state shows that the container is waiting for an operation to finish. For example, it could be mounting the volumes or downloading the container image. A container can be in this state because of failure as well. Failing to download the container image is one example. Waiting is the default state of a container.

- **Terminated**: This state specifies that the container is no longer running. This can be because of an error, or it can indicate that the container successfully finished.

- **Running**: This state indicates that the container is running without any issues.

These are the most important fields to check when something is not working right in the Pod. As mentioned earlier, a combination of all this information should be evaluated to understand the root cause better. In the next section, we will touch on the auto-recovery concept in Kubernetes as it is useful for our application to become operational again without our action.

Auto Recovery

Auto recovery or self-healing means the capability of healing when the application encounters a problem. To make this more clear, sometimes it is just enough to restart an application to make it operational again. Kubernetes provides a way to configure this so that in certain situations, it restarts the application, solving the problem and eliminating the need for us to fix the issue.

One way to ensure auto recovery in Kubernetes is through using the controllers whenever possible. Instead of manually creating Pods, the appropriate controller object (such as a Deployment, DaemonSet, or Job) should be utilized. This way, when failure occurs, the controller tries its best to match the desired state as soon as possible. For example, when one of the Pods managed by a Deployment becomes unhealthy, it will be replaced by a new Pod immediately so that your application won't be affected by this failure. This is much more effective and resilient than manually trying to keep the system running.

Kubernetes provides a way of checking the health of the application regularly by probing for its liveness and readiness.

Health checks

Two different health checks can be set for a Pod in Kubernetes. These are **liveness** and **readiness** probes.

Liveness Probe

This informs Kubernetes that the containers are running, and that the application is generally in a healthy status. It always returns **success** if not set. Whenever this probe fails, Kubernetes restarts the respective containers to make them run again.

Setting a liveness probe is not a must if the containers can exit with failure when they are not healthy. In that case, Kubernetes will already restart them if the restart policy allows. However, if you want to specify another reason for Kubernetes to restart the containers in case of failures, you can utilize this. For example, when your application cannot connect to a database anymore, it does not necessarily need to crash, but you can use liveness probes for it to be killed and restarted to solve the problem.

A liveness probe can be one of these three types: a command, HTTP check, or TCP check. Its configuration resides under spec/containers.

Here's a sample configuration for setting a command as a liveness probe:

```
livenessProbe:
  exec:
    command:
    - cat
    - /tmp/healthy
  initialDelaySeconds: 5
  periodSeconds: 5
```

Once a command probe is set, this command will be executed every five seconds (defined by **periodSeconds**) to check the health status. If the command fails, the respective container will be restarted. In the preceding code, **initialDelaySeconds** also determines the amount of time to wait before the first check.

Alternatively, you can set an HTTP liveness probe. In this case, an HTTP GET request is sent to the provided port through the provided path:

```
livenessProbe:
  httpGet:
    path: /healthz
    port: 8080
  initialDelaySeconds: 3
  periodSeconds: 3
```

Just like in the command, you can set **periodSeconds** to determine the interval of the check and **initialDelaySeconds** to determine the amount of time before the first check.

Any result code between 200 and 400 (200 and 400 included) is regarded as a success. If it returns any other code, the container will be restarted.

The last alternative is to set a TCP liveness probe. In this way, Kubernetes will check whether it is possible to open a socket to the specified port. If it succeeds, the container is regarded as healthy, and it is restarted if not:

```
livenessProbe:
  tcpSocket:
    port: 8080
  initialDelaySeconds: 15
  periodSeconds: 20
```

'er probe types, you can set **periodSeconds** to determine the interval
.d **initialDelaySeconds** to determine the amount of time before the first

are two more important configurations that you can set, which are
.ureThreshold and **successThreshold**. The first one, that is, **failureThreshold**,
determines the number of failed probes necessary before restarting the Pod. For
example, if you set it to three, a failing probe does not immediately cause the Pod to
restart till the third attempt. The next one, which is **successThreshold**, determines the
number of successful probes until the Pod is marked as healthy.

Readiness Probe

This informs Kubernetes that the containers are ready to serve incoming requests. This
way, the respective **Services** start directing traffic to this Pod by adding it to the load
balancer. It always returns **success** if not set. Whenever this probe fails, the Pod is taken
out of the available Pod list in the Service, and the traffic is cut immediately.

A readiness probe can be set to the same condition as the liveness probe if the
application does not need a startup time before accepting requests. If it needs some
time, for example, to connect to the other services before serving the traffic, you can
utilize the readiness probe. Hence, the related Service won't send any traffic until the
readiness probe succeeds.

Readiness probes are set in an identical way to the liveness probes. The configuration
also resides under spec/containers. The only difference is the use of **readinessProbe**
instead of **livenessProbe**:

```
readinessProbe:
  exec:
    command:
    - cat
    - /tmp/healthy
  initialDelaySeconds: 5
  periodSeconds: 5
```

Like liveness probes, you can set a readiness probe by a command, HTTP check, or a
TCP check. Furthermore, you can set **periodSeconds** to determine the interval of the
check and **initialDelaySeconds** to determine the amount of time before the first check.
You can also set the **failureThreshold** and **successThreshold** fields, as explained in the
Liveness Probe section.

In the next section, we present an exercise on how to use the liveness and readiness probes for a Pod in Kubernetes.

Exercise 21: Using Liveness and Readiness Probes in Kubernetes

In this exercise, we aim to practice how to create liveness and readiness probes for a Pod in Kubernetes. We'll be observing the events of the Pod to see how they affect the life cycle:

1. Create a file named **probe-pod.yaml** using the following Pod definition. We set a liveness probe as a command, which will check whether a file named **healthy** exists. In the same way, we also set a readiness probe as a command, which will check whether a file named **ready** exists:

```
apiVersion: v1
kind: Pod
metadata:
  name: probe-pod
spec:
  containers:
  - name: test
    image: busybox
    args:
    - /bin/sh
    - -c
    - touch /healthy; touch /ready; sleep 20; rm -rf /ready; sleep 40; rm
-rf /healthy; sleep 100
    livenessProbe:
      exec:
        command:
        - cat
        - /healthy
      initialDelaySeconds: 3
      periodSeconds: 5
    readinessProbe:
      exec:
        command:
        - cat
        - /ready
      initialDelaySeconds: 3
      periodSeconds: 5
```

2. Create a new namespace called **lesson-8** and deploy **probe-pod.yaml** to this namespace:

```
$ kubectl create ns lesson-8
$ kubectl create -f probe-pod.yaml -n lesson-8
```

This is as shown in *Figure* 8.3:

```
/devops $ kubectl create ns lesson-8
namespace/lesson-8 created
/devops $
/devops $ kubectl create -f probe-pod.yaml -n lesson-8
pod/probe-pod created
/devops $
```

Figure 8.3: Creating the lesson-8 namespace and deploying the probe-pod

3. Observe the Pod readiness using the watch option of **kubectl get pods** as shown in *Figure* 8.4:

```
$ kubectl get pods -n lesson-8 -w
```

```
/devops $ kubectl get pods -n lesson-8 -w
NAME         READY    STATUS     RESTARTS    AGE
probe-pod    1/1      Running    0           9s
probe-pod    0/1      Running    0           36s
^C/devops $
```

Figure 8.4: Observing the Pod readiness

Since we have the **healthy** and **ready** files from the beginning, the Pod starts healthy (without any restarts) and ready (**Ready 1/1**). After 20 seconds, we remove the **ready** file, which leads to the failed readiness probe. As a result of the readiness probe failure, the Pod is not listed as **Ready** anymore. This will cause the Pod not to receive traffic from the Service anymore.

4. Observe the Pod liveness using the watch option of **kubectl get pods** again:

```
$ kubectl get pods -n lesson-8 -w
```

```
/devops $ kubectl get pods -n lesson-8 -w
NAME         READY    STATUS     RESTARTS    AGE
probe-pod    0/1      Running    0           53s
probe-pod    0/1      Running    1           1m
probe-pod    1/1      Running    1           1m
^C/devops $
```

Figure 8.5: Observing the Pod liveness

After 40 more seconds, we remove the **healthy** file, which leads to the failed liveness probe. As a result of the liveness probe failure, the Pod is restarted.

5. Observe the Pod events using **kubectl describe**:

```
$ kubectl describe pod probe-pod -n lesson-8
```

```
Events:
  Type      Reason               Age             From                                    Message
  ----      ------               ---             ----                                    -------
  Normal    Scheduled            4m              default-scheduler                       Successfully
assigned probe-pod to gke-prow-suakbas-default-pool-ba3d1a45-hdpn
  Normal    SuccessfulMountVolume 4m             kubelet, gke-default-pool-bsda213-hdpn  MountVolume.S
etUp succeeded for volume "default-token-q77xq"
  Normal    Pulling              3m (x2 over 4m) kubelet, gke-default-pool-bsda213-hdpn  pulling image
 "busybox"
  Normal    Killing              3m              kubelet, gke-default-pool-bsda213-hdpn  Killing conta
iner with id docker://test:Container failed liveness probe.. Container will be killed and recreated.
  Normal    Pulled               3m (x2 over 4m) kubelet, gke-default-pool-bsda213-hdpn  Successfully
pulled image "busybox"
  Normal    Created              3m (x2 over 4m) kubelet, gke-default-pool-bsda213-hdpn  Created conta
iner
  Normal    Started              3m (x2 over 4m) kubelet, gke-default-pool-bsda213-hdpn  Started conta
iner
  Warning   Unhealthy            2m (x4 over 4m) kubelet, gke-default-pool-bsda213-hdpn  Liveness prob
e failed: cat: can't open '/healthy': No such file or directory
  Warning   Unhealthy            2m (x11 over 4m) kubelet, gke-default-pool-bsda213-hdpn Readiness pro
be failed: cat: can't open '/ready': No such file or directory
```

Figure 8.6: Events of the probe-pod

At the end of the page, you'll see the events for this Pod. Pay attention, particularly to the last two lines. They inform you about the liveness and readiness probe failures. As you practice, this will be the easiest way to understand what's wrong with a Pod.

6. You can delete the Pod now using **kubectl delete**:

```
$ kubectl delete -f probe-pod.yaml -n lesson-8
```

In this exercise, we saw how we can set the liveness and readiness probes. We also observed what happens when these probes fail. In the following section, we'll see another Kubernetes feature providing another way to make it clear why a Pod is terminated.

Creating a Termination Log

Kubernetes provides a nice feature to understand why the application running inside the Pod is terminated. You can make your application write down the reason of termination to a pre-defined path, **/dev/termination-log** is the default, so that you can see the termination reason quickly by checking the Pod definition. You can determine a different location by setting the **terminationMessagePath** field of a container.

Here's a sample Pod writing the termination reason to the **/termination-log** path:

```
apiVersion: v1
kind: Pod
metadata:
  name: termination-pod
spec:
  containers:
  - name: termination
    image: busybox
    command: ["/bin/sh"]
    args: ["-c", "sleep 20 && echo Done sleeping > /termination-log"]
    terminationMessagePath: "/termination-log"
```

When this Pod exits after 20 seconds, you can check the Pod definition to see the termination reason by executing the **kubectl get** command:

```
$ kubectl get pod termination-pod -o yaml
```

Here's a sample output showing the termination message:

```
apiVersion: v1
kind: Pod
...
    lastState:
      terminated:
        containerID: ...
        exitCode: 0
        finishedAt: ...
        message: |
          Done sleeping

      ...
```

In the next section, we will go over several handy commands that we can make use of while troubleshooting a problem in Kubernetes.

Handy Commands for Troubleshooting

The first step to solve a problem is always figuring out what's wrong. To see what a problem with an application's Pods could be, you can use a couple of **kubectl** commands. Let's check them one by one. The most handy command is **kubectl describe**.

kubectl describe

This command provides you with all the information for the current state of a Pod and of the containers running inside the Pod.

Here, you can see the sample output from a **kubectl describe** call:

```
$ kubectl describe pod <pod-name>
```

The Pod status is as shown:

```
Status:         Running
IP:             10.44.0.30
Controlled By:  ReplicaSet/test-76656f9f8
Containers:
  test:
    Container ID:
docker://9c020c544611fd5c2be4f42bbd89f65934fd8d9e6e14ab32d5a9a517a5fee717
      Image:        suakbas/lesson08:v1
      Port:         8888/TCP
      Host Port:    0/TCP
      Args:
        --enable=false
      State:          Running
        Started:      Wed, 20 Mar 2019 10:36:03 +0100
      Ready:          True
      Restart Count:  0
  Conditions:
    Type           Status
    Initialized    True
    Ready          True
    PodScheduled   True
```

Running **kubectl describe** provides you with detailed information about the Pod and the containers, as shown earlier. What is important to check here is whether the containers are in running state, the restart count, and the Pod conditions. This information can show you what's going on with your application.

kubectl get

In the case of a problem, you may want to check whether the configuration of your application Pods is correct. You can easily do this using **kubectl get**.

This command provides the Pod definition of the application with a little high-level information about the status of the Pod:

```
$ kubectl get pod <pod-name> -o yaml
```

You can also get the current status of the Pods by adding the **-w** option to the **kubectl get** command. This way, you can see what's happening in real time, and this can give insights to solve the problem:

```
$ kubectl get pods -w
```

Another useful option for **kubectl get** is **-o wide**, which will show the nodes on which the Pods are running and the IP addresses of the Pods. This information can be useful to detect a problematic node and determine which Pods can be affected:

```
$ kubectl get pods -o wide
```

There is one more useful option of **kubectl get**, which is to check the events in the cluster. This can save a lot of time as it allows you to see all the events from the cluster together. Hence, you can get the health of a cluster:

```
$ kubectl get events
```

kubectl logs

You can check the logs of the Pod using **kubectl log**:

```
$ kubectl logs <pod-name>
```

It has a handy option to reach the logs of the previously crashed container by specifying the **--previous** flag:

```
$ kubectl logs --previous <pod-name>
```

kubectl exec

Another way to debug a problem is by getting into the container using **kubectl exec**:

```
$ kubectl exec -it <pod-name> bin/bash
```

You can alternatively run a command inside the container without necessarily opening a shell:

```
$ kubectl exec -it <pod-name> -- printenv
```

This command will print the environment variables set in the container. For all these commands, you can also specify the container name using the **-c** option if the Pod has more than one container:

```
$ kubectl logs <pod-name> -c <container-name>
```

Other Handy Commands

While troubleshooting an issue, an alternate way is to run a **busybox** Pod in the cluster and access the interactive shell. This way, you can be in the same environment with your application Pods and can interact with them. For example, you can test sending requests from inside the cluster:

```
$ kubectl run busybox --image=busybox -i -- sh
```

There is another handy command in **kubectl** called **attach**, which you can use to attach to the running process inside the container:

```
$ kubectl attach <pod-name> -i
```

You can also use the **kubectl port-forward** command to forward the specified port in the container to the specified one in the local machine. This way, you can quickly test interacting with your application over the port:

```
$ kubectl port-forward <pod-name> <local-port>:<container-port>
```

The **kubectl top** command shows the resource usage of the Pods. You can easily see whether there is any conspicuous resource consumption such as CPU and memory, which could be the root cause of a bigger problem:

```
$ kubectl top pods --containers
```

Action Commands

After figuring out what's wrong and coming up with the solution, you can apply this to the cluster using a handful amount of commands to update a Kubernetes resource. You can use any one of the following three commands to update a resource in Kubernetes:

- Use **kubectl apply -f** to apply the changes you make in the object's definition file:

      $ kubectl apply -f <file-wt-correct-resource>

- Use **kubectl edit** to make the changes in a text editor:

      $ kubectl edit <resource-type> <resource-name>

- Use **kubectl patch** to change only a field of the object:

      $ kubectl patch <resource-type> <resource-name> -p <updated-field>

Suggestions for Some Common Problems

There might be plenty of reasons why your application is not healthy. Here are some of the common problems and how you can understand the reasons behind them. We will also suggest some solutions to these problems.

Lack of Resources

If a Pod is in the Pending state for a long time, it could mean that it couldn't be scheduled to a node. There could be many reasons, but the most common one is that you don't have enough resources left in the cluster. You can confirm this by checking the conditions of the Pod by running **kubectl describe**. If this is the case, you need to either increase the number of available resources or free the current resources by deleting other Pods:

    $ kubectl describe pod <pod-name>

Also, you can use **kubectl top nodes** to see whether the nodes are having capacity issues. It shows the resource usage of the nodes:

    $ kubectl top nodes

> **Note**
>
> To run this command on Minikube, ensure that the **metrics-server** addon is enabled:
>
> $ minikube addons enable metrics-server

This command will show you the resource usage, whereas the following one will show the capacity:

```
$ kubectl get nodes -o jsonpath='{range .items[*]}{.metadata.name} {.status.
capacity} {"\n"}{end}'
```

By using both, you can check whether there is a resource issue with the nodes.

Image Pull Failure

If the Pod is in the Waiting state for a long time, it could mean that the container images take a long time to be downloaded or cannot be downloaded at all. You can confirm this by running **kubectl describe** and checking the conditions. In this case, you need to check whether the specified image is correct and can be downloaded. You can use a simple **docker pull** command to check whether you can download the image by yourself.

In the next section, we will practice troubleshooting a Pod failure using several **kubectl** commands.

Exercise 22: Fixing a Pod Failure in Kubernetes

In this exercise, we will use **kubectl** commands to troubleshoot a problem with a Pod in Kubernetes:

Note

To do this exercise on Minikube, ensure that the **metrics-server** addon is enabled:

$ minikube addons enable metrics-server

1. Create a file named **test-pod.yaml** using the following Pod definition:

```
apiVersion: v1
kind: Pod
metadata:
  name: test-pod
spec:
  containers:
  - name: test
    image: busybo
    command: ["/bin/sh"]
    args: ["-c", "sleep 99999"]
```

2. Deploy the Pod in the **lesson-8** namespace using **kubectl create**:

```
$ kubectl create -f test-pod.yaml -n lesson-8
```

```
/devops $ kubectl create -f test-pod.yaml -n lesson-8
pod/test-pod created
/devops $
```

Figure 8.7: Deploying the test-pod

3. Check whether the Pod is running successfully:

```
$ kubectl get pods -n lesson-8
```

```
/devops $ kubectl get pods -n lesson-8
NAME        READY     STATUS          RESTARTS    AGE
test-pod    0/1       ErrImagePull    0           7s
/devops $
```

Figure 8.8: Checking the test-pod status

As you see, the Pod fails to run. We can also see the cause of the problem in the status field. However, let's pretend that we don't know what this status stands for and inspect the problem further using several **kubectl** commands.

4. Check the resource usage of the Pod to check whether excessive usage could be the source of the problem:

   ```
   $ kubectl top pods -n lesson-8
   ```

```
/devops $ kubectl top pods -n lesson-8
W0324 20:50:34.156835   72205 top_pod.go:263] Metrics not available for pod lesson-8/test-pod, age: 2m0.149757152s
error: Metrics not available for pod lesson-8/test-pod, age: 2m0.149757152s
/devops $
```

Figure 8.9: Checking the resource usage

As you see, resource usage is not even available as the Pod didn't run at all, which means excessive resource usage cannot be the problem.

5. Check the Pod logs to see what's happening with the application:

   ```
   $ kubectl logs test-pod -n lesson-8
   ```

```
/devops $ kubectl logs test-pod -n lesson-8
Error from server (BadRequest): container "test" in pod "test-pod" is waiting to start: image can't be pulled
/devops $
```

Figure 8.10: Checking the logs of test-pod

As you see from the logs, the container inside the Pod is still waiting to start because of the reason: **image can't be pulled**. Now that we know there is something wrong with the image, let's check the Pod details to figure out the problem.

6. Use **kubectl describe** to see the Pod details, including the states and the conditions:

```
$ kubectl describe pod test-pod -n lesson-8
```

```
Start Time:   Sun, 24 Mar 2019 20:48:34 +0100
Labels:       <none>
Annotations:  <none>
Status:       Pending
IP:           10.44.1.47
Containers:
  test:
    Container ID:
    Image:        busybo
    Image ID:
    Port:         <none>
    Host Port:    <none>
    Command:
      /bin/sh
    Args:
      -c
      sleep 99999
    State:        Waiting
      Reason:     ImagePullBackOff
    Ready:        False
    Restart Count: 0
    Environment:  <none>
    Mounts:
      /var/run/secrets/kubernetes.io/serviceaccount from default-token-q77xq (ro)
Conditions:
  Type            Status
  Initialized     True
  Ready           False
  PodScheduled    True
Volumes:
  default-token-q77xq:
    Type:         Secret (a volume populated by a Secret)
    SecretName:   default-token-q77xq
    Optional:     false
QoS Class:        BestEffort
Node-Selectors:   <none>
Tolerations:      node.kubernetes.io/not-ready:NoExecute for 300s
                  node.kubernetes.io/unreachable:NoExecute for 300s
Events:
  Type      Reason                Age           From                                        Message
  ----      ------                ----          ----                                        -------
  Normal    Scheduled             3m            default-scheduler                           Successfully assigned test-pod to gke-
default-pool-ba3d1a45-hdpn
  Normal    SuccessfulMountVolume 3m            kubelet, gke-default-pool-ba3d1a45-hdpn     MountVolume.SetUp succeeded for volume "d
efault-token-q77xq"
  Normal    Pulling               2m (x4 over 3m) kubelet, gke-default-pool-ba3d1a45-hdpn   pulling image "busybo"
  Warning   Failed                2m (x4 over 3m) kubelet, gke-default-pool-ba3d1a45-hdpn   Failed to pull image "busybo": rpc error:
 code = Unknown desc = Error response from daemon: repository busybo not found: does not exist or no pull access
  Warning   Failed                2m (x4 over 3m) kubelet, gke-default-pool-ba3d1a45-hdpn   Error: ErrImagePull
  Normal    BackOff               1m (x6 over 3m) kubelet, gke-default-pool-ba3d1a45-hdpn   Back-off pulling image "busybo"
  Warning   Failed                1m (x6 over 3m) kubelet, gke-default-pool-ba3d1a45-hdpn   Error: ImagePullBackOff
/devops $
```

Figure 8.11: Object details for test-pod

The overall status of the Pod is Pending, and the container is in the **Waiting state**. We check the Pod conditions to see that Pod is successfully scheduled and initialized, but it is not ready. Finally, we check the events at the end of the page and see that Pod complains saying the image **does not exist or no pull access** (see the highlighted event under **Events** at the end of the *Figure 8.11*). We realize that the image name should have been **busybox** instead of **busybo**.

7. Let's fix the image name in the file that was the source of the problem so that when someone else is using the same file in the future, they won't have this problem:

```
$ vi test-pod.yaml
# Fix the image name to busybox and exit the file using ':wq'. This will
save your changes.
```

```
/devops $ vi test-pod.yaml
/devops $
```

Figure 8.12: Opening the text editor

8. Apply the fix to the cluster:

```
$ kubectl apply -f test-pod.yaml -n lesson-8
```

```
/devops $ kubectl apply -f test-pod.yaml -n lesson-8
pod/test-pod configured
/devops $
```

Figure 8.13: Modifying the test-pod

9. Check whether the Pod runs successfully after the fix:

```
$ kubectl get pods -n lesson-8
```

```
/devops $ kubectl get pods -n lesson-8
NAME        READY    STATUS     RESTARTS    AGE
test-pod    1/1      Running    0           10m
/devops $
```

Figure 8.14: Checking the test-pod status

As you see, the problem is fixed, and the Pod is running without any issues now.

10. You can delete the Pod now using **kubectl delete**:

```
$ kubectl delete -f test-pod.yaml -n lesson-8
```

In this exercise, we practiced different commands while troubleshooting an application in Kubernetes. In the end, we fix the problem and reflect the changes in such a way that the problem will not happen in the future again.

In the next section, we mention another vital point of where to ask, in case you cannot solve a problem by yourself.

Community

.., o solve a problem alone or within the company is sometimes not enough. Someone else could have experienced the same problem and already provided a solution somewhere online. You can go over the existing or closed issues in the Kubernetes GitHub repository (https://github.com/kubernetes/kubernetes) to find out whether a related issue has already been solved before. If you cannot find the solution to your problem, you can create a new issue, or you can always ask for help in Stack Overflow using the **kubernetes** tag (https://stackoverflow.com/questions/tagged/kubernetes). Also, don't hesitate to post a question on Kubernetes Slack channels (https://kubernetes.slack.com). Kubernetes has one of the most active communities, and it wouldn't take long for someone to pick up and answer your question.

Also, you can take a look at the debugging section of the official Kubernetes website (https://kubernetes.io/docs/tasks/debug-application-cluster/debug-application-introspection/) for the most up-to-date information for troubleshooting your applications in Kubernetes.

In the next section, we will practice our learnings in a problem similar to real-life situations by performing an activity.

Activity 9: Troubleshooting an Application in Kubernetes

Imagine that you are a nightly on-call DevOps engineer maintaining the health of the applications deployed for your company. There is an application that is behaving strangely by exiting all the time. You check the logs for the application, but the information there is not sufficient to understand the problem. Luckily, your team decoupled the configurations from the source code, and you can configure the logging level to get more verbose logs. After changing the logging level, you figure out what the problem can be and take some actions to fix it. In the end, you verify that the application is running without any issues by checking the logs.

> **Note**
>
> To complete this activity, you can use Minikube or a real cluster.

Perform the following steps to complete this activity:

1. Create a Pod definition file that uses the **suakbas/lesson08:v1** image and is consuming the **LOG_LEVEL** and **ENABLE_CONNECTION** environment variables from a ConfigMap named **app-config**. Name the file as **pod.yaml**.

2. Create a ConfigMap with the **LOG_LEVEL** field set to **INFO** and **ENABLE_CONNECTION** set to **No**. Name the file as **configmap.yaml**.

3. Deploy the ConfigMap and the Pod to the **lesson-8** namespace. Then, check whether the Pod is running.

4. Try to figure out why the Pod is constantly terminating instead of running. Use **kubectl logs** to check the logs of the application.

5. Change the log level by updating the **LOG_LEVEL** field from the ConfigMap to 'DEBUG'.

6. Use **kubectl logs** again to check more verbose logs.

7. Check the set environment variables using **kubectl exec**.

8. Fix the problem by setting **ENABLE_CONNECTION** to **Yes** by updating the **configmap.yaml** file. Apply the updated file to the cluster.

9. Check the logs to verify the solution.

10. You can clean up everything now by removing the namespace.

> **Note**
>
> The solution to this activity can be found on page 333.

In this activity, we practiced several **kubectl** commands to troubleshoot an application. We also see the importance of logging in finding out how an application is behaving and to help determine the root cause of a problem. We completed an exercise where we used different logging levels and configured them by utilizing environment variables. This way, we practiced the same steps that you would take in a real-life situation. In the next section, we summarize the learning of this chapter.

Summary

In this chapter, we first explored troubleshooting in general and saw why it is an important concept. We looked at several aspects for troubleshooting applications effectively, including identifying the problem, adding tests to prevent the chances of the problem occurring again, documenting the solution to tackle it easily if it occurs again, using monitoring tools, and logging more efficiently to understand the underlying issues quickly.

Later, we moved to troubleshooting in Kubernetes. We explained some key concepts such as the Pod life cycle. We went through the many different conditions and states that a Pod can have. We also saw what each of these conditions and states mean and what issues they indicate. After that, we continued with the auto recovery topic. We introduced two health checks in Kubernetes, liveness and readiness probes, and we also practiced utilizing them through an exercise.

We then continued by creating a termination log from an application to make it possible to understand why a Pod terminated. We proceeded to the **kubectl** commands, which are most helpful while troubleshooting a problem. We covered many commands such as **kubectl logs**, **kubectl exec**, and **kubectl port-forward**. Then, we checked some suggestions to avoid some of the common problems encountered by an application running on Kubernetes. We then used these commands via an exercise to troubleshoot a Pod failure.

Finally, in the last section, we introduced the communication channels to the Kubernetes community. We then continued with an activity where we made use of different logging levels and fixed a problem using **kubectl** commands. In the next chapter, we will explore monitoring and alerting in Kubernetes.

Monitoring Applications in Kubernetes

Learning Objectives

By the end of this chapter, you will be able to:

- Explain the importance of monitoring
- List the tools for monitoring resources on Kubernetes
- Explore ways to create alert rules on Prometheus and dashboards on Grafana
- Use Alertmanager to receive alert notifications on Slack

This chapter introduces various techniques to monitor infrastructures and applications by using the most commonly used tools in Kubernetes

Monitoring

In the previous chapter, *Troubleshooting Applications in Kubernetes*, we explored ways to troubleshoot our applications quickly in the event of a problem. Now we're moving one step further in detecting any potential problems before they occur with the help of monitoring, which is about observing and determining the behavior of a system.

Nowadays, companies need to ensure high levels of customer satisfaction in order to stay competitive in the market. Particularly for websites, it is important to be functional and provide an excellent service 24/7. In spite of this, many companies still embrace a reactive approach in order to tackle any issues that may occur; that is, they wait for problems to occur before attempting to tackle and fix them. This causes system downtime and can lead to customer frustration.

Formerly, the source code of an application was mostly static; that's why sophisticated tools were not necessary to monitor applications in real time. Instead, it was enough to collect statistical information in order to gain an understanding of how users were consuming a product. This was then mostly used to develop a brand-new product or to implement an improvement for the next big release in upcoming months. However, in the DevOps era, it is usually an everyday practice to deploy a new version of an application to a production environment, that is, once all the tests are green. With this change, it is now vital to continually watch for any issues in real time and provide solutions as quickly as possible.

With the evolution of DevOps, monitoring has become a part of the daily life of application developers. In the pre-DevOps era, this was usually the responsibility of the operations team, but now it is the responsibility of the entire team. This allows a team to maintain a system's productivity and systematically detect potential problems early on in the project life cycle so that preventive actions can be taken to tackle problems quickly.

Nowadays, software usually depends on many other resources, such as external services and databases. Any problems related to these other resources could quickly destroy the value brought by your application. That's why they should be continuously monitored, and any problems should be detected as soon as possible.

Furthermore, monitoring an application provides significant information, such as about the performance of the application. Particularly with microservices, there are now many independent services that make a lot of API calls in a distributed environment. Due to this, it is tricky to detect any problems manually. Additionally, there are many metrics generated by these systems that refer to quantitative measurements for software. This makes it necessary to have a monitoring tool that can automatically watch the overall health of systems by monitoring these metrics and notifying you in the event of a problem.

Although monitoring can touch on many operational aspects in DevOps, we will be focusing on two types of monitoring: **infrastructure monitoring** and **application performance monitoring** (APM).

Infrastructure Monitoring

Infrastructure monitoring refers to analyzing servers (or any other devices that are included in a system) to detect the overall status. It includes basic but important server metrics such as memory, CPU, and disk performance. This provides timely information, so that if a device is being overloaded in terms of resources, then the resources can be increased before it causes an issue. Additionally, the information obtained by monitoring the infrastructure can be used to increase the efficiency of the system. You can determine the under- or over-utilized system elements and take appropriate actions to use them as efficiently as possible.

Application Performance Monitoring (APM)

APM consists of tracking the performance of the internal assets of an application. These can be metrics such as request queue processing times, garbage collection, and page load times. This provides us with essential information to understand any problems and find areas to improve – even before customers themselves become aware of them. For example, if a problem is not easily detectable, monitoring the calls within an application makes it easier to see precisely what the application is doing rather than going through the source code. You can also explore whether there is an inefficient pattern, such as two microservices making too many calls between them. In such cases, it may make more sense to bring those services together into one microservice to increase application performance:

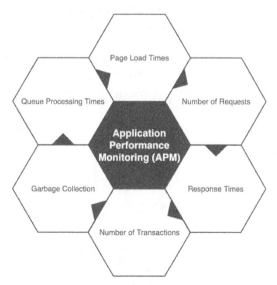

Figure 9.1: Sample metrics for APM

APM also enables us to understand how customers are using software so that we can engage more actively with them and provide solutions to improve their overall experience.

Apart from these monitoring tasks, there are some other key aspects of monitoring, such as alerting and tools. In the next section, we will go through these aspects in detail.

Alerting

Alerting refers to being notified if there is a problem or any unusual activity within a system or an application. These alerts can be in various forms, such as emails, SMS messages, or chat notifications. An alerting tool plays a vital role as an early warning system about the current health status of a system or an application. Later, in the *Monitoring Applications in Kubernetes* section, we will demonstrate how to enable alerting for a cluster and how to receive alert notifications.

Tools

There are many monitoring tools available in the market today. It can be difficult to compare and find the best tool for your case, so you should determine the requirements that you need in a monitoring system before obtaining a tool.

You can either have one tool for everything or you can combine many tools to work together to realize a monitoring system. In the end, you must have a running system that should be capable of performing the following:

- All the metrics in a system can be gathered and aggregated.
- Alerting should be provided; it should have the necessary capabilities for your case, such as sending emails or sending resolved messages.
- Visualization should be available; it should allow you to customize dashboards to your needs. You should be able to visualize as much as possible in order to see application trends and detect any problems early on.

The tools in the market usually provide many more features, but these three features are necessary to achieve a useful monitoring system.

In the next section, we will demonstrate how to achieve a capable monitoring system in Kubernetes.

Monitoring Applications in Kubernetes

In this section, we will explore how to monitor infrastructures and applications by using the most commonly used tools in Kubernetes. We will also discover how we can expose our custom metrics from these applications and set up alert notifications so that we will have a fully capable monitoring system.

We will start with **Prometheus** as a tool for collecting metrics from a cluster and **Alertmanager** as an alert notifier. Then, we'll continue with **Grafana** as the visualizer tool for the metrics obtained by Prometheus. Finally, we'll complete the system by configuring a Slack channel to receive these alert notifications.

Prometheus

Prometheus is an open source monitoring and alerting system. It periodically collects real-time data from the configured applications and stores them in a database in timely order, also called time series data. Prometheus has a querying language called **Prometheus Query Language** (**PromQL**), which enables the user to select and aggregate data obtained from metrics.

PromQL allows the user to write many complex queries, just like any other querying language using different operators. You can create a query by using only the metric name. By doing so, the query behaves like a selector and returns all the data collected by that particular metric, just like a `Select * from <table>` query in MySQL. You can then use labels in curly braces (`{}`) to filter out the results. Additionally, you can use the many functions provided to derive some kind of meaning from the data. For example, using the `sum` function, you can aggregate all the results to find the total number of values for a metric.

PromQL is also used to create alert rules. An alert rule is a configuration that includes a Boolean expression provided by the user, which is periodically checked against the metrics data. If the expression returns `false`, then an alert is fired. If there is a receiver configured by the user for this particular alert, then an alert notification is sent. We will discuss this in more detail in the *Alertmanager* section.

Here is a simple alert rule that is defined by using a `PromQL` query in the `expr` field:

```
- name: pod-container-not-running-rule

    rules:

    - alert: PodContainerNotRunning

      expr: (kube_pod_container_status_running { namespace="default",
container="test" } == 0)

      for: 30s
      labels:
```

```
        severity: warning
    annotations:
        description: "{{$labels.namespace}}/{{$labels.pod}} is not running"
        summary: "Test container is not running"
```

This query in the expression field selects all the containers in the running status from the **default** namespace along with the containers called **test**. This expression will return **false** if there is no container called **test** in the **default** namespace and it will trigger an alert.

Prometheus has a pull model for getting metrics, which requires the services to have a **/metrics** endpoint so that it can periodically fetch the metrics from there. Therefore, you need to expose a **/metrics** endpoint from every service where you provide only plain text data. Then, Prometheus obtains them by sending an HTTP request.

Prometheus, as a system, is composed of several components; these are as follows:

- The Prometheus server: This is responsible for collecting metrics.

- The exporters: These are the supporting servers, which are used to export existing metrics from well-known services such as Kubernetes.

- Alertmanager: This is responsible for sending alerts.

- Pushgateway: This is responsible for collecting metrics from short-lived jobs.

Prometheus comes with a built-in UI, where you can see and use the exposed metrics to make queries using PromQL. You can start by writing a metric name that will trigger the suggestions through autocomplete and from there you can explore more metrics. Finally, after writing the full metric name and any configuration values inside the brackets, you can click on **Execute** to see the measurements aggregated from this metric:

Figure 9.2: The query page on the Prometheus UI

The installation of Prometheus by Helm, which will be practiced in the first exercise later, deploys two ConfigMaps: **prometheus-server** and **prometheus-alertmanager**. The **prometheus-server** ConfigMap holds all the configurations needed for the Prometheus server and the alert rules. Therefore, to add a new alert rule, the **alerts** field in this ConfigMap should be modified.

Here is the initial state of the alerts field:

```
apiVersion: v1
data:
  alerts: |
    {}
```

Figure 9.3: The initial state of the alerts field

This is how the **alerts** field should look after configuring a sample alert:

```
apiVersion: v1
data:
  alerts: |
    groups:
    - name: pod-container-not-running-rule
      rules:
      - alert: PodContainerNotRunning
        expr: (kube_pod_container_status_running { namespace="default", container="test" } == 0)
        for: 30s
        labels:
          severity: warning
        annotations:
          description: "{{$labels.namespace}}/{{$labels.pod}} is not running"
          summary: "Test container is not running"
```

Figure 9.4: The state of the alerts field after configuring a sample alert

In the next section, we will dig deeper into one of the components, called **Alertmanager**. This is important for sending alerting notifications.

Alertmanager

Alertmanager comes as an independent module within the Prometheus system. It is responsible for sending alert notifications based on the firing alerts in Prometheus. It supports many receivers out of the box, such as email clients, Slack (https://slack.com), VictorOps (https://victorops.com/), and WeChat (https://www.wechat.com).

Here is a sample configuration for a **slack** receiver:

```
- name: "slack"
  slack_configs:
  - channel: "test"
    send_resolved: true
    api_url: "<webhook-url>"
    title: "{{ .CommonAnnotations.description }}"
    text: "Description: {{ .CommonAnnotations.description }}"
```

Here, an alerting notification can be customized and enriched using different fields; for example, an explanatory title and text field can be added. Many other fields that can be used for customizing the notification can be found at https://prometheus.io/docs/alerting/configuration/#slack_config.

Here is a sample configuration for an email receiver:

```
- name: email_config
  email_configs:
  - to: 'to@test.com'
    from: 'from@test.com'
    smarthost: 'smtp.test.com:587'
    auth_username: 'from@test.com'
    auth_password: '<password>'
    auth_secret: 'admin@test.com'
    auth_identity: 'admin@test.com'
```

Just like the **slack** receiver, this can also be enriched by utilizing many more fields from https://prometheus.io/docs/alerting/configuration/#email_config.

Additional configurations for all the other receivers, such as VictorOps and WeChat, can be found at https://prometheus.io/docs/alerting/configuration/.

The ConfigMap named **prometheus-alertmanager**, deployed by the installation of Prometheus, holds the configurations for Alertmanager, such as all the receiver information. So, to add a new receiver, the `receivers` field in this ConfigMap should be modified.

Here is the initial state of the `receivers` field in the **prometheus-alertmanager** ConfigMap:

```
receivers:
- name: default-receiver
```

Figure 9.5: The initial state of the receivers field

This is how the `receivers` field in the **prometheus-alertmanager** ConfigMap should look after configuring a sample Slack receiver:

```
receivers:
- name: default-receiver
- name: "slack"
  slack_configs:
  - channel: "test"
    send_resolved: true
    api_url: "<webhook-url>"
    title: "{{ .CommonAnnotations.description }}"
    text: "Description: {{ .CommonAnnotations.description }}"
```

Figure 9.6: The state of the receivers field after configuring a sample slack receiver

We will learn how to obtain and fill in these fields, especially the API URL, in the Slack section.

In the next section, we will explore Grafana, which is used to visualize all the metrics we obtained with Prometheus on nice dashboards and graphs.

Grafana

Even though Prometheus provides a UI where you can inspect metrics, it is difficult to visualize this information with nice dashboards or graphs. That's where Grafana comes into play; Grafana is called a metric analytics and visualization suite. Just like Prometheus, Grafana is also open source. Alongside other data stores, such as Elasticsearch (https://github.com/elastic/elasticsearch) and **InfluxDB** (https://github.com/influxdata/influxdb), Prometheus is a supported data source in Grafana for obtaining metrics data.

Grafana provides many features that can be used to visualize monitored data by creating custom dashboards. A dashboard consists of many panels visualizing a particular metric in a graph. In addition to creating a custom dashboard, there are a lot of free dashboards that you can get from the Grafana marketplace (https://grafana. com/dashboards). It also comes with out-of-the-box authentication and authorization, which means that it is highly convenient to share these dashboards publicly, if necessary. These dashboards can also be stored in version control as they are plain JSON files:

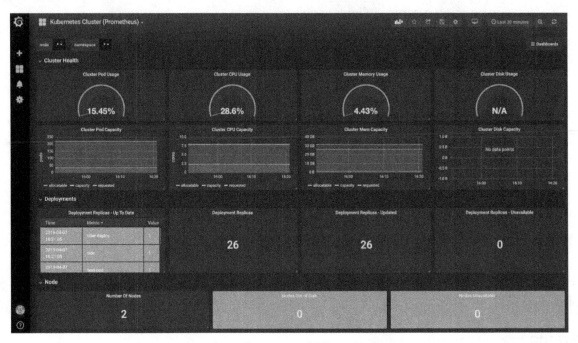

Figure 9.7: A sample dashboard in Grafana

Creating a Dashboard in Grafana

Although there are already plenty of dashboards in the Grafana marketplace, you may want to create your own custom dashboard as well. To achieve this, Grafana offers you many different panel types, such as a graph, a table, or a panel showing a single stat. You can create all the panels that you need and collect them together in a dashboard. We will observe how to create a custom dashboard in the following exercise.

In the next exercise, we will demonstrate how to install Prometheus and Grafana. We will even install our first dashboards in Grafana.

Exercise 23: Installing Prometheus and Grafana

In this exercise, we will go through the installation of Prometheus and Grafana using their Helm charts. Then, we will add Prometheus as a data source in Grafana. Finally, we will create a custom dashboard and import an existing one to see the current status of the Kubernetes cluster.

> **Note**
>
> To complete this exercise, please use a real cluster. You can obtain a managed Kubernetes cluster on Google Kubernetes Engine.

Perform the following steps to complete this exercise:

1. Create the **lesson-9** namespace:

```
$ kubectl create ns lesson-9
```

```
/devops $ kubectl create ns lesson-9
namespace/lesson-9 created
/devops $
```

Figure 9.8: Creating the lesson-9 namespace

2. Install Prometheus using the **stable/prometheus** Helm chart:

```
$ helm install stable/prometheus --name prometheus --namespace lesson-9
```

```
/devops $ helm install stable/prometheus --name prometheus --namespace lesson-9
NAME:    prometheus
LAST DEPLOYED: Sun Apr  7 14:33:53 2019
NAMESPACE: lesson-9
STATUS: DEPLOYED

RESOURCES:
==> v1beta1/DaemonSet
NAME                       DESIRED   CURRENT   READY   UP-TO-DATE   AVAILABLE   NODE SELECTOR   AGE
prometheus-node-exporter   2         2         0       2            0           <none>          1s

==> v1beta1/Deployment
NAME                           DESIRED   CURRENT   UP-TO-DATE   AVAILABLE   AGE
prometheus-alertmanager        1         1         1            0           1s
prometheus-kube-state-metrics  1         1         1            0           1s
prometheus-pushgateway         1         1         1            0           1s
prometheus-server              1         1         1            0           1s

==> v1beta1/ClusterRoleBinding
NAME                           AGE
prometheus-kube-state-metrics  1s
prometheus-server              1s

==> v1/PersistentVolumeClaim
NAME                      STATUS    VOLUME     CAPACITY   ACCESS MODES   STORAGECLASS   AGE
prometheus-alertmanager   Pending   standard   2s
prometheus-server         Pending   standard   2s

==> v1/ServiceAccount
NAME                           SECRETS   AGE
prometheus-alertmanager        1         2s
prometheus-kube-state-metrics  1         1s
prometheus-node-exporter       1         1s
prometheus-pushgateway         1         1s
prometheus-server              1         1s

==> v1beta1/ClusterRole
NAME                           AGE
prometheus-kube-state-metrics  1s
prometheus-server              1s

==> v1/Service
NAME                           TYPE        CLUSTER-IP      EXTERNAL-IP   PORT(S)    AGE
prometheus-alertmanager        ClusterIP   10.47.246.151   <none>        80/TCP     1s
prometheus-kube-state-metrics  ClusterIP   None            <none>        80/TCP     1s
prometheus-node-exporter       ClusterIP   None            <none>        9100/TCP   1s
```

Figure 9.9: Installing Prometheus using Helm

3. Check the pods to see whether there are any problems:

```
$ kubectl get pods -n lesson-9
```

```
/devops $ kubectl get pods -n lesson-9
NAME                                              READY    STATUS     RESTARTS    AGE
prometheus-alertmanager-5c4d9d9fdf-gp8wm          2/2      Running    0           1m
prometheus-kube-state-metrics-79965f8ddd-qls9j    1/1      Running    0           1m
prometheus-node-exporter-29cxh                    1/1      Running    0           1m
prometheus-node-exporter-lcwmp                    1/1      Running    0           1m
prometheus-pushgateway-5dc5444dbd-p5vj9           1/1      Running    0           1m
prometheus-server-f4696b766-qd68p                 2/2      Running    0           1m
/devops $
```

Figure 9.10: Checking the pods in the lesson-9 namespace

4. Export **POD_NAME** to a variable and then use it while port-forwarding (kubectl port-forward) in order to access the Prometheus UI:

```
$ export POD_NAME=$(kubectl get pods -n lesson-9 -l
"app=prometheus,component=server" -o jsonpath="{.items[0].metadata.name}")
$ kubectl port-forward $POD_NAME 9090 -n lesson-9
```

```
/devops $ kubectl port-forward prometheus-server-f4696b766-qd68p 9090 -n lesson-9
Forwarding from 127.0.0.1:9090 -> 9090
Forwarding from [::1]:9090 -> 9090
```

Figure 9.11: Port-forwarding the Prometheus server to reach the UI

5. Open a browser and go to **http://localhost:9090** to see the Prometheus UI:

Figure 9.12: The Prometheus UI

Being able to access the Prometheus UI and view the preceding screen means that our Prometheus installation was successful. Now, let's continue with the installation of Grafana on a new Terminal. Keep this Terminal open to use it later in the activity.

6. Install Grafana using the **stable/grafana** Helm chart on a new Terminal:

```
$ helm install stable/grafana --name grafana --namespace lesson-9
```

```
/devops $ helm install stable/grafana --name grafana --namespace lesson-9
NAME:    grafana
LAST DEPLOYED: Sun Apr  7 14:39:22 2019
NAMESPACE: lesson-9
STATUS: DEPLOYED

RESOURCES:
==> v1beta1/PodSecurityPolicy
NAME     DATA  CAPS   SELINUX   RUNASUSER  FSGROUP   SUPGROUP  READONLYROOTFS  VOLUMES
grafana  false RunAsAny RunAsAny RunAsAny  RunAsAny  false               configMap,emptyDir,projected,secret,downwardAPI
,persistentVolumeClaim

==> v1/ServiceAccount
NAME     SECRETS  AGE
grafana  1        0s

==> v1/ClusterRoleBinding
NAME                       AGE
grafana-clusterrolebinding 0s

==> v1beta1/Role
NAME     AGE
grafana  0s

==> v1beta1/RoleBinding
NAME     AGE
grafana  0s

==> v1/Service
NAME     TYPE       CLUSTER-IP      EXTERNAL-IP  PORT(S)  AGE
grafana  ClusterIP  10.47.251.212   <none>       80/TCP   0s

==> v1beta2/Deployment
NAME     DESIRED  CURRENT  UP-TO-DATE  AVAILABLE  AGE
grafana  1        1        1           0          0s

==> v1/Pod(related)
NAME                     READY  STATUS            RESTARTS  AGE
grafana-7bc7f5766-zptqm  0/1    ContainerCreating 0         0s

==> v1/Secret
NAME     TYPE    DATA  AGE
grafana  Opaque  3     0s

==> v1/ConfigMap
NAME     DATA  AGE
grafana  1     0s
```

Figure 9.13: Installing Grafana using Helm

7. Check the pods to see whether there are any problems:

```
$ kubectl get pods -n lesson-9
```

```
/devops $ kubectl get pods -n lesson-9
NAME                                          READY  STATUS   RESTARTS  AGE
grafana-7bc7f5766-zptqm                       1/1    Running  0         58s
prometheus-alertmanager-5c4d9d9fdf-gp8wm      2/2    Running  0         6m
prometheus-kube-state-metrics-79965f8ddd-qls9j 1/1   Running  0         6m
prometheus-node-exporter-29cxh                1/1    Running  0         6m
prometheus-node-exporter-lcwmp                1/1    Running  0         6m
prometheus-pushgateway-5dc5444dbd-p5vj9       1/1    Running  0         6m
prometheus-server-f4696b766-qd68p             2/2    Running  0         6m
/devops $
```

Figure 9.14: Checking the pods in the lesson-9 namespace

8. Take a look at the secret named **grafana** in order to obtain the username and password for Grafana UI:

```
$ kubectl get secret grafana -n lesson-9 -o yaml
```

```
/devops $ kubectl get secret grafana -n lesson-9 -o yaml
apiVersion: v1
data:
  admin-password: Qm83S0R4ekFPVGM2ekhwZTJnS2V2OGc5ZXc0RXhDVElGd2RTS0YwOQ==
  admin-user: YWRtaW4=
  ldap-toml: ""
kind: Secret
metadata:
  creationTimestamp: 2019-04-07T12:39:23Z
  labels:
    app: grafana
    chart: grafana-1.22.1
    heritage: Tiller
    release: grafana
  name: grafana
  namespace: lesson-9
  resourceVersion: "14503878"
  selfLink: /api/v1/namespaces/lesson-9/secrets/grafana
  uid: 2c1bb629-5932-11e9-bd98-42010a9c01eb
type: Opaque
/devops $
```

Figure 9.15: Checking the contents of Grafana secret

9. Decode the username and password as follows:

```
$ echo '<admin-user-value>' | base64 -D
$ echo '<admin-password-value>' | base64 -D
```

```
/devops $ echo 'YWRtaW4=' | base64 -D
admin
/devops $ echo 'Qm83S0R4ekFPVGM2ekhwZTJnS2V2OGc5ZXc0RXhDVElGd2RTS0YwOQ==' | base64 -D
Bo7KDxzAOTc6zHpe2gKev8g9ew4ExCTIFwdSKF09
/devops $
```

Figure 9.16: Decoding the Grafana username and password

Note

To decode secrets using **base64**, use the **-D** option in macOS or **-d** in Linux.

10. Export **POD_NAME** to a variable and use it while port-forwarding in order to access the Grafana UI:

    ```
    $ export POD_NAME=$(kubectl get pods -n lesson-9 -l "app=grafana" -o
    jsonpath="{.items[0].metadata.name}")
    $ kubectl port-forward $POD_NAME 3000 -n lesson-9
    ```

    ```
    /devops $ kubectl port-forward grafana-7bc7f5766-zptqm 3000 -n lesson-9
    Forwarding from 127.0.0.1:3000 -> 3000
    Forwarding from [::1]:3000 -> 3000
    ```

    Figure 9.17: Port-forwarding the Grafana pod to reach the UI

11. From the browser, go to **http://localhost:3000** to see the Grafana UI. Enter the username and password you obtained in the previous step to log in:

Figure 9.18: The Grafana login page

At this point, we have both Prometheus and Grafana installed successfully.

12. To add Prometheus as a data source, click on **Add data source**:

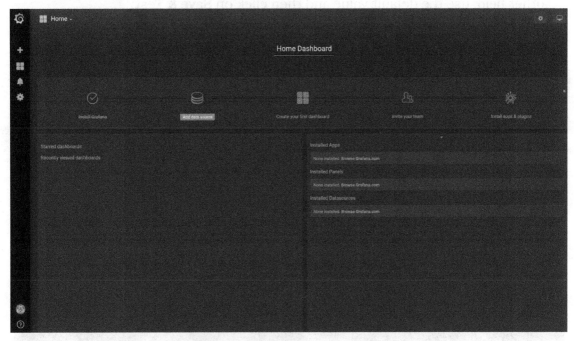

Figure 9.19: The Grafana home page

13. From the data source types, select **Prometheus**, as follows:

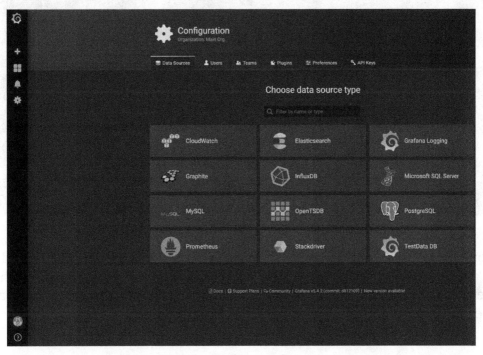

Figure 9.20: The Grafana configuration page

14. As the URL, enter `http://prometheus-server.lesson-9.svc.cluster.local`. For the other field, use the default value and then click on **Save & Test**:

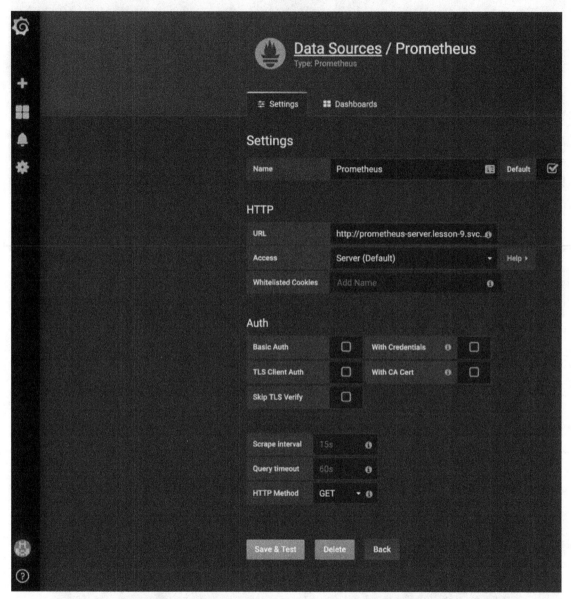

Figure 9.21: Adding Prometheus as a data source in Grafana

Now that both Prometheus and Grafana are installed, and Prometheus is added as a data source in Grafana, we have the complete monitoring system. As the next step, let's create a custom dashboard in Grafana to start monitoring the health of the cluster.

15. To create a custom dashboard, click on the plus (**+**) sign and choose **Dashboard**:

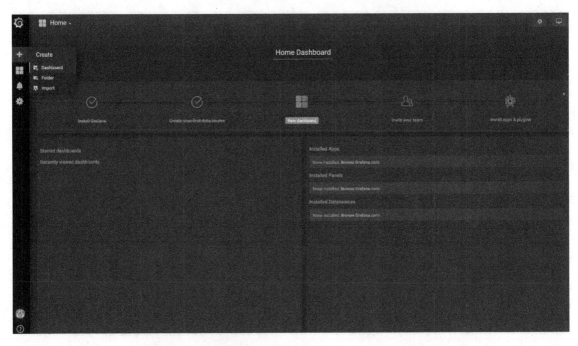

Figure 9.22: Creating a custom dashboard in Grafana

16. Choose **Graph** as the panel type that we want to create for this dashboard:

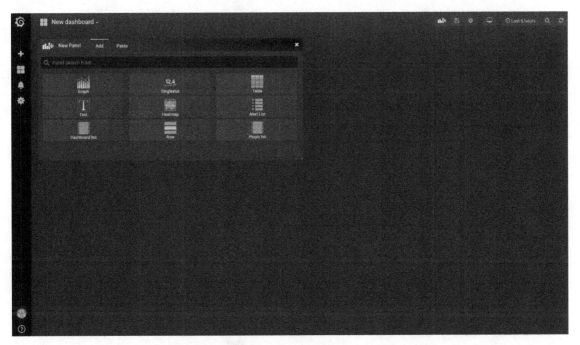

Figure 9.23: Adding a graph panel to the dashboard

17. Click on **Panel Title** and then click on **Edit**:

Figure 9.24: Editing a graph panel

18. Choose **Prometheus** as the data source and enter **kube_node_status_capacity_ cpu_cores** in the text field to see the current capacity status of the CPUs for the nodes:

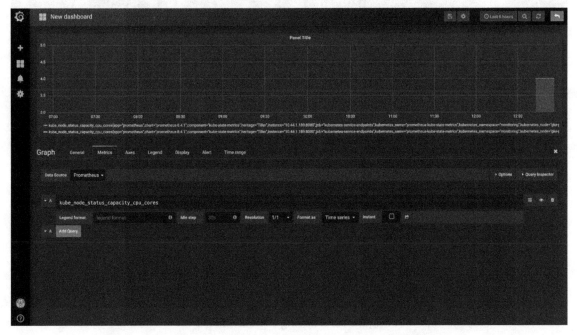

Figure 9.25: Creating a panel to see the current node CPU capacity

19. To save this dashboard, click on the **Save** button in the top-right panel. Enter a name and then click on **Save**:

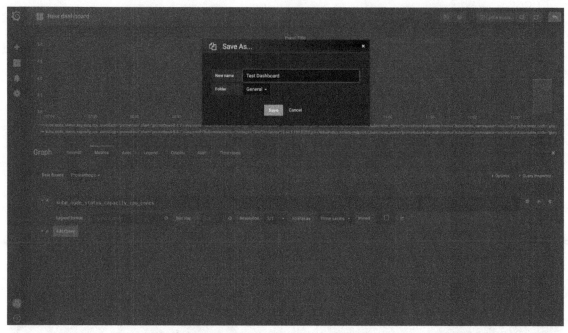

Figure 9.26: Saving the dashboard

Now your dashboard is ready:

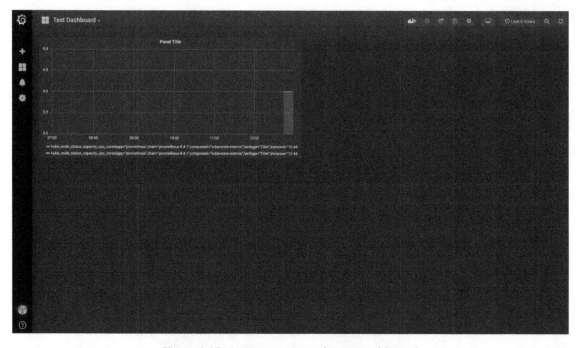

Figure 9.27: A custom-created Test Dashboard

We have seen how to create a new custom dashboard. Now, let's also import an already available dashboard from the marketplace, called Kubernetes Cluster:

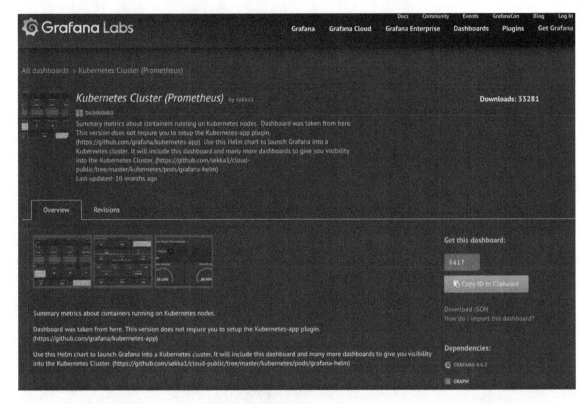

Figure 9.28: The Kubernetes Cluster dashboard in the Grafana marketplace

> **Note**
>
> You can read more about the Kubernetes Cluster dashboard at https://grafana.com/dashboards/6417.

20. To add the Kubernetes Cluster dashboard to your Grafana instance, click on the plus sign (+) on the left and then click on **Import**:

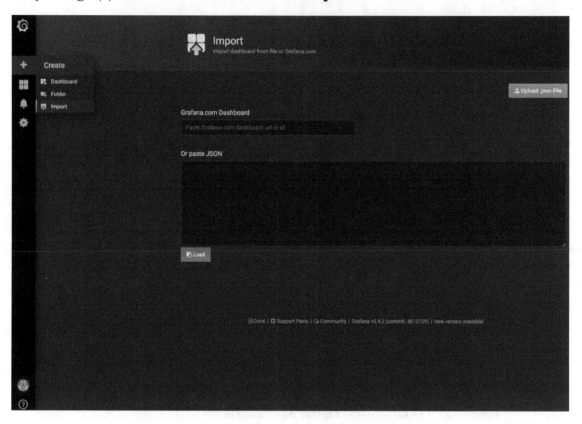

Figure 9.29: Grafana's Import dashboard page

21. On this page, enter the dashboard ID for the Kubernetes Cluster, which is **6417**, and then click on the *Tab* key for Grafana to obtain the dashboard details. Then, click on **Import**:

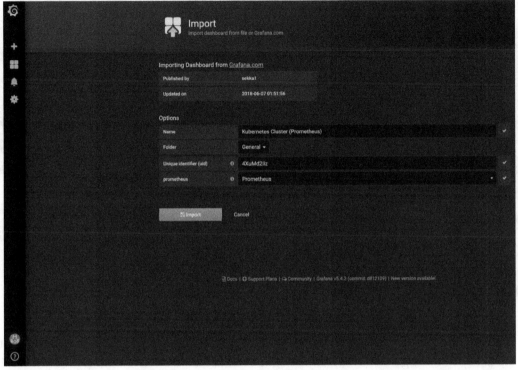

Figure 9.30: Importing the Kubernetes Cluster dashboard

22. Go back to the home page and choose **Kubernetes Cluster** as the dashboard you want to see in the top-left menu:

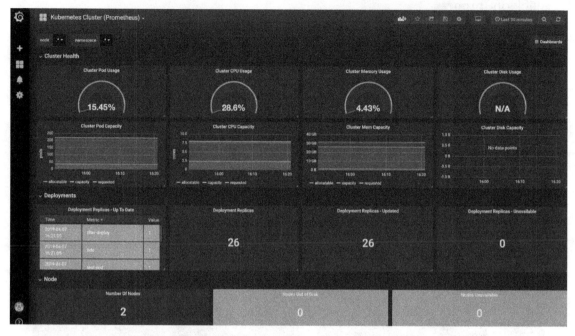

Figure 9.31: The Kubernetes Cluster dashboard in Grafana

Now we have the Kubernetes Cluster dashboard showing various essential metrics, such as CPU usage and memory usage, in order to view the current health status of the cluster.

In this exercise, we installed Prometheus and Grafana so that we have a complete monitoring system, which is capable of collecting metrics and showing them on a dashboard in real time.

In the following section, we will demonstrate how to expose custom metrics from our applications.

Custom Metrics

Prometheus provides client libraries for many languages, such as Go, Java, and Python, to expose custom metrics that can be read by the Prometheus server. You need to create a **/metrics** endpoint from your application for Prometheus to read the custom metrics. Additionally, for the Prometheus server to discover your application, you need to add this annotation to your pod: **prometheus.io/scrape: true**.

Here is how it will look in the pod definition:

```
metadata:

  annotations:

    prometheus.io/scrape: "true"
```

These custom metrics can be categorized under APM. They can be anything that would be valuable for you to monitor for the application. For example, for a financial institution, the number of transactions can be really valuable, whereas, for a messaging application, the number of messages in the queue can be much more valuable. After determining the needs of the application, you can use the appropriate client library for your application to expose the metric.

In the following exercise, we will see how a sample custom metric can be exposed in Go code using Prometheus' Go client. We will explore how the metric we exposed will be picked up by Prometheus and will become available for queries.

Exercise 24: Exposing a Custom Metric in Prometheus

In this exercise, we will explore a sample Go application, which exposes a sample custom metric in Prometheus. Then, we will deploy this application to the cluster and look at how the custom metric read by Prometheus can become available for queries.

Perform the following steps to complete this exercise:

1. Take a look at the following Go code to see a sample metric being exposed. This code is used to create the **suakbas/lesson09:v1** Docker image.

   Here, in this code, a sample custom metric, **number_of_incrementals**, is simply calculated by incrementing a number variable every second. To create the metric, the **NewCounter** function from Prometheus' Go client library is used. We expose the **/metrics** endpoint for Prometheus to read this metric:

   ```
   package main

   import (
       "net/http"
       "time"

       "github.com/prometheus/client_golang/prometheus"
       "github.com/prometheus/client_golang/prometheus/promauto"
       "github.com/prometheus/client_golang/prometheus/promhttp"
   )
   ```

```go
func main() {
    numOfInc := promauto.NewCounter(prometheus.CounterOpts{
        Name: "number_of_incrementals",
        Help: "The number of incrementals",
    })

    go func() {
        for {
            numOfInc.Inc()
            time.Sleep(1 * time.Second)
        }
    }()

    http.Handle("/metrics", promhttp.Handler())
    http.ListenAndServe(":3000", nil)
}
```

2. Create a file named **deploy.yaml** using the following **Deployment** and **Service** definitions:

```
$ vi deploy.yaml
```

Copy and paste the following definitions and close the file using **wq**:

```yaml
apiVersion: apps/v1
kind: Deployment
metadata:
  name: metric-app
spec:
  replicas: 1
  selector:
    matchLabels:
      app: metric
  template:
    metadata:
      annotations:
        prometheus.io/scrape: "true"
      labels:
        app: metric
```

```
    spec:
      containers:
      - image: suakbas/lesson09:v1
        imagePullPolicy: Always
        name: metric
        ports:
        - containerPort: 3000


    ---


    apiVersion: v1
    kind: Service
    metadata:
      name: metric-svc
    spec:
      ports:
      - port: 3000
      selector:
        app: metric
```

3. Deploy the **Deployment** and the **Service** to the cluster:

```
$ kubectl apply -f deploy.yaml -n lesson-9
```

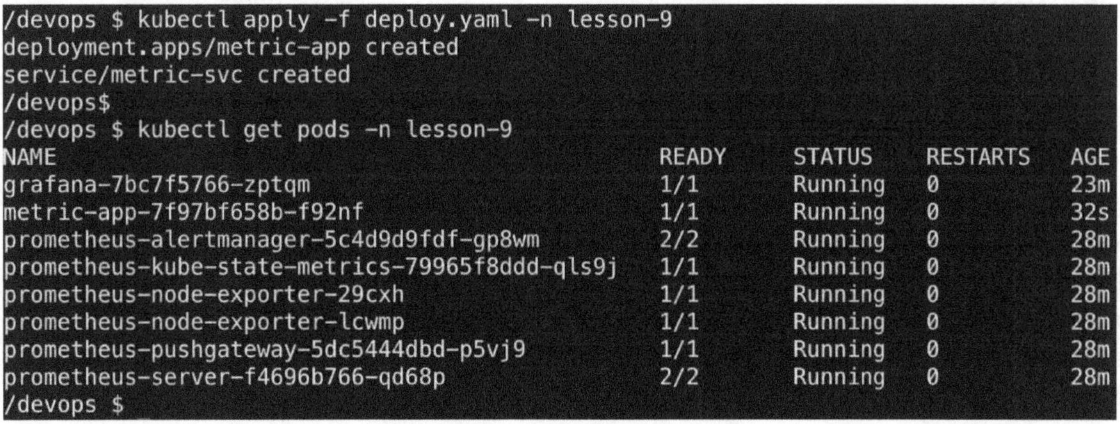

```
/devops $ kubectl apply -f deploy.yaml -n lesson-9
deployment.apps/metric-app created
service/metric-svc created
/devops$
/devops $ kubectl get pods -n lesson-9
NAME                                          READY   STATUS    RESTARTS   AGE
grafana-7bc7f5766-zptqm                       1/1     Running   0          23m
metric-app-7f97bf658b-f92nf                   1/1     Running   0          32s
prometheus-alertmanager-5c4d9d9fdf-gp8wm      2/2     Running   0          28m
prometheus-kube-state-metrics-79965f8ddd-qls9j 1/1    Running   0          28m
prometheus-node-exporter-29cxh                1/1     Running   0          28m
prometheus-node-exporter-lcwmp                1/1     Running   0          28m
prometheus-pushgateway-5dc5444dbd-p5vj9       1/1     Running   0          28m
prometheus-server-f4696b766-qd68p             2/2     Running   0          28m
/devops $
```

Figure 9.32: Deploying metric-app

4. Go to the Prometheus UI and enter the sample metric (**number_of_ incrementals**) in the query field to see the results:

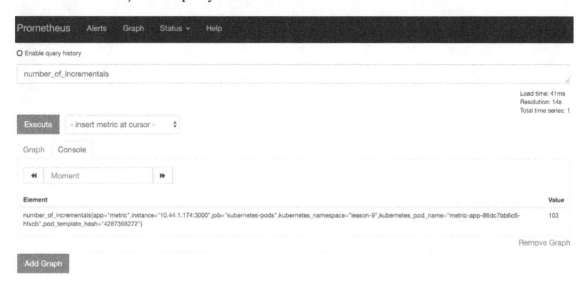

Figure 9.33: Querying number_of_incrementals in the Prometheus UI

As you can see from the Prometheus UI, **number_of_incrementals** becomes available to be queried. We can see the value in the bottom-right of the UI as **103** in this call.

> **Note**
>
> **scrape_interval** determines the interval for Prometheus to read the metric data and it is set to one minute by default. This means that the data will be updated after each minute.

In this exercise, we learned how to expose custom metrics from a Go application. We also saw how to enable Prometheus to read custom metrics from our application by exposing an endpoint. We can now use this custom metric for various purposes, such as creating an alert or creating a monitoring dashboard, to be able to observe how it changes over time.

In the next section, we will explore some of the critical metrics exposed by Kubernetes.

Exposed Metrics in Kubernetes

Kubernetes provides many out-of-the-box metrics that can be collected by Prometheus. For this, Kubernetes' system has a service called **kube-state-metrics** (https://github.com/kubernetes/kube-state-metrics), which listens to the Kubernetes API server and produces metrics to inform you about the current status of the objects. These metrics provide information on the current health status of the cluster nodes and the other Kubernetes resources, such as pods and services. Some of the key metrics are explained here:

- **kube_pod_info**: This provides detailed information about the pods, such as the pod name, namespace, and the node name that the pod is running on.

- **kube_pod_status_ready**: This enables you to check whether the pod is in **Ready** status.

- **kube_pod_container_status_running**: This enables you to check whether the container has a **Running** status.

- **kube_node_status_condition**: This provides information about the current condition of the node.

- **kube_endpoint_address_available**: This enables you to check whether an endpoint address is currently available:

Figure 9.34: Querying kube_pod_container_status_running for the lesson-9 namespace and the container metric

These are just a few helpful metrics used in typical cases. You can see the list of all the exposed metrics at https://github.com/kubernetes/kube-state-metrics/tree/master/docs#exposed-metrics.

So far, we have learned about the available metrics, how to create custom metrics, and how to create alerts and alert rules. In the following section, we will explore a communication tool called Slack, which we will use for sending alert notifications.

Slack

Slack is a commonly used, modern communication tool. It provides many features, such as creating purpose-specific channels or creating a thread under a message for the related discussion. Slack uses the workspace concept, which allows the overall environment to communicate within a particular group of people, such as the team members of a particular project. Each channel inside a workspace is used to separate communication into more specific topics. For example, a company can have a workspace that has sales and development channels.

Since it is easy to use and provides many functionalities, Slack has become one of the most common communication tools in the workplace. It even offers free usage, with some limitations, such as up to 10,000 free messages. Many open source communities, such as Kubernetes, have Slack workspaces that are active. This is the most convenient way to reach out to the people behind open source projects:

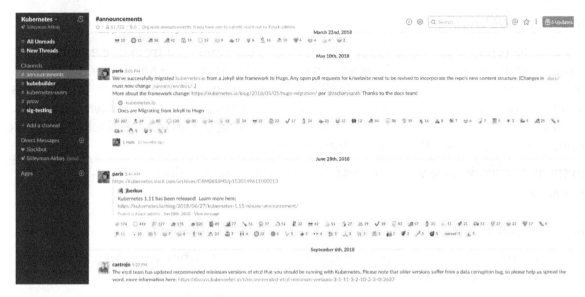

Figure 9.35: A screenshot from the Kubernetes Slack workspace

> **Note**
>
> You can check out the Kubernetes Slack workspace at https://kubernetes.slack.com.

Slack can also be used as a **ChatOps** tool, which is a new concept, referring to the use of a chat medium as the primary communication tool to handle incidents quickly and efficiently. Slack can be configured to receive webhooks (or event notifications) from monitoring tools, so this makes it a great tool to be used for ChatOps. In this way, you can receive failure notifications in a Slack channel and start a discussion right there under the notification. Put simply, imagine that an incident occurred in the live system and a monitoring tool sent an alert to a Slack channel created for tracking specific issues coming from this system. Only the relevant people, who are members of this channel, will be notified. Furthermore, a discussion can take place right in the channel for that specific alert; even an immediate call can be started right from the channel.

We will now explore more about Incoming Webhooks.

Incoming Webhooks

A webhook refers to a web callback, which sends real-time data from one application to another. Incoming Webhooks is a handy feature in Slack that enables you to send messages from another application to Slack. When you enable this feature, it generates a unique URL that is used for sending JSON-typed messages to a particular Slack channel. You can create an Incoming Webhook by going to **Customize Slack | Configure Apps** – we will practice this later, in the activity.

In the next exercise, we will demonstrate how to sign up for Slack and create a workspace.

Exercise 25: Signing Up for Slack and Creating a Workspace

In this exercise, we will sign up for Slack and create a new workspace, which will be used later to receive alert notifications:

1. Open a browser and go to https://slack.com/. Enter your email address on the home page and then click on **GET STARTED**:

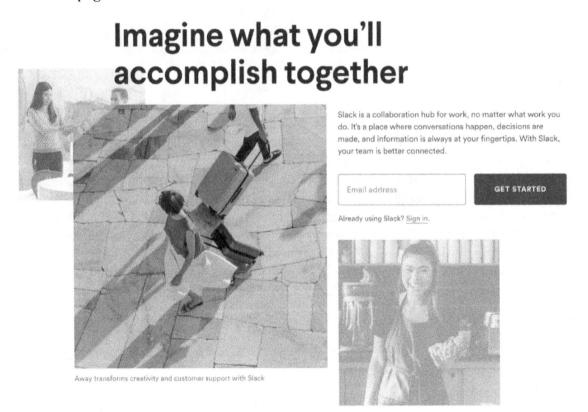

Figure 9.36: Signing up on slack.com

2. Select the **Create a new workspace** option, as follows:

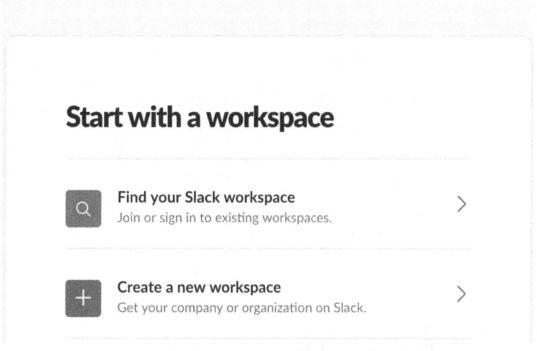

Figure 9.37: Choosing a Slack workspace

3. This will send a code to your email address; enter the code and then proceed. On the next page, you will be asked to fill in the name of your company or team. You can enter a fake name for this exercise:

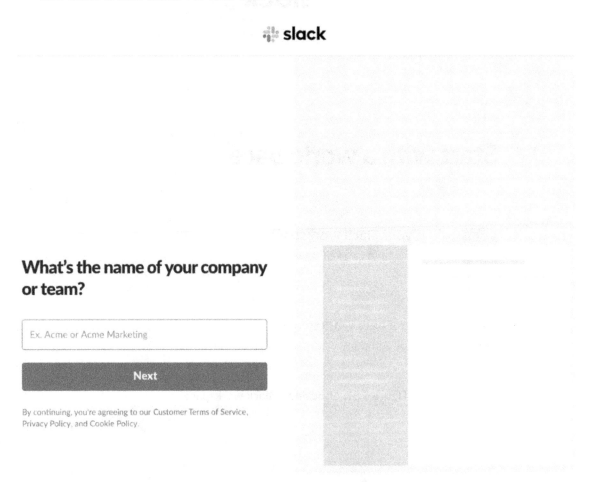

Figure 9.38: Entering the company name in Slack

4. On the next page, you will be asked the project name of your team. Enter **DevOps** and then click on **Next**; this will also create a **DevOps** channel for you:

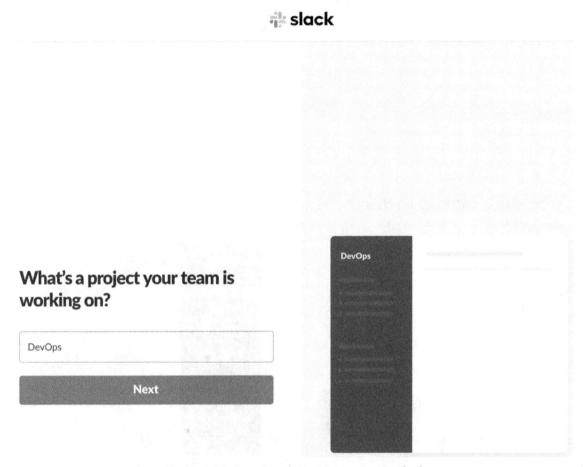

Figure 9.39: Entering the project name in Slack

5. Then, you will be asked to send out invitations, which you can skip by clicking on **skip for now**:

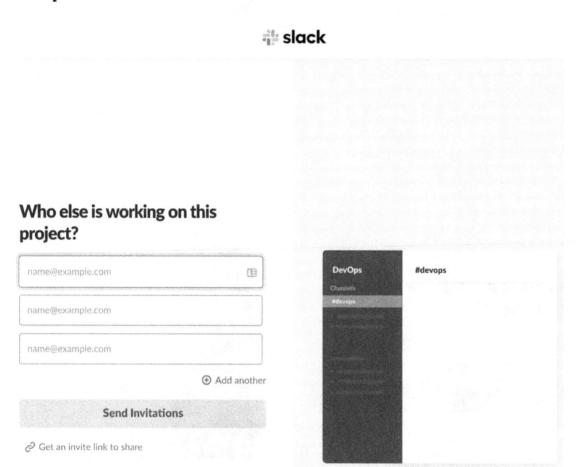

Figure 9.40: Inviting people to the Slack workspace

6. Finally, your workspace is ready! Click on **See Your Channel in Slack** to proceed:

Figure 9.41: The workspace creation success page in Slack

7. Now you can see the Slack UI. On the left-hand side, you can find all the channels; a **DevOps** channel has already been created because we entered **DevOps** as the team's project name:

Figure 9.42: The DevOps channel on Slack

In this exercise, we signed up to Slack and created our workspace. You can even invite your colleagues to the workspace to use it as an easy communication channel. It is essential that you complete this exercise as, during the activity, we will use this workspace to receive alert messages.

In the following activity, we will practice creating an alert and configuring Alertmanager to receive alert notifications for that alert in Slack. For this, we will enable Incoming Webhooks in Slack. Finally, we will examine the alert notification when the test pod is not running.

Activity 10: Setting Up Alert Notifications in Kubernetes

Imagine that you have an application running in production that occasionally stops working for various reasons. You only realize that the application is not working when a customer representative calls you to complain. You are frustrated about the situation, and the company reputation is at risk. You want to receive real-time notifications from the application whenever there is a problem so that you can fix it immediately to avoid creating customer dissatisfaction. To achieve this, you create an alert rule and configure Alertmanager to send notifications to a Slack channel so that you can quickly notice the problems and fix them.

> **Note**
>
> To complete this activity, you must first complete all the exercises in this chapter.

Execute the following steps to complete this activity:

1. Create an Incoming Webhook for the **devops** channel. Click on your username and then click on **Customize Slack**.

2. On the next page, click on **Configure Apps**, which will direct you to the **App Directory** page; here, search for **Incoming Webhooks**.

3. Click on **Add Configuration**.

4. Select the channel that you want to set for the alerting notifications and then click on **Add Incoming WebHooks integration**.

5. From the resulting page, note down the Webhook URL that will be used to configure `Alertmanager`.

6. Prepare an alert rule in Prometheus.

7. Modify the `prometheus-server` ConfigMap to specify this alert.

8. Create a Slack receiver in Alertmanager.

9. Modify the **prometheus-alertmanager** ConfigMap to add the Slack receiver.

10. Check the Prometheus UI to see whether the alert is visible on Prometheus.

11. Create a file named **pod.yaml** using the pod definition, which has a mistake in the image name written as **busybo** instead of **busybox**.

12. Deploy the test pod; then, check to see the error.

13. Check the Prometheus UI to see whether the alert is firing.

14. Check the **devops** channel in Slack to see the alert notification.

15. Fix the image to be **busybox**.

16. Check the **devops** channel in Slack again to see the resolved notification.

17. To clean up the environment, you can delete the **lesson-9** namespace.

> **Note**
>
> The solution to this activity can be found on Page 337.

In this activity, we explored how we can set up an alert rule in Prometheus and configure Alertmanager to send notifications for this alert to a Slack channel. To achieve this, we also demonstrated how to enable Incoming Webhooks in Slack. We examined the notification in the Slack channel while the pod was not working, and we saw the resolved notification when the pod returned to a healthy state.

Summary

In this chapter, we first explored the concept of monitoring in general, and examined why it is essential to have a monitoring system. Then, we introduced infrastructure monitoring and APM as the two main categories of monitoring. We also discussed alerting and tools within the monitoring context.

We then continued with monitoring in Kubernetes. We demonstrated the most common monitoring tools available in Kubernetes. We started with Prometheus, which is used to collect metrics from the infrastructure and application. We continued with Alertmanager as a component of Prometheus, which is responsible for sending alert notifications to many supported receivers, such as Slack and email clients. Next, we discussed Grafana as the tool used to visualize metrics through graphs and dashboards. We then installed Prometheus and Grafana and also installed our first dashboard to check the status of the Kubernetes cluster. With all of these topics, we explored how to create a capable monitoring system in Kubernetes.

In this chapter, we also concluded the *Introduction to DevOps with Kubernetes* course. Throughout this course, we have explored the basics of DevOps practices and Kubernetes primitives. We covered creating clusters locally or on the cloud. Then, we learned about configuration, secret, and storage management for your applications. We explored how to update and scale an application in many different ways. We also went through troubleshooting practices that are used heavily in Kubernetes, so that you understand how to handle a problem quickly. Finally, we set up a monitoring system in Kubernetes to be able to monitor and receive alert notifications in the event of a problem. With all of these topics, we aimed to equip you with the necessary skills for using Kubernetes in all of your DevOps practices.

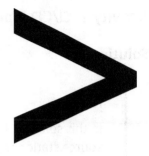

Appendix

About

This section is included to assist the students to perform the activities present in the book. It includes detailed steps that are to be performed by the students to complete and achieve the objectives of the book.

Chapter 1: Introduction to DevOps

Activity 1: CI/CD Pipeline for the DevOps Blog

Solution:

> **Note**
>
> In this solution, Hugo is used to generate website content. Hugo is a popular open-source static site generator that provides speed and flexibility. Documentation and further information is available on the official website: https://gohugo.io

Perform the following steps to complete this activity:

1. Create a file with the name `.travis.yml` in the master branch of the repository. Configure `.travis.yml` as follows:

   Use **go** with version **1.11.x** as the Travis-CI worker language:

   ```
   language: go
   go:
     - 1.11.x
   ```

   Install Hugo (https://GitHub.com/gohugoio/hugo) using the "**go get GitHub.com/gohugoio/hugo**" command:

   ```
   install:
     - go get GitHub.com/gohugoio/hugo
   ```

   Install the **beautifulhugo** theme by creating a **themes/beautifulhugo** folder and cloning it from the GitHub repository: **https://GitHub.com/halogenica/beautifulhugo.git**

   Generate blog content with the **hugo --theme beautifulhugo** command:

   ```
   script:
     - mkdir -p themes/beautifulhugo && git clone https://GitHub.com/
   halogenica/beautifulhugo.git themes/beautifulhugo
     - hugo --theme beautifulhugo
   ```

Use the **deploy** block of Travis-CI with the provider pages and the **GITHUB_TOKEN** environment variable defined in the exercises.

The deployment should be configured to run only the **master** branch, as follows:

```
deploy:
  provider: pages
  skip_cleanup: true
  GitHub_token: $GITHUB_TOKEN
  local_dir: public
  on:
    branch: master
```

2. Commit the **.travis.yml** file into the **master** branch:

```
git add .travis.yml
git commit -m "travis file added"
git push origin master
```

3. Trigger a build in Travis-CI for the **master** branch:

Figure 1.45: Triggering the build in Travis-CI

Select the **master** branch and fill the details:

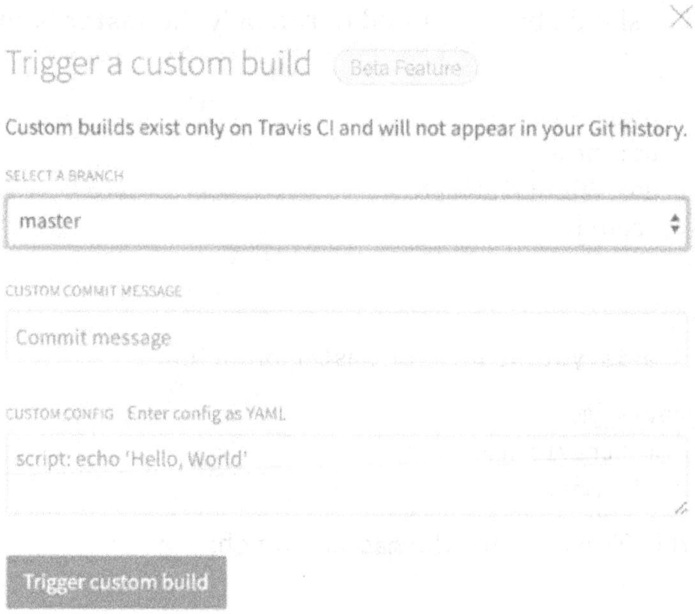

Figure 1.46: Triggering the build in Travis-CI

4. Add a new blog post to the **content/post** folder. An example of blog content could be as follows, in a file named **2019-02-02-kubernetes-scale.md**:

```
---
title: Scaling My Kubernetes Deployment
date: 2019-02-02
tags: ["kubernetes", "code"]
---

Scaling my Kubernetes deployment

<!--more-->

'''sh
    $ kubectl scale deployments/kubernetes-bootcamp --replicas=4
'''

Now, check whether it is scaled up:
```

```sh
$ kubectl get deployments
NAME                 DESIRED   CURRENT   UP-TO-DATE   AVAILABLE   AGE
kubernetes-bootcamp  4         4         4            4           26s

$ kubectl get pods -o wide
NAME                                    READY     STATUS      RESTARTS
AGE        IP             NODE
kubernetes-bootcamp-5c69669756-9jhz9    1/1       Running     0
3s         172.18.0.7     minikube
kubernetes-bootcamp-5c69669756-lrjwz    1/1       Running     0
3s         172.18.0.5     minikube
kubernetes-bootcamp-5c69669756-slht6    1/1       Running     0
3s         172.18.0.6     minikube
kubernetes-bootcamp-5c69669756-t4pcs    1/1       Running     0
28s        172.18.0.4     minikube
```

5. Wait for Travis-CI to trigger an automated build with the new material:

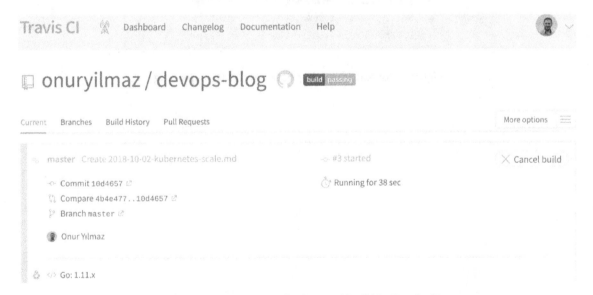

Figure 1.47: Automated triggered build in Travis-CI

6. Check for the blog on the browser for the new content once the build is completed:

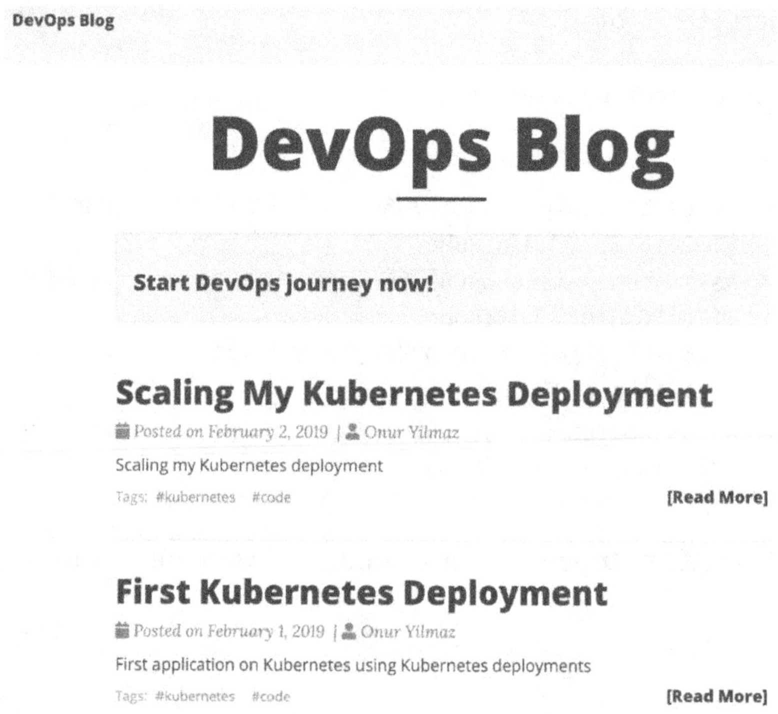

Figure 1.48: Automated updates in the DevOps blog

7. Move the **Connect CI/CD pipeline** item to **Done** on the project board created in *Exercise 1.*

> **Note**
>
> A complete pipeline solution in `.travis.yml` is available as follows:

```
language: go
go:
  - 1.11.x
install:
  - go get GitHub.com/gohugoio/hugo
script:
  - mkdir -p themes/beautifulhugo && git clone https://GitHub.com/
halogenica/beautifulhugo.git themes/beautifulhugo
  - hugo --theme beautifulhugo
deploy:
  provider: pages
  skip_cleanup: true
  GitHub_token: $GITHUB_TOKEN
  local_dir: public
  on:
    branch: master
```

Chapter 2: Introduction to Microservices and Containers

Activity 2: Installing a WordPress Blog and Database Using Docker

Solution:

Perform the following steps to complete this activity:

1. Create a folder named **data**. This folder will keep the stateful state of the database in the next steps:

   ```
   mkdir data
   ```

2. Start a MySQL container using the official Docker image and the following specifications:

   Use the **data** folder from Step 1 as the database file. Publish port **3306** to the local system. Set the **MYSQL_ROOT_PASSWORD** environment variable as **rootPassword**. Set the **MYSQL_DATABASE** environment variable as **database**. Set the **MYSQL_USER** environment variable as **user**. Set the **MYSQL_PASSWORD** environment variable as **password**. Use **mysql** as the name of the container. Use the **mysql:5.7** container image:

   ```
   docker run \
   -v ${PWD} /data/:/var/lib/mysql \
   -p 3306:3306 \
   -e MYSQL_ROOT_PASSWORD=rootPassword \
   -e MYSQL_DATABASE=database \
   -e MYSQL_USER=user \
   -e MYSQL_PASSWORD=password \
   --name mysql \
    mysql:5.7
   ```

Wait for the MySQL container to be ready using a similar logline to **[Note] mysqld: ready for connections**:

```
2019-03-05T11:43:39.639820Z 0 [Warning] 'user' entry 'root@localhost' ignored in --skip-name-resolve mode.
2019-03-05T11:43:39.639887Z 0 [Warning] 'user' entry 'mysql.session@localhost' ignored in --skip-name-resolve mode.
2019-03-05T11:43:39.639902Z 0 [Warning] 'user' entry 'mysql.sys@localhost' ignored in --skip-name-resolve mode.
2019-03-05T11:43:39.640603Z 0 [Warning] 'db' entry 'performance_schema mysql.session@localhost' ignored in --skip-name-resolve mode.
2019-03-05T11:43:39.640661Z 0 [Warning] 'db' entry 'sys mysql.sys@localhost' ignored in --skip-name-resolve mode.
2019-03-05T11:43:39.641214Z 0 [Warning] 'proxies_priv' entry '@ root@localhost' ignored in --skip-name-resolve mode.
2019-03-05T11:43:39.688124Z 0 [Warning] 'tables_priv' entry 'user mysql.session@localhost' ignored in --skip-name-resolve mode.
2019-03-05T11:43:39.688174Z 0 [Warning] 'tables_priv' entry 'sys_config mysql.sys@localhost' ignored in --skip-name-resolve mode.
2019-03-05T11:43:39.867024Z 0 [Note] Event Scheduler: Loaded 0 events
2019-03-05T11:43:39.867704Z 0 [Note] mysqld: ready for connections.
Version: '5.7.25'  socket: '/var/run/mysqld/mysqld.sock'  port: 3306  MySQL Community Server (GPL)
```

Figure 2.24: The start of the MySQL container

3. Start a WordPress container using the following specification:

Publish port **80** of the container to port **8080** of the host system. Link the **mysql** container using the **db** name. Set the **WORDPRESS_DB_HOST** environment variable as **db:3306**. Set the **WORDPRESS_DB_NAME** environment variable as **database**. Set the **WORDPRESS_DB_USER** environment variable as **user**. Set the **WORDPRESS_DB_PASSWORD** environment variable as **password**. Use **WordPress** as the name of the container. Use the **latest** WordPress container image:

```
docker run \
-p 8080:80 \
--link=mysql:db \
-e WORDPRESS_DB_HOST=db:3306 \
-e WORDPRESS_DB_NAME=database \
-e WORDPRESS_DB_USER=user \
-e WORDPRESS_DB_PASSWORD=password \
--name WordPress \
 WordPress:latest
```

4. Open **http://localhost:8080** in the browser and fill out the popular WordPress setup form:

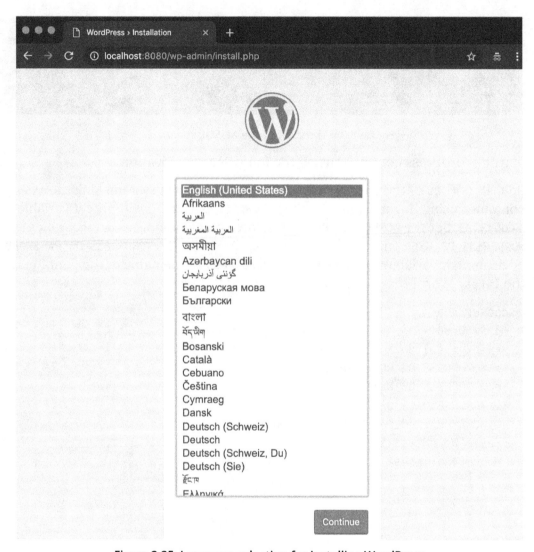

Figure 2.25: Language selection for installing WordPress

Add the necessary details like **Sub Title**, **Password** etc:

Figure 2.26: The admin setup for installing WordPress

5. Open **http://localhost:8080** in the browser and check that your new blog is running in the containers:

Figure 2.27: The home page of the WordPress blog

6. Stop the running containers and remove the data folder:

```
docker stop WordPress mysql
docker rm WordPress mysql
rm -rf ${PWD} /data
```

Chapter 3: Introduction to Kubernetes

Activity 3: Installing a WordPress Blog and Database on Kubernetes

Solution:

Perform the following steps to complete this activity:

1. Create a two-container stateful set definition inside the **wordpress-database.yaml** file with the following specifications:

   The nme should be **wordpress-database** and the replica count should be set to **1**. The database container should have the name of **database** and use the container image of **mysql:5.7**. Publish the container to port **3306** and mount the **data** volume to the **/var/lib/mysql** path. In addition, set the following environment variables:

Name	Value
MYSQL_ROOT_PASSWORD	rootPassword
MYSQL_DATABASE	database
MYSQL_USER	user
MYSQL_PASSWORD	password

Figure 3.24: Environment variables

Create a blog container with the name **blog** using the **latest** WordPress container image and publish the container to port **80**. In addition, set the following environment variables:

Name	Value
WORDPRESS_DB_HOST	127.0.0.1:3306
WORDPRESS_DB_NAME	database
WORDPRESS_DB_USER	user
WORDPRESS_DB_PASSWORD	password

Figure 3.25: Environment variables

Include a volume claim with the name **data** and **1GB** storage.

The stateful set description as YAML for the specification is as follows:

```
apiVersion: apps/v1beta2
kind: StatefulSet
metadata:
  name: wordpress-database
spec:

//[...]

  volumeClaimTemplates:
  - metadata:
      name: data
    spec:
      resources:
        requests:
          storage: 1Gi
```

Note

The entire stateful set description as YAML for the specification can be found at https://github.com/TrainingByPackt/Introduction-to-DevOps-with-Kubernetes/blob/master/Lesson03/wordpress-database.yaml

2. Deploy the **wordpress-database** stateful set into the Kubernetes cluster:

```
kubectl apply -f wordpress-database.yaml
```

```
/devops $ kubectl create -f wordpress-database.yaml
statefulset "wordpress-database" created
/devops $ █
```

Figure 3.26: Deploying stateful set

3. Check the status of the **wodpress-database-0** pod and wait until it is ready:

```
kubectl get pods wordpress-database-0
```

```
/devops $ kubectl get pods wordpress-database-0
NAME                     READY    STATUS     RESTARTS    AGE
wordpress-database-0     2/2      Running    0           54s
/devops $ █
```

Figure 3.27: Pod status

Ready 2/2 and **Running** indicate that both blog and database containers are running for the **wodpress-database-0** pod.

4. Create a proxy to the local system from the blog container using the **port-forward** command of **kubectl**:

```
kubectl port-forward wordpress-database-0 8080:80
```

```
/devops $ kubectl port-forward wordpress-database-0 8080:80
Forwarding from 127.0.0.1:8080 -> 80
```

Figure 3.28: Port forwarding with kubectl

5. Open the forwarded address in the browser and fill in the WordPress setup form:

Figure 3.29: Language selection – WordPress Install

Add the necessary information on the admin setup page to proceed:

Figure 3.30: Admin setup – WordPress Install

6. Open the forwarded address in the browser and check that your new blog is running in the containers:

Figure 3.31: Home page – WordPress blog

7. Stop the port forwarding that we started in step 4, and remove the stateful set:

```
kubectl delete -f wordpress-database.yaml
```

```
/devops $ kubectl delete -f wordpress-database.yaml
statefulset "wordpress-database" deleted
/devops $
```

Figure 3.32: Cleanup

Chapter 4: Creating a Kubernetes Cluster

Activity 4: Migrating a Running Application in Kubernetes Cluster

Solution:

Perform the following steps to complete this activity:

1. Run a sample web application with six replicas in the cluster:

   ```
   kubectl run hello-world --image=gcr.io/google-samples/hello-app:1.0
   --replicas=6
   ```

Figure 4.30: Creating hello-world application

2. Check the status of pods of the sample web application and their nodes:

   ```
   kubectl get pods -o wide
   ```

Figure 4.31: Pods and their nodes of the hello-world application

3. Create a node pool in GCP with a larger memory:

   ```
   gcloud container node-pools create high-memory-pool --cluster=devops \
     --machine-type=n1-highmem-2 --num-nodes=2
   ```

Figure 4.32: Node pool creation

4. Wait until all nodes are **Ready** in the cluster:

```
kubectl get nodes --label-columns=beta.kubernetes.io/instance-type
```

```
mail_@cloudshell:~ (devops-236913)$ kubectl get nodes --label-columns=beta.kubernetes.io/instance-type
NAME                                          STATUS   ROLES    AGE   VERSION          INSTANCE-TYPE
gke-devops-default-pool-c42afc38-1hkz         Ready    <none>   6h    v1.11.7-gke.12   n1-standard-1
gke-devops-default-pool-c42afc38-d3hs         Ready    <none>   6h    v1.11.7-gke.12   n1-standard-1
gke-devops-default-pool-c42afc38-sdd7         Ready    <none>   6h    v1.11.7-gke.12   n1-standard-1
gke-devops-high-memory-pool-033d3312-ctmr     Ready    <none>   1m    v1.11.7-gke.12   n1-highmem-2
gke-devops-high-memory-pool-033d3312-f3s8     Ready    <none>   1m    v1.11.7-gke.12   n1-highmem-2
mail_@cloudshell:~ (devops-236913)$
```

Figure 4.33: Kubernetes nodes after pool creation

5. Mark the nodes in the default node pool as unschedulable and make Kubernetes move the workloads from the default node pool:

```
for node in $(kubectl get nodes -l cloud.google.com/gke-nodepool=default-
pool -o=name); do
    kubectl drain --ignore-daemonsets "$node";
done
```

```
mail_@cloudshell:~ (devops-236913)$ for node in $(kubectl get nodes -l cloud.google.com/gke-nodepool=default-pool -o=name); do
>    kubectl drain --ignore-daemonsets "$node";
> done
node/gke-devops-default-pool-c42afc38-1hkz cordoned
WARNING: Ignoring DaemonSet-managed pods: fluentd-gcp-v3.2.0-rgkv4
pod/l7-default-backend-7ff48cffd7-wndhp evicted
pod/kube-dns-autoscaler-67c97c87fb-2d2jc evicted
pod/hello-world-764ccf8958-12vs8 evicted
pod/hello-world-764ccf8958-55t7r evicted
pod/event-exporter-v0.2.3-85644fcdf-jwrkn evicted
pod/fluentd-gcp-scaler-8b674f786-bp2ct evicted
pod/kube-dns-7df4cb66cb-c9gpk evicted
node/gke-devops-default-pool-c42afc38-d3hs cordoned
WARNING: Ignoring DaemonSet-managed pods: fluentd-gcp-v3.2.0-6f5j2
pod/hello-world-764ccf8958-tfksh evicted
pod/hello-world-764ccf8958-98nqf evicted
pod/hello-world-764ccf8958-zh88q evicted
pod/kube-dns-7df4cb66cb-58mkl evicted
node/gke-devops-default-pool-c42afc38-sdd7 cordoned
WARNING: Ignoring DaemonSet-managed pods: fluentd-gcp-v3.2.0-ncmj5
pod/metrics-server-v0.2.1-fd596d746-mftwh evicted
pod/hello-world-764ccf8958-mwrkp evicted
pod/heapster-v1.6.0-beta.1-5b47fd8bbc-zwkjd evicted
mail_@cloudshell:~ (devops-236913)$
```

Figure 4.34: Output of the kubectl drain for default pool

6. Check the status of nodes:

```
kubectl get nodes --label-columns=beta.kubernetes.io/instance-type
```

Figure 4.35: Kubernetes nodes after cordon and drain

7. Ensure that the pods of the sample application are moved to new nodes:

```
kubectl get pods -o wide
```

Figure 4.36: Pods and their nodes of the hello-world application

8. Remove the default node pool:

```
gcloud container node-pools delete default-pool --cluster devops
```

Figure 4.37: Node pool deletion

9. Verify that the nodes from the default node pool are removed from the cluster:

    ```
    kubectl get nodes --label-columns=beta.kubernetes.io/instance-type
    ```

```
mail_@cloudshell:~ (devops-236913)$ kubectl get nodes --label-columns=beta.kubernetes.io/instance-type
NAME                                       STATUS      ROLES     AGE    VERSION          INSTANCE-TYPE
gke-devops-high-memory-pool-033d3312-ctmr  Ready       <none>    7m     v1.11.7-gke.12   n1-highmem-2
gke-devops-high-memory-pool-033d3312-f3s8  Ready       <none>    7m     v1.11.7-gke.12   n1-highmem-2
mail_@cloudshell:~ (devops-236913)$
```

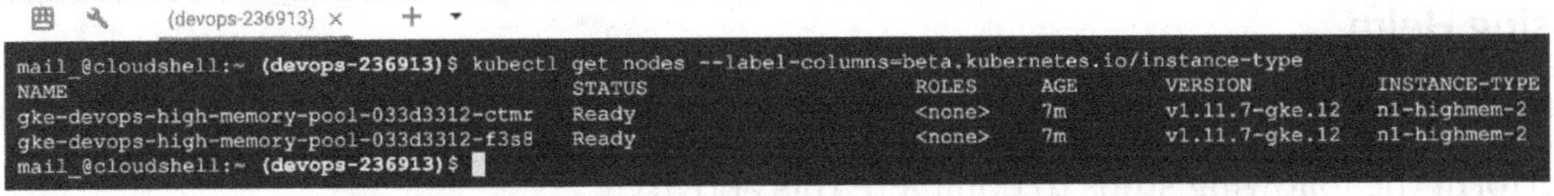

Figure 4.38: Kubernetes nodes after node pool deletion

10. If you do not plan to use this Kubernetes cluster in the following chapters or the future, remove the Kubernetes cluster:

    ```
    gcloud container clusters delete devops
    ```

```
mail_@cloudshell:~ (devops-236913)$ gcloud container clusters delete devops
The following clusters will be deleted.
 - [devops] in [us-west1-a]

Do you want to continue (Y/n)?  Y

Deleting cluster devops...done.
Deleted [https://container.googleapis.com/v1/projects/devops-236913/zones/us-west1-a/clusters/devops].
mail_@cloudshell:~ (devops-236913)$
```

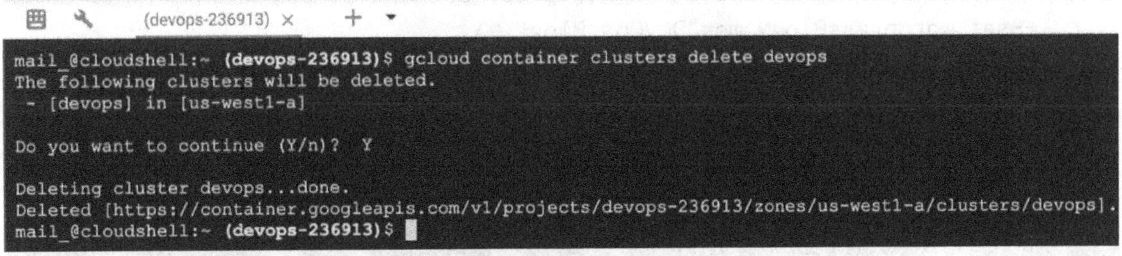

Figure 4.39: Cluster deletion

Chapter 5: Deploy an Application to Kubernetes

Activity 5: Installing and Scaling a WordPress Blog in Kubernetes Using Helm

Solution:

Perform the following steps to complete this activity:

1. Install the WordPress **helm** chart. The release name should be **devops-blog** and the username should be **admin**. Use **devops** as your password and **DevOps Blog** as the blog name:

```
helm install --name devops-blog \
--set wordpressUsername=admin,wordpressPassword=devops \
--set wordpressBlogName="DevOps Blog" \
stable/wordpress
```

```
/devops $ helm install --name devops-blog  --set wordpressUsername=admin,wordpressPassword=devops --set wordpressBlogName="DevOps Blog"  stable/wordpress
NAME:   devops-blog
E0417 23:32:35.408470    3939 portforward.go:303] error copying from remote stream to local connection: readfrom tcp4 127.0.0.1:53691->127.0.0.1:53694: write
  tcp4 127.0.0.1:53691->127.0.0.1:53694: write: broken pipe
LAST DEPLOYED: Wed Apr 17 23:32:35 2019
NAMESPACE: default
STATUS: DEPLOYED

RESOURCES:
==> v1/Secret
NAME                    TYPE    DATA  AGE
devops-blog-mariadb     Opaque  2     0s
devops-blog-wordpress   Opaque  1     0s

==> v1/ConfigMap
NAME                        DATA  AGE
devops-blog-mariadb         1     0s
devops-blog-mariadb-tests   1     0s

==> v1/PersistentVolumeClaim
NAME                    STATUS  VOLUME                                      CAPACITY  ACCESS MODES  STORAGECLASS  AGE
devops-blog-wordpress   Bound   pvc-50cddc7c-6158-11e9-887b-080027b3f752    10Gi      RWO           standard      0s

==> v1/Service
NAME                    TYPE          CLUSTER-IP      EXTERNAL-IP  PORT(S)                       AGE
devops-blog-mariadb     ClusterIP     10.111.31.87    <none>       3306/TCP                      0s
devops-blog-wordpress   LoadBalancer  10.107.229.89   <pending>    80:32598/TCP,443:31137/TCP    0s

==> v1/Deployment
NAME                    DESIRED  CURRENT  UP-TO-DATE  AVAILABLE  AGE
devops-blog-wordpress   1        1        1           0          0s

==> v1beta1/StatefulSet
NAME                  DESIRED  CURRENT  AGE
devops-blog-mariadb   1        1        0s

==> v1/Pod(related)
NAME                                   READY  STATUS            RESTARTS  AGE
devops-blog-wordpress-549f7b4f49-5k74b  0/1    ContainerCreating  0        0s
devops-blog-mariadb-0                   0/1    Pending            0        0s


NOTES:
1. Get the WordPress URL:

  NOTE: It may take a few minutes for the LoadBalancer IP to be available.
        Watch the status with: 'kubectl get svc --namespace default -w devops-blog-wordpress'
  export SERVICE_IP=$(kubectl get svc --namespace default devops-blog-wordpress --template "{{ range (index .status.loadBalancer.ingress 0) }}{{.}}{{ end }}"
)
  echo "WordPress URL: http://$SERVICE_IP/"
  echo "WordPress Admin URL: http://$SERVICE_IP/admin"

2. Login with the following credentials to see your blog

  echo Username: admin
  echo Password: $(kubectl get secret --namespace default devops-blog-wordpress -o jsonpath="{.data.wordpress-password}" | base64 --decode)

/devops $
```

Figure 5.25: Helm installation of the WordPress chart

With successful installation, the output lists all the resources installed alongside the WordPress chart.

2. Wait until all the pods are running and are ready:

```
kubectl get pods
```

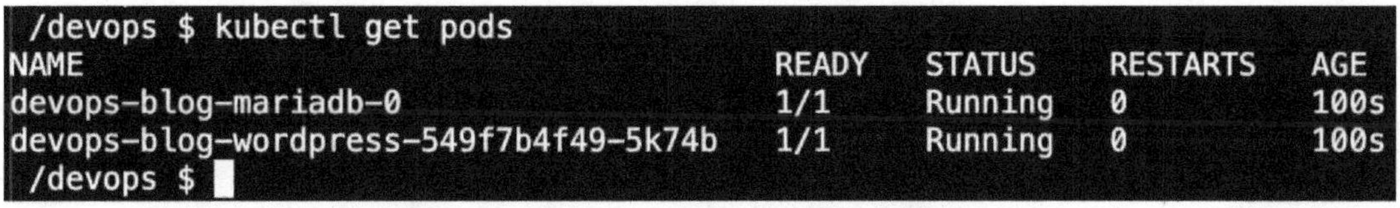

```
/devops $ kubectl get pods
NAME                                         READY   STATUS    RESTARTS   AGE
devops-blog-mariadb-0                        1/1     Running   0          100s
devops-blog-wordpress-549f7b4f49-5k74b       1/1     Running   0          100s
/devops $ █
```

Figure 5.26: The WordPress installation pods

3. Open the home page of WordPress and check that it is installed successfully.

    The URL can be found using the following commands:

```
# Google Kubernetes Engine installation
kubectl get svc devops-blog-wordpress -o jsonpath='{.status.loadBalancer.
ingress[0].hostname}'


# Minikube installation
minikube service devops-blog-wordpress --url
```

```
/devops $ minikube service devops-blog-wordpress --url
http://192.168.99.100:32598
http://192.168.99.100:31137
/devops $ █
```

Figure 5.27: Minikube service Ips

WordPress homepage is as shown below:

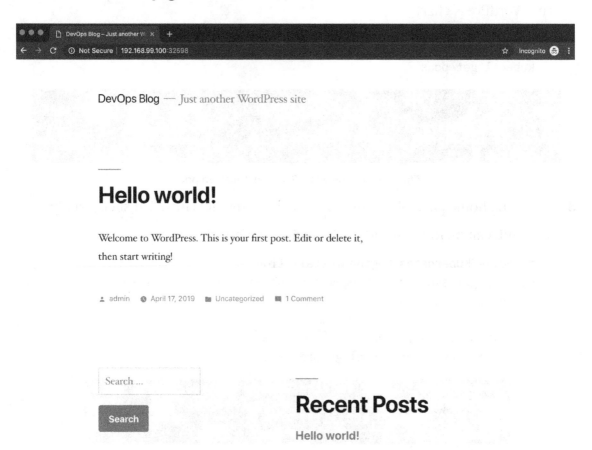

Figure 5.28: Home page of the WordPress blog

4. Scale the WordPress instances to three, as follows:

```
helm upgrade devops-blog --set replicaCount=3 stable/wordpress
```

```
/devops $ helm upgrade devops-blog --set replicaCount=3 stable/wordpress
Release "devops-blog" has been upgraded. Happy Helming!
LAST DEPLOYED: Wed Apr 17 23:45:20 2019
NAMESPACE: default
STATUS: DEPLOYED

RESOURCES:
==> v1/Service
NAME                     TYPE          CLUSTER-IP      EXTERNAL-IP   PORT(S)                       AGE
devops-blog-mariadb      ClusterIP     10.111.31.87    <none>        3306/TCP                      12m
devops-blog-wordpress    LoadBalancer  10.107.229.89   <pending>     80:32598/TCP,443:31137/TCP    12m

==> v1/Deployment
NAME                    DESIRED  CURRENT  UP-TO-DATE  AVAILABLE  AGE
devops-blog-wordpress   3        3        3           1          12m

==> v1beta1/StatefulSet
NAME                  DESIRED  CURRENT  AGE
devops-blog-mariadb   1        1        12m

==> v1/Pod(related)
NAME                                       READY  STATUS             RESTARTS  AGE
devops-blog-wordpress-66488fc656-b5s8k     1/1    Running            0         7m29s
devops-blog-wordpress-66488fc656-sddd8     0/1    ContainerCreating  0         0s
devops-blog-wordpress-66488fc656-wt79x     0/1    ContainerCreating  0         0s
devops-blog-mariadb-0                      1/1    Running            0         12m

==> v1/Secret
NAME                     TYPE     DATA  AGE
devops-blog-mariadb      Opaque   2     12m
devops-blog-wordpress    Opaque   1     12m

==> v1/ConfigMap
NAME                        DATA  AGE
devops-blog-mariadb         1     12m
devops-blog-mariadb-tests   1     12m

==> v1/PersistentVolumeClaim
NAME                     STATUS  VOLUME                                      CAPACITY  ACCESS MODES  STORAGECLASS  AGE
devops-blog-wordpress    Bound   pvc-50cddc7c-6158-11e9-887b-080027b3f752    10Gi      RWO           standard      12m


NOTES:
1. Get the WordPress URL:

   NOTE: It may take a few minutes for the LoadBalancer IP to be available.
        Watch the status with: 'kubectl get svc --namespace default -w devops-blog-wordpress'
   export SERVICE_IP=$(kubectl get svc --namespace default devops-blog-wordpress --template "{{ range (index .status.loadBalancer.ingress 0) }}{{.}}{{ end }}")
   echo "WordPress URL: http://$SERVICE_IP/"
   echo "WordPress Admin URL: http://$SERVICE_IP/admin"

2. Login with the following credentials to see your blog

   echo Username: user
   echo Password: $(kubectl get secret --namespace default devops-blog-wordpress -o jsonpath="{.data.wordpress-password}" | base64 --decode)

/devops $ []
```

Figure 5.29: Upgrading the Helm chart installation

5. Check the status of the pods with three instances:

```
kubectl get pods
```

```
/devops $ kubectl get pods
NAME                                       READY   STATUS    RESTARTS   AGE
devops-blog-mariadb-0                      1/1     Running   0          13m
devops-blog-wordpress-66488fc656-b5s8k     1/1     Running   0          8m38s
devops-blog-wordpress-66488fc656-sddd8     1/1     Running   0          69s
devops-blog-wordpress-66488fc656-wt79x     1/1     Running   0          69s
 /devops $ █
```

Figure 5.30: WordPress installation pods

6. Check that the home page is still accessible in the browser:

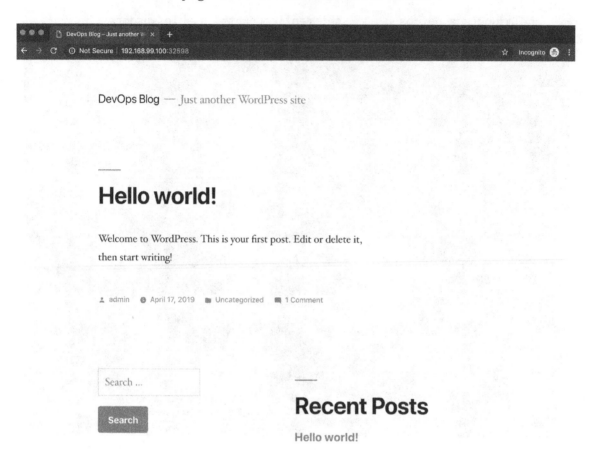

Figure 5.31: Home page of the WordPress blog

7. Delete the WordPress installation:

```
helm delete --purge devops-blog
```

```
/devops $ helm delete --purge devops-blog
release "devops-blog" deleted
/devops $
```

Figure 5.32: Deleting the WordPress installation

Chapter 6: Configuration and Storage Management in Kubernetes

Activity 6: Updating Configurations on the Fly

Solution:

Perform the following steps to complete this activity:

1. We created a ConfigMap named **app-config** and a secret named **token** earlier in the chapter. Please include them in your solution. Create a pod definition file that consumes this ConfigMap and the secret:

```
apiVersion: v1
kind: Pod
metadata:
  name: config-secret-pod
spec:
  containers:
  - name: content
    image: busybox
    command: [ "sh", "-c"]
    args:
    - while true; do
        echo -en '\n';
        echo Current environment is 'cat /configurations/environment';
        echo Used token is 'cat /secrets/token';
        sleep 10;
      done;
    volumeMounts:
    - name: config-volume
      mountPath: "/configurations"
    - name: secret-volume
      mountPath: "/secrets"
  volumes:
  - name: config-volume
    configMap:
      name: app-config
  - name: secret-volume
    secret:
      secretName: token
```

2. Deploy the pod:

```
$ kubectl apply -f Pod.yaml -n lesson-6
```

```
/devops $ kubectl apply -f Pod.yaml -n lesson-6
pod/config-secret-pod created
/devops $
```

Figure 6.18: Deploying config-secret-pod to the cluster

3. Make sure that the pod is running and check the logs to see the current environment coming from ConfigMap and the token coming from the secret:

```
$ kubectl get pods -n lesson-6
$ kubectl logs config-secret-pod -n lesson-6
```

```
/devops $ kubectl get pods -n lesson-6
NAME                READY       STATUS      RESTARTS    AGE
config-secret-pod   1/1         Running     0           17s
/devops $
/devops $ kubectl logs config-secret-pod -n lesson-6

Current environment is test
Used token is b83f7d3cc64efc58

Current environment is test
Used token is b83f7d3cc64efc58

Current environment is test
Used token is b83f7d3cc64efc58

Current environment is test
Used token is b83f7d3cc64efc58
/devops $
```

Figure 6.19: Checking the logs of config-secret-pod

4. Replace the current environment variable set by the **app-config** ConfigMap:

```
$ kubectl create configmap app-config -n lesson-6 --from-
literal=environment=prod -o yaml --dry-run | kubectl replace -f -
```

```
/devops $ kubectl create configmap app-config -n lesson-6 --from-literal=environment=prod -o yaml --dry-run | kube
ctl replace -f -
configmap/app-config replaced
/devops $
```

Figure 6.20: Replacing the content of app-config to set the environment as prod

5. Check the logs to see the updated environment information:

```
$ kubectl logs config-secret-pod -n lesson-6
```

```
Current environment is test
Used token is b83f7d3cc64efc58

Current environment is test
Used token is b83f7d3cc64efc58

Current environment is prod
Used token is b83f7d3cc64efc58

Current environment is prod
Used token is b83f7d3cc64efc58
```

Figure 6.21: Checking the logs of config-secret-pod to see the change

> **Note**
>
> It may take up to a few minutes for the pod to get the changes.

6. Generate and encode a 32-byte token:

```
$ openssl rand -hex 32
```

```
/devops $ openssl rand -hex 32
04d39a77b0cec29e4850280c408da5ad5325eec0ae8ce57e1b6bb5b6987b58e1
/devops $
```

Figure 6.22: Creating a 32-byte random token

> **Note**
>
> The token generated will be different for you.

7. Replace the current token set by the secret:

```
$ kubectl create secret generic token -n lesson-6 --from-
literal=token=<new-token> -o yaml --dry-run | kubectl replace -f -
```

```
/devops $ kubectl create secret generic token -n lesson-6 --from-literal=token=04d39a77b0cec29e4850280c408da5ad5325ee
c0ae8ce57e1b6bb5b6987b58e1 -o yaml --dry-run | kubectl replace -f -
secret/token replaced
/devops $
```

Figure 6.23: Replacing the content of the secret with the new token

8. Recheck the logs to see the updated token:

```
Current environment is prod
Used token is b83f7d3cc64efc58

Current environment is prod
Used token is b83f7d3cc64efc58

Current environment is prod
Used token is 04d39a77b0cec29e4850280c408da5ad5325eec0ae8ce57e1b6bb5b6987b58e1

Current environment is prod
Used token is 04d39a77b0cec29e4850280c408da5ad5325eec0ae8ce57e1b6bb5b6987b58e1
```

Figure 6.24: Checking the logs of config-secret-pod to see the change

Activity 7: Running a Persistent Database on Kubernetes

Solution:

Perform the following steps to complete this activity:

1. Create a **Deployment** definition file for MySQL, which uses a secret for the user password and a Volume using a PVC:

```yaml
apiVersion: apps/v1
kind: Deployment
metadata:
  name: mysql-deployment
  labels:
    app: mysql
spec:
  replicas: 1
  selector:
    matchLabels:
      app: mysql
  template:
    metadata:
      labels:
        app: mysql
    spec:
      containers:
      - image: mysql:5.6
        name: mysql-container
        env:
        - name: MYSQL_ROOT_PASSWORD
```

```
    valueFrom:
      secretKeyRef:
        name: mysql-secret
        key: password
  ports:
  - containerPort: 3306
    name: mysql-port
  volumeMounts:
  - name: mysql-volume
    mountPath: /var/lib/mysql
volumes:
- name: mysql-volume
  persistentVolumeClaim:
    claimName: mysql-pvc
```

2. Create a service definition file for your deployment:

```
apiVersion: v1
kind: Service
metadata:
  name: mysql-svc
spec:
  ports:
  - port: 3306
  selector:
    app: mysql
```

3. Generate a password and deploy a secret using the password as a literal to the cluster:

```
$ openssl rand -hex 8
$ kubectl create secret generic mysql-secret --from-
literal=password=<generated-password> -n lesson-6
```

```
/devops $ openssl rand -hex 8
b980a92aa2c3cebb
```

```
/devops $ kubectl create secret generic mysql-secret --from-literal=password=b980a92aa2c3cebb -n lesson-6
secret/mysql-secret created
```

Figure 6.25: Creating a random token and a secret using the token

4. Create a PVC that requests 20GB of storage and deploy it to the cluster. Then, check whether PV is automatically created by Kubernetes and bound to the PVC:

```
$ kubectl apply -f mysql-pvc.yaml -n lesson-6
$ kubectl get pvc -n lesson-6
```

```
apiVersion: v1
kind: PersistentVolumeClaim
metadata:
  name: mysql-pvc
spec:
  accessModes:
    - ReadWriteOnce
  resources:
    requests:
      storage: 20Gi
```

```
/devops $ kubectl apply -f mysql-pvc.yaml -n lesson-6
persistentvolumeclaim/mysql-pvc created
/devops $
/devops $ kubectl get pvc -n lesson-6
NAME        STATUS    VOLUME                                      CAPACITY   ACCESS MODES   STORAGECLASS   AGE
mysql-pvc   Bound     pvc-bfa79332-3aca-11e9-bd98-42010a9c01eb    20Gi       RWO            standard       14s
```

Figure 6.26: Deploying a MySQL PVC to the cluster and seeing whether it's bound

5. Deploy MySQL Deployment and Service to the cluster:

```
$ kubectl apply -f mysql-deployment.yaml -n lesson-6
$ kubectl apply -f mysql-svc.yaml -n lesson-6
```

```
/devops $ kubectl apply -f mysql-deployment.yaml -n lesson-6
deployment.apps/mysql-deployment created
/devops $
/devops $ kubectl apply -f mysql-svc.yaml -n lesson-6
service/mysql-svc created
/devops $
```

Figure 6.27: Deploying MySQL Deployment and Service to the cluster

6. Check whether the pod is running and verify that MySQL works properly by trying to access the server:

```
$ kubectl get pods -n lesson-6
```

```
/devops $ kubectl get pods -n lesson-6
NAME                                READY    STATUS     RESTARTS   AGE
mysql-deployment-7f6df7bb79-dbp6m   1/1      Running    0          39s
/devops $
```

Figure 6.28: Checking whether the MySQL pod is running

```
$ kubectl run -it --rm --image=mysql:5.6 mysql-test -n lesson-6 -- mysql
-h mysql-svc -p<generated-password>
# Press enter
```

```
/devops $ kubectl run -it --rm --image=mysql:5.6 mysql-test -n lesson-6 -- mysql -h mysql-svc -pb980a92aa2c3cebb
If you don't see a command prompt, try pressing enter.

mysql>
```

Figure 6.29: Running another pod as a client to test the health of MySQL server

Chapter 7: Updating and Scaling an Application in Kubernetes

Activity 8: Enabling Autoscaling and Performing a Rolling Update

Solution:

Perform the following steps to complete this activity:

1. Create a deployment definition file that uses the **suakbas/lesson07:v1** image and has the RollingUpdate strategy type set; this application does a CPU-intensive operation:

```
apiVersion: apps/v1
kind: Deployment
metadata:
  name: lesson07-deployment
spec:
  replicas: 1
  strategy:
    type: RollingUpdate
  selector:
    matchLabels:
      app: lesson07
  template:
    metadata:
      labels:
        app: lesson07
    spec:
      containers:
      - image: suakbas/lesson07:v1
        imagePullPolicy: Always
        name: lesson07
        resources:
          requests:
            memory: "500m"
            cpu: "250m"
```

2. Deploy the deployment and check whether the pod is running:

```
$ kubectl apply -f deployment.yaml -n lesson-7
$ kubectl get pods -n lesson-7
```

```
/devops $ kubectl apply -f deployment.yaml -n lesson-7
deployment.apps/lesson07-deployment created
/devops $
/devops $ kubectl get pods -n lesson-7
NAME                                  READY    STATUS     RESTARTS   AGE
lesson07-deployment-59dcd9dd-d68p4    1/1      Running    0          7s
/devops $
```

Figure 7.21: Deploying the lesson07-deployment to the cluster

3. Create a **HorizontalPodAutoscaler** for this deployment using the **suakbas/lesson07:v1** image, which has two as the minimum number of pods and five as the maximum. It should also have a CPU percentage target of 50%:

```
$ kubectl autoscale deployment lesson07-deployment --min=2 --max=5
--cpu-percent=50 -n lesson-7
```

```
/devops $ kubectl autoscale deployment lesson07-deployment --min=2 --max=5 --cpu-percent=50 -n lesson-7
horizontalpodautoscaler.autoscaling/lesson07-deployment autoscaled
/devops $
```

Figure 7.22: Setting an HPA for the deployment

4. Check the **HorizontalPodAutoscaler** for the deployment using the **suakbas/lesson07:v1** image to see the current status:

```
$ kubectl get hpa -n lesson-7
```

```
/devops $ kubectl get hpa -n lesson-7
NAME                  REFERENCE                        TARGETS    MINPODS   MAXPODS   REPLICAS   AGE
lesson07-deployment   Deployment/lesson07-deployment   399%/50%   2         5         4          3m
/devops $
```

Figure 7.23: Checking the HPA details

5. Check the pods to see whether they are scaled up and are running without any problems:

```
$ kubectl get pods -n lesson-7
```

```
/devops $ kubectl get pods -n lesson-7
NAME                                  READY    STATUS     RESTARTS   AGE
lesson07-deployment-dc8d64ff8-4w9ff   1/1      Running    0          3m
lesson07-deployment-dc8d64ff8-bscjx   1/1      Running    0          3m
lesson07-deployment-dc8d64ff8-rggwk   1/1      Running    0          5m
lesson07-deployment-dc8d64ff8-xt9g8   1/1      Running    0          4m
/devops $
```

Figure 7.24: Checking whether the pods run without any problems

6. Perform a rolling update by changing the used image to **suakbas/lesson07:v2**. This application just sleeps, which relieves the CPU; then, check whether the rolling update has finished successfully:

```
$ kubectl set image deployment/lesson07-deployment lesson07=suakbas/
lesson07:v2 --record -n lesson-7
```

```
$ kubectl rollout status deployment/lesson07-deployment -n lesson-7
```

```
/devops $ kubectl set image deployment/lesson07-deployment lesson07=suakbas/lesson07:v2 --record -n lesson-7
deployment.extensions/lesson07-deployment image updated
/devops $
/devops $ kubectl rollout status deployment/lesson07-deployment -n lesson-7
deployment "lesson07-deployment" successfully rolled out
/devops $
```

Figure 7.25: Performing a rolling update

7. Recheck the **HorizontalPodAutoscaler** that you created before to see the current status after the update. Watch the change in the number of pods and check the latest status after a few minutes:

```
$ kubectl get hpa -n lesson-7
$ kubectl get pods -n lesson-7
```

```
/devops $ kubectl get hpa -n lesson-7
NAME                  REFERENCE                          TARGETS    MINPODS   MAXPODS   REPLICAS   AGE
lesson07-deployment   Deployment/lesson07-deployment     0%/50%     2         5         5          8m
/devops $
/devops $kubectl get pods -n lesson-7 -w
NAME                                  READY    STATUS        RESTARTS    AGE
lesson07-deployment-5746b7647f-8xkl8  1/1      Running       0           2m
lesson07-deployment-5746b7647f-djkdv  1/1      Running       0           2m
lesson07-deployment-5746b7647f-kn9vt  1/1      Running       0           2m
lesson07-deployment-5746b7647f-mpsvp  1/1      Running       0           2m
lesson07-deployment-5746b7647f-wvs8d  1/1      Running       0           2m
lesson07-deployment-5746b7647f-wvs8d  1/1      Terminating   0           3m
lesson07-deployment-5746b7647f-8xkl8  1/1      Terminating   0           3m
lesson07-deployment-5746b7647f-djkdv  1/1      Terminating   0           3m
lesson07-deployment-5746b7647f-8xkl8  0/1      Terminating   0           3m
lesson07-deployment-5746b7647f-wvs8d  0/1      Terminating   0           3m
lesson07-deployment-5746b7647f-djkdv  0/1      Terminating   0           3m
lesson07-deployment-5746b7647f-8xkl8  0/1      Terminating   0           3m
lesson07-deployment-5746b7647f-8xkl8  0/1      Terminating   0           3m
lesson07-deployment-5746b7647f-wvs8d  0/1      Terminating   0           3m
lesson07-deployment-5746b7647f-wvs8d  0/1      Terminating   0           3m
lesson07-deployment-5746b7647f-djkdv  0/1      Terminating   0           3m
lesson07-deployment-5746b7647f-djkdv  0/1      Terminating   0           3m

^C/devops $ kubectl get hpa -n lesson-7
NAME                  REFERENCE                          TARGETS    MINPODS   MAXPODS   REPLICAS   AGE
lesson07-deployment   Deployment/lesson07-deployment     0%/50%     2         5         2          11m
/devops $
```

Figure 7.26: Checking the HPA details and the pods

8. Clean up the environment by removing the namespace:

```
$ kubectl delete ns lesson-7
```

Chapter 8: Troubleshooting Applications in Kubernetes

Activity 9: Troubleshooting an Application in Kubernetes

Solution:

Perform the following steps to complete this activity:

1. Create a Pod definition file that uses the **suakbas/chapter08:v1** image and is consuming the **LOG_LEVEL** and **ENABLE_CONNECTION** environment variables from a ConfigMap named **app-config**. Name the file as **pod.yaml**:

```
apiVersion: v1
kind: Pod
metadata:
  name: app
spec:
  containers:
  - name: app
    image: suakbas/lesson08:v1
    env:
      - name: LOG_LEVEL
        valueFrom:
          configMapKeyRef:
            name: app-config
            key: log-level
      - name: ENABLE_CONNECTION
        valueFrom:
          configMapKeyRef:
            name: app-config
            key: enable-connection
```

2. Create a ConfigMap with the **LOG_LEVEL** field set to **INFO** and **ENABLE_CONNECTION** set to **No**. Name the file as **configmap.yaml**:

```
apiVersion: v1
kind: ConfigMap
metadata:
  name: app-config
data:
  log-level: "INFO"
  enable-connection: "No"
```

3. Deploy the ConfigMap and the Pod to the **lesson-8** namespace:

```
$ kubectl create -f configmap.yaml -n lesson-8
$ kubectl create -f pod.yaml -n lesson-8
```

```
/devops $ kubectl create -f configmap.yaml -n lesson-8
configmap/app-config created
/devops $
/devops $ kubectl create -f pod.yaml -n lesson-8
pod/app created
/devops $
```

Figure 8.15: Deploying the ConfigMap app-config and the Pod app

Check whether the Pod is running:

```
$ kubectl get pods -n lesson-8
```

```
/devops $ kubectl get pods -n lesson-8
NAME      READY      STATUS            RESTARTS    AGE
app       0/1        CrashLoopBackOff  3           1m
/devops $
```

Figure 8.16: Checking the app status

4. Try to figure out why the Pod is constantly terminating instead of running. Use **kubectl logs** to check the logs of the application:

```
$ kubectl logs app -n lesson-8
```

```
/devops $ kubectl logs app -n lesson-8
{"level":"info","msg":"Application is starting..","time":"2019-03-25T20:41:23Z"}
{"level":"info","msg":"Application is exiting..","time":"2019-03-25T20:41:23Z"}
/devops $
```

Figure 8.17: Getting the logs of the app

As you see, the logging level does not allow you to understand the problem. Let's try changing the logging level to debug.

5. Change the log level by updating the **LOG_LEVEL** field from the ConfigMap to **DEBUG**:

```
$ kubectl edit configmap app-config -n lesson-8
```

```
/devops $ kubectl edit configmap app-config -n lesson-8
configmap/app-config edited
/devops $
```

Figure 8.18: Modifying the app-config

6. Use **kubectl logs** again to check more verbose logs:

> **Note**
>
> Since we consume the ConfigMap values as environment variables, we need to restart the Pod to get the latest changes either by waiting for the next restart or by deleting/re-creating the Pod.

```
$ kubectl logs app -n lesson-8
```

```
/devops $ kubectl logs app -n lesson-8
{"level":"info","msg":"Application is starting..","time":"2019-03-25T21:01:23Z"}
{"level":"debug","msg":"ENABLE_CONNECTION set to [No]","time":"2019-03-25T21:01:23Z"}
{"level":"info","msg":"Application is exiting..","time":"2019-03-25T21:01:23Z"}
bash-3.2$
/devops $
```

Figure 8.19: Checking the logs of app

Now, we have more information to understand the problem. It seems that the **ENABLE_CONNECTION** environment variable is set to **No**. Let's confirm this by checking inside the Pod.

7. Check the set environment variables using **kubectl exec**:

```
$ kubectl exec app -n lesson-8 -- printenv
```

```
/devops $ kubectl exec app -n lesson-8 -- printenv
PATH=/go/bin:/usr/local/go/bin:/usr/local/sbin:/usr/local/bin:/usr/sbin:/usr/bin:/sbin:/bin
HOSTNAME=app
LOG_LEVEL=DEBUG
ENABLE_CONNECTION=No
KUBERNETES_PORT=tcp://10.47.240.1:443
KUBERNETES_PORT_443_TCP=tcp://10.47.240.1:443
KUBERNETES_PORT_443_TCP_PROTO=tcp
KUBERNETES_PORT_443_TCP_PORT=443
KUBERNETES_PORT_443_TCP_ADDR=10.47.240.1
KUBERNETES_SERVICE_HOST=10.47.240.1
KUBERNETES_SERVICE_PORT=443
KUBERNETES_SERVICE_PORT_HTTPS=443
GOLANG_VERSION=1.11.6
GOPATH=/go
HOME=/root
/devops $
```

Figure 8.20: Printing the environment variables inside the app

> **Note**
>
> Since the application will keep crashing because of the problem, you may need to execute this command multiple times to print the environment variables successfully.

We confirm that **ENABLE_CONNECTION** is set to **No**.

8. Fix the problem by setting **ENABLE_CONNECTION** to **Yes** by updating the **configmap. yaml** file. Apply the updated file to the cluster:

```
apiVersion: v1
kind: ConfigMap
metadata:
  name: app-config
data:
  log-level: "INFO"
  enable-connection: "Yes"
$ kubectl apply -f configmap.yaml -n lesson-8
```

```
/devops $ kubectl apply -f configmap.yaml -n lesson-8
configmap/app-config configured
/devops $
```

Figure 8.21: Modifying app-config

9. Check the logs to verify the solution:

> **Note**
>
> Since we consume the ConfigMap values as environment variables, we need to restart the Pod to get the latest changes either by waiting for the next restart or by deleting/re-creating the Pod.

```
$ kubectl logs app -n lesson-8
```

```
/devops $ kubectl logs app -n lesson-8
{"level":"info","msg":"Application is starting..","time":"2019-03-25T21:22:21Z"}
{"level":"info","msg":"Application is running..","time":"2019-03-25T21:22:21Z"}
/devops $
```

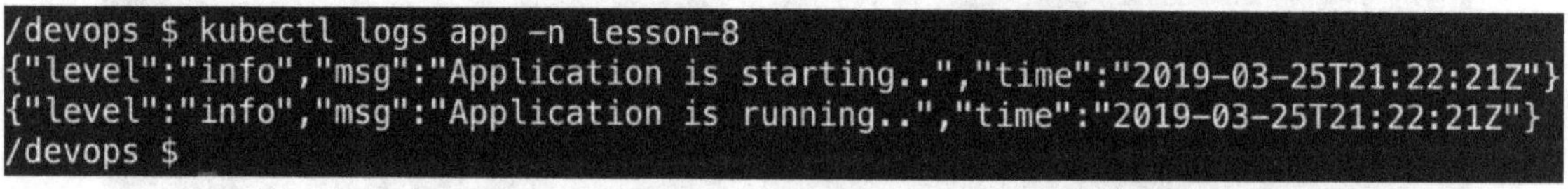

Figure 8.22: Checking the logs of the app

10. You can clean up everything now by removing the namespace:

```
$ kubectl delete ns lesson-8
```

Chapter 9: Monitoring Applications in Kubernetes

Activity 10: Setting Up Alert Notifications in Kubernetes

Solution:

Perform the following steps to complete this activity:

1. Create an **Incoming Webhook** for the **devops** channel. Click on your username and then click on **Customize Slack**:

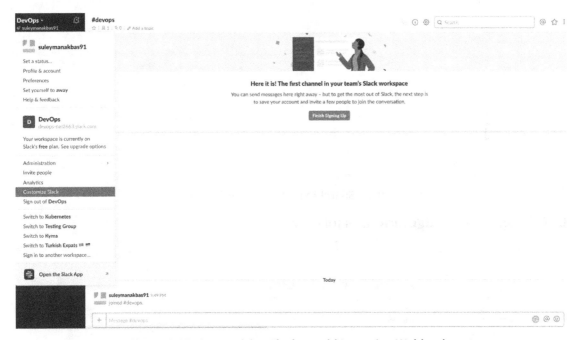

Figure 9.43: Customizing Slack to add Incoming Webhooks

2. On the next page, click on **Configure Apps**, which will direct you to the following screen. Here, search for **Incoming Webhooks**, as follows:

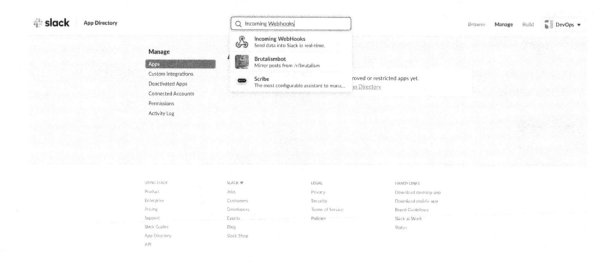

Figure 9.44: Searching for Incoming Webhooks

3. Click on **Add Configuration**, as follows:

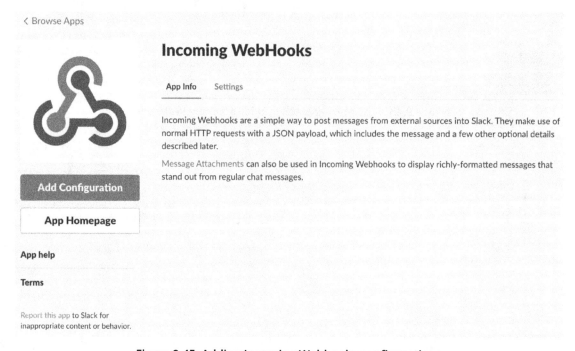

Figure 9.45: Adding Incoming Webhooks configurations

4. Select the channel that you want to set for the alerting notifications, and then click on **Add Incoming WebHooks integration**:

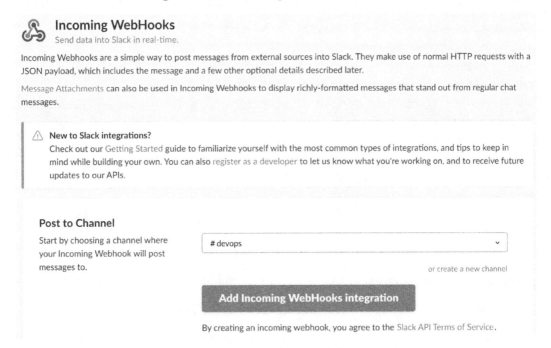

Figure 9.46: Adding Incoming Webhooks to the devops channel

5. From the resulting page, note down the Webhook URL that will be used to configure Alertmanager:

Figure 9.47: The generated Webhook URL

If you can see the Webhook URL already generated, this means that everything was successful. Please take a note of this URL.

6. Prepare an alert rule in Prometheus.

   Here is an alert rule that you can use to check the status of the **test** container:

   ```
   groups:
     - name: test-pod-not-running-rule
       rules:
       - alert: TestPodNotRunning
         expr: (kube_pod_container_status_running { namespace="lesson-9",
   container="test" } == 0)
         for: 30s
         labels:
           severity: critical
         annotations:
           description: "{{$labels.namespace}}/{{$labels.pod}} is not
   running"
           summary: "{{$labels.pod}} is not running"
   ```

7. Modify the **prometheus-server** ConfigMap to specify this alert:

   ```
   $ kubectl edit configmap prometheus-server -n lesson-9
   ```

   > **Note**
   >
   > **kubectl edit** uses **Vim** as the default text editor. If you want to use another one, such as **nano**, you can set the **KUBE_EDITOR** environment variable with the name of your favorite text editor. For example, you can set **nano** as the default text editor as follows:
   >
   > **$ export KUBE_EDITOR="nano"**

   > **Note**
   >
   > Copy the alert rule from the previous step and paste it under alerts, as shown in the following screenshot:

   ```
   /devops $ kubectl edit configmap prometheus-server -n lesson-9
   configmap/prometheus-server edited
   /devops $
   ```

   Figure 9.48: Modifying the prometheus-server ConfigMap

This is how it should look after pasting the alert rule under **alerts** from the previous step:

```
apiVersion: v1
data:
  alerts: |
    groups:
    - name: test-pod-not-running-rule
      rules:
      - alert: TestPodNotRunning
        expr: (kube_pod_container_status_running { namespace="lesson-9", container="test" } == 0)
        for: 30s
        labels:
          severity: critical
        annotations:
          description: "{{$labels.namespace}}/{{$labels.pod}} is not running"
          summary: "{{$labels.pod}} is not running"
```

Figure 9.49: Adding the new alert rule

8. Create a Slack receiver in Alertmanager:

    Here is a Slack receiver that you can use to configure Alertmanager:

    ```
    receivers:
    - name: "slack"
      slack_configs:
      - channel: "devops"
        send_resolved: true
        api_url: <Webhook_URL>
        title: "{{ .CommonAnnotations.description }}"
        text: "Description: {{ .CommonAnnotations.description }}"
    route:
      routes:
      - match:
          alertname: TestPodNotRunning
        receiver: "slack"
    ```

9. Modify the **prometheus-alertmanager** ConfigMap to add the Slack receiver:

```
$ kubectl edit configmap prometheus-alertmanager -n lesson-9
```

> **Note**
>
> Copy the receiver from the previous step and paste it under **receivers**, as shown in the following screenshot:

```
/devops $ kubectl edit configmap prometheus-alertmanager -n lesson-9
configmap/prometheus-alertmanager edited
/devops $
```

Figure 9.50: Modifying the prometheus-alertmanager ConfigMap

Here is how it should look after pasting the receiver from the previous step under **receivers**:

```
apiVersion: v1
data:
  alertmanager.yml: |
    global: {}
    receivers:
    - name: default-receiver
    - name: "slack"
      slack_configs:
      - channel: "devops"
        send_resolved: true
        api_url: "https://hooks.slack.com/services/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"
        title: "{{ .CommonAnnotations.description }}"
        text: "Description: {{ .CommonAnnotations.description }}"
    route:
      routes:
      - match:
          alertname: TestPodNotRunning
        receiver: "slack"
      group_interval: 5m
      group_wait: 10s
      receiver: default-receiver
      repeat_interval: 3h
```

Figure 9.51: Adding the Slack receiver

10. Check the Prometheus UI to see whether the alert is visible on Prometheus:

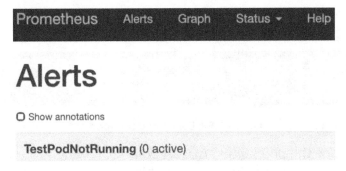

Figure 9.52: The Prometheus Alerts page

This shows that we successfully created an alert rule, and it is not firing any alerts yet.

11. Create a file named **pod.yaml** using the following **Pod** definition, which has a mistake in the image name, written as **busybo** instead of **busybox**.

```
$ vi pod.yaml
```

> **Note**
>
> Copy and paste the following Pod definition and exit with **wq**.

Here is the **Pod** definition with the **busybo** image:

```
apiVersion: v1
kind: Pod
metadata:
  name: test-pod
spec:
  containers:
  - name: test
    image: busybo
    command: ["/bin/sh"]
    args: ["-c", "sleep 99999"]
```

12. Deploy **test-pod**; then, check to see the error:

```
$ kubectl apply -f pod.yaml -n lesson-9
$ kubectl get pod test-pod -n lesson-9
```

```
/devops $ kubectl apply -f pod.yaml -n lesson-9
pod/test-pod created
/devops $
```

Figure 9.53: Deploying test-pod

Here, you can see the pod status, **ImagePullBackOff**, which refers to a problem where the image cannot be downloaded; this is because the **busybo** image does not really exist:

```
/devops $ kubectl get pod test-pod -n lesson-9
NAME        READY    STATUS            RESTARTS    AGE
test-pod    0/1      ImagePullBackOff  0           1m
/devops $
```

Figure 9.54: Checking whether the test-pod is running

13. Check the Prometheus UI to see whether the alert is firing; note that it could take about a minute to see the alert firing:

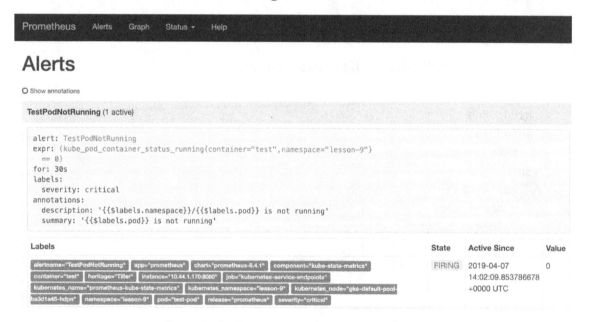

Figure 9.55: The activated alert in Prometheus

14. Check the **devops** channel on Slack to see the alert notification:

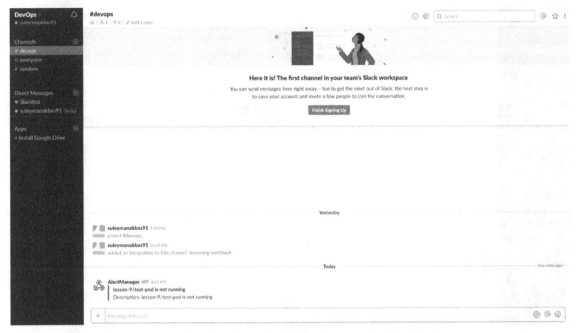

Figure 9.56: the alerting notification received in Slack

15. Fix the image to be **busybox**:

```
$ kubectl set image pod/test-pod test=busybox -n lesson-9
$ kubectl get pod test-pod -n lesson-9
```

```
/devops $ kubectl set image pod/test-pod test=busybox -n lesson-9
pod/test-pod image updated
/devops $
/devops $ kubectl get pod test-pod -n lesson-9
NAME        READY      STATUS      RESTARTS    AGE
test-pod    1/1        Running     0           4m
/devops $
```

Figure 9.57: Fixing the test-pod image

16. Check the **devops** channel on Slack again to see the resolved notification:

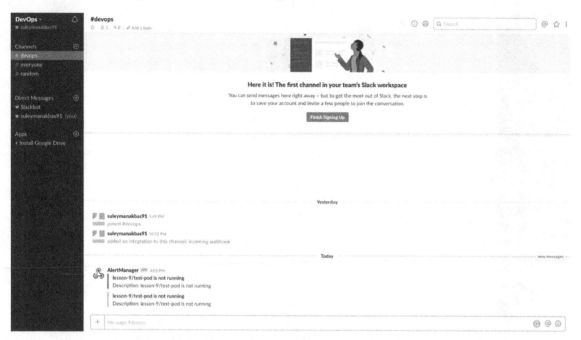

Figure 9.58: The resolved notification received in Slack

Here, take a closer look at the colors on the left-hand side of the notifications. Red corresponds to the failure notification, whereas green refers to the resolved notification.

17. To clean up the environment, you can delete the **lesson-9** namespace:

```
$ kubectl delete ns lesson-9
```

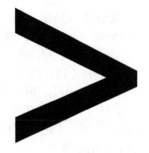

Index

About

All major keywords used in this book are captured alphabetically in this section. Each one is accompanied by the page number of where they appear.

A

abstracted:140
access: 22-23, 58, 69,
    78, 81-82, 93, 96,
    139-141, 147, 165-166,
    177, 182-183, 186, 230,
    241, 246, 265, 268
accessible: 45-46, 141, 149
acquaint:69
activate: 118, 121
active: 3, 15, 18-19, 70,
    113, 143, 190, 193,
    195-196, 248, 284
activities: 5, 33,
    124, 126-127
activity: 33-36, 42, 61-62,
    64-65, 92, 94-95, 100,
    124, 126, 130, 147-149,
    175-176, 185-186,
    219-221, 248-250, 256,
    265, 286, 292-294
addons: 242-243
address: 40, 79, 95,
    102-103, 118, 140,
    177, 283, 286, 288
adhering: 212, 218
adopted: 4, 42, 177
advanced: 115, 118, 190
aliases:84
alibaba: 41, 73
amazon: 53, 70, 113, 116
analysis: 4, 18
analyzed: 112-113, 130
analyzing: 112, 255
android:43
annotate: 131, 133
annotation: 131, 278
ansible: 78, 152
api-driven:73
apiversion: 85-87,
    89-90, 140, 155-159,

161, 168-172, 177-180,
    182-184, 197-202,
    204-205, 207, 213,
    215, 218, 235, 238,
    244, 280-281
app-config: 155-156,
    158-161, 175, 249
applied: 186, 213
applies:112
approach: 2, 4, 6, 32, 40,
    100, 114, 224, 254
apt-get: 52, 54
assets: 226, 255
automate: 84, 152
automated: 18, 20-22,
    33, 35-36, 152
automation: 3, 21, 29,
    34, 101, 117, 134,
    152, 176-177, 197
autoscale:218
autoscaler: 218-221, 224

B

backing:185
backlog: 6, 8-9, 12-13
banking: 29, 40
bankruptcy:165
branch: 17, 30, 33-35
browser: 18, 31, 35, 61,
    65, 79, 95, 102-103,
    149, 265, 268, 286
bug-fixing:40
building: 21, 36, 51, 53-55,
    66, 70, 84-85, 87, 100,
    139, 152, 163, 209
built-in: 153, 158, 163,
    166, 171, 177, 181, 186,
    213, 218, 221, 258

C

chapter: 1, 3, 9, 34, 36, 42,
    62, 65-66, 69-70, 77, 96,
    99-100, 127, 129-130,
    136, 140, 145, 147, 149,
    151, 174-175, 185-186,
    189-190, 206, 209-210,
    212-213, 219-221,
    223-224, 226, 249-250,
    253-254, 293-295
charts: 129, 143-144,
    147, 263
checked: 8, 15, 25, 46-47,
    57, 78, 114-116, 250, 257
checking: 24, 72-73, 78,
    81-82, 95, 162-163, 173,
    205, 208, 216-217, 226,
    231-232, 237, 242-245,
    247-248, 265-267
client: 26, 43, 45-46,
    49, 56, 66, 78, 83,
    85, 130, 135, 143,
    145-146, 278-279
clients: 259, 294
closed: 7, 19, 248
closer:41
cluster: 33, 53, 69-78,
    81-85, 87-88, 90,
    95, 99-102, 107-109,
    111-116, 118, 120-121,
    123-127, 130, 132,
    134-136, 138-141, 143,
    145-147, 149, 155, 162,
    168-170, 175, 180-186,
    205-206, 210, 212-213,
    215, 218-221, 229,
    240-242, 247-249,
    256-257, 263, 270,
    275-279, 281, 283, 294
clusterip:202
clusters: 27, 33, 70-71, 74,

CPSIA information can be obtained
at www.ICGtesting.com
Printed in the USA
BVHW011137080420
577186BV00005B/115